composition STUDIES

Volume 49, Number 3
Fall 2021

Editors
Matthew Davis
Kara Taczak

Book Review Editor
Jason Chew Kit Tham

Managing Editor
Megan Busch

Content Editors
Mike Haen
Callie Kostelich
Emma Kostopoulos
Alex McAdams
Clare Sully-Stendahl

Blog Editors
Lauren Fusilier
Megan Von Bergen

Social Media Editors
Nitya Pandey
Annmarie Steffes

Editorial Assistant
Anna Aldrich

Editorial Consultant
Bob Mayberry

Former Editors
Gary Tate
Bob Mayberry
Christina Murphy
Peter Vandenberg
Ann George
Carrie Leverenz
Brad E. Lucas
Jennifer Clary-Lemon
Laura R. Micciche

Advisory Board
Sheila Carter-Tod
 Virginia Tech University

Chen Chen
 Winthrop University

David Green
 Howard University

Christina LaVecchia
 Neumann University

Michael McCamley
 University of Delaware

Cruz Medina
 Santa Clara University

Jessica Nastal-Dema
 Prairie State College

Melissa Berry Pearson
 Northeastern University

Annette Harris Powell
 Bellarmine University

Margaret Price
 The Ohio State University

Nathalie Singh-Corcoran
 West Virginia University

Darci Thoune
 University of Wisconsin-La Crosse

SUBSCRIPTIONS

Composition Studies is published twice each year (May and November). Annual subscription rates: Individuals $25 (Domestic), $30 (International), and $15 (Students). To subscribe online, please visit https://compstudiesjournal.com/subscriptions/.

BACK ISSUES

Back issues, five years prior to the present, are freely accessible on our website: https://compstudiesjournal.com/archive/. If you don't see what you're looking for, contact us. Also, recent back issues are now available through Amazon.com. To find issues, use the advanced search feature and search on "Composition Studies" (title) and "Parlor Press" (publisher).

BOOK REVIEWS

Assignments are made from a file of potential book reviewers. If you are interested in writing a review, please contact our Book Review editor at Jason.Tham@ttu.edu.

JOURNAL SCOPE

The oldest independent periodical in the field, *Composition Studies* publishes original articles relevant to rhetoric and composition, including those that address teaching college writing; theorizing rhetoric and composing; administering writing programs; and, among other topics, preparing the field's future teacher-scholars. All perspectives and topics of general interest to the profession are welcome. We also publish Course Designs, which contextualize, theorize, and reflect on the content and pedagogy of a course. CFPs, announcements, and letters to the editor are most welcome. *Composition Studies* does not consider previously published manuscripts, unrevised conference papers, or unrevised dissertation chapters.

SUBMISSIONS

For submission information and guidelines, see https://compstudiesjournal.com/submissions/.

Direct all correspondence to:

> Matthew Davis, Co-Editor
> Department of English
> UMass Boston
> 100 Morrissey Blvd
> Boston MA 02125–3393
> compstudiesjournal@gmail.com

Composition Studies is grateful for the support of the University of Massachusetts Boston and the University of Denver.

© 2021 by Matthew Davis and Kara Taczak, Co-Editors

Production and distribution is managed by Parlor Press, www.parlorpress.com.

ISSN 1534–9322.

Cover art by Wafaa Razeq.

https://compstudiesjournal.com/

composition STUDIES

Volume 49, Number 3
Fall 2021

Contents

From the Editors: 2021, in Words   8

At a Glance

Teaching, Writing, Gaming   14
    Richard Colby, Matthew S. S. Johnson, and Rebekah Shultz Colby

Articles

Are We Overlooking (and Underselling) the Writing Capstone Course?   16
    Timothy Ballingall and Brad Lucas

"Sometimes I Forget I'm in an Online Class!" Why Place Matters for Meaningful Student Online Writing Experiences   38
    Felicita Arzu Carmichael

"How am I Supposed to Watch a Little Piece of Paper?" Literacy and Learning Under Duress   56
    Carrie Hall

Tracing Ableism's Rhetorical Circulation through an Analysis of Composition Mission Statements   74
    Kristin C. Bennett

Course Design

Global Efforts to Professionalize Online Literacy Instructors: GSOLE's Basic OLI Certification   101
    Amy Cicchino, Kevin DePew, Jason Snart, and Scott Warnock

ENGL 1100 Contextualized: Designing a FYW Course for Guided Pathways   118
    Nancy Pine

Where We Are

Writing in the West African Context   133
    Linford O. Lamptey and Roland Dumavor

Something of Our Own to Say: Writing Pedagogy in India   139
    Anuj Gupta and Anannya Dasgupta

Transforming the Teaching of Writing from a Skills-Based Approach to a Knowledge Construction Approach in a University in Singapore   145
    Radhika Jaidev

Writing Instruction and Writing Research in Denmark 150
Kristine Kabel and Jesper Bremholm

Teaching of Writing in Hong Kong: Where Are We? 155
Icy Lee

Weh Wi Deh / Veh Vi Is / Where We Are: Teaching and Researching Academic Writing in the Caribbean 160
Vivette Milson-Whyte, Raymond Oenbring, and Brianne Jaquette

(Re)Writing the Middle East: Tension, Engagement, and Rhetorical Translanguaging 165
Emma Moghabghab

On the Teaching of University Writing in Latin America 171
Natalia Ávila Reyes and Federico Navarro

Writing Instruction in Australia 176
Susan E. Thomas

Book Reviews 182

Literacy and Pedagogy in an Age of Misinformation and Disinformation, ed. by Tara Lockhart, et al. 182
  Reviewed by Christine Wilson

PARS in Practice: More Resources and Strategies for Online Writing Instructors, ed. by Jessie Borgman and Casey McArdle 186
  Reviewed by Omar Yacoub

The Anti-Racist Writing Workshop: How to Decolonize the Creative Classroom, by Felicia Rose Chavez 190
  Reviewed by Siara Schwartzlow

Speaking Up, Speaking Out: Lived Experiences of Non-Tenure-Track Faculty in Writing Studies, ed. by Jessica Edwards, Meg McGuire, and Rachel Sanchez 194
  Reviewed by Stacy Wittstock

Sixteen Teachers Teaching: Two-Year College Perspectives, ed. by Patrick Sullivan 199
  Reviewed by Bethany Sweeney

Empowering the Community College First-Year Composition Teacher: Pedagogies and Policies, ed. by Meryl Siegal and Betsy Gilliland 203
  Reviewed by Katherine Daily O'Meara

Style and the Future of Composition Studies, ed. by Paul Butler, Brian Ray, and Star Medzerian Vanguri 207
  Reviewed by Roberto S. Leon

Contributors 211

TCU PH.D. IN RHETORIC AND COMPOSITION

PROGRAM. One of the founding programs in rhetoric and composition. Scholarly innovation, professional development, excellent job placement, well-endowed library, state-of-the-art Center for Digital Expression, and graduate certificates in New Media; Women and Gender Studies; and Comparative Race and Ethnic Studies.

FACULTY. Nationally recognized teacher-scholars in literacy studies, composition, modern rhetoric, women's rhetoric, digital rhetoric, and writing program administration.

TEACHING. 1-1 teaching loads, small classes, extensive pedagogy and technology training, and administrative fellowships in writing program administration and new media.

FUNDING. Generous five-year graduate instructorships, competitive stipends, travel support, and prestigious fellowship opportunities.

EXPERIENCE. Mid-sized liberal arts university setting nestled in the vibrant, culturally rich Dallas-Fort Worth metroplex.

eng.tcu.edu

From the Editors: 2021, in Words

Our editorial introductions so far tried have tried to capture the prevailing personal, professional, and social atmosphere with metaphors and eloquently composed intros. In truth, though, the task has eluded us. Things seem to have moved so rapidly in the last few years that we wonder if the world is rotating faster on its axis. It has also eluded us because these short pages are hardly the place for all the thoughts, feelings, and emotions running tirelessly through our beings. Nevertheless, we find ourselves at the end of another difficult year, yet again compelled to attempt it. One one hand, we're slightly hopeful–we're vaccinated; and also distressed—few, if any, of the issues raised in our previous introdcutions are resolved, and it seems that the omicron variant awaits. As teachers and researchers, we are interested in how words frame experience, impact learning, build reflective capacity, and promote growth. (Key terms are an important part of our research on transfer and often provide a conceptual foundation–a heuristic, if you will–for how students understand writing situations; so it's a wonder we haven't brought them into our editorials sooner!)

So we found ourselves wondering . . . what words are others using to frame the current moment?

For many, a "word of the year" helps set the tone for an annual moment of reflection. These terms are often chosen by some combination of editorial decision and search frequency, so they provide a kind of rough metric for both the interest in and impact of lexical items each year. How might those annual "word of the year" choices—both in the US and abroad—work as a heuristic for thinking about 2021?

Because this "moment" has lasted for almost two years now, we thought we'd start by looking at the words of year for 2020. Where we've been seems pretty clear: the American Dialect Society chose "Covid" as its word of the year in 2020. Merriam-Webster and Dictionary.com both chose "pandemic," and Collins Dictionary chose "lockdown." As a rebuff to what she saw as word-of-the-year negativity, Arianna Huffington, the one-time independent newswoman turned behavioral technology guru, announced that "resilience" was her 2020 word of the year. Oxford UP Languages, for their part, found 2020 so difficult to frame that, instead of a word of the year, they produced an entire language report. Internationally, things looked pretty similar: Macquarie Dictionary in Australia chose both "rona" (as in Corona) and "doomscrolling." The Australian National Dictionary Centre chose "iso" (as in, self-isolation). The Society for German Language (or Gesellschaft für deutsche Sprache) chose "Corona-Pandemie," which needs little translation. Our favorite international contribution for 2020, however, was from the Danish Language Council (or

Dansk Sprognævn): samfundssinn, which means "putting the concern of society higher than one's own interests."

In other words, in 2020 you might have doomscrolled while iso'ing from the rona pandemic, trying to remain resilient out of samfundssinn.

The words for 2021, we hoped, would provide more reason for optimism . . . or at least a reframing of our individual and collective responses to the recent past. The American Dialect Society choice is not yet published, but Merriam-Webster chose "vaccine" and, similarly, Oxford UP Languages chose "vax." The Collins Dictionary chose "NFT"—an acronym for non-fungible token—which narrowly beat out climate anxiety, double-vaxxed, hybrid working, and pingdemic (as in, when an app notifies you of pandemic-related news), among others. Cambridge Dictionary chose "perseverance" for 2021, explicitly linking that choice to the collective response to the global problems of the year and to the landing of an eponymous NASA Rover on Mars. The hope, Cambridge's announcement said, was to capture "the undaunted will of people across the world to never give up, despite the many challenges of the last 12 months" (Glennon). Highlighting collective response of another solidaristic kind, Dictionary.com chose "allyship" for 2021. Internationally, the mood shifted a bit as well. In Germany, the choice was "Wellenbrecher"–literally a breakwater, aka the measures necessary to fend off a wave of infections. In Australia, it was "strollout" (as in, a very slow rollout of vaccines) for both the Australian National Dictionary Centre and Macquarie Dictionary. Despite our enjoyment of samfundssinn in 2020, the Danes have yet to announce their choice for 2021.

Because of this small heuristic experiment, we no longer feel so alone in our inability to capture the current moment. Perhaps it's difficult to capture because it is so . . . dispersed and unequally distributed. Perhaps it's because we are all experiencing it differently. To test that theory, we asked family, friends, colleagues, and students what their "word of the year" might be: the answers ranged from the wildly optimistic to mournfully tired. The lesson we take from these words of the year and from talking with family, friends, colleagues, and students is of the importance of taking care of our mental, emotional, and physical wellbeing.

That will be the topic of the next special issue. We're thrilled to announce that Stacey Cochran and Susan Miller-Cochran will guest edit the next digital, open-access, issue for summer 2022. The title of the issue will be "Teaching Writing to Increase Student and Teacher Well-Being," and a CFP will be ready for you soon–so keep an eye out!

At A Glance

This issue's At A Glance is "Teaching, Writing, Gaming" by Richard Colby, Matthew S. S. Johnson, and Rebekah Shultz Colby. This gamified research poster outlines ways of thinking about games and their possible influence and impact on writing classrooms: as sites of writing and learning; as possibilities for teaching strategies; and as a way of thinking about teaching and learning. Most helpfully, this text provides three accompanying sets of key terms and a substantial bibliography for following up on the poster's ideas. It also serves as a nice entrée into the authors' new book, *The Ethics of Playing, Researching, and Teaching Games in the Writing Classroom* (2021).

Articles

The first article in this issue, "Are We Overlooking (and Underselling) the Writing Capstone Course?" by Timothy Ballingall and Brad Lucas, offers a content analysis of 54 writing capstone syllabi from 44 different institutions while highlighting course descriptions, outcomes, and assigned readings. Their findings suggest that "the writing capstone is, primarily, a qualitatively different course from the rest of the curriculum, neither just another course nor a professional-development after-thought." And yet, they find, capstone courses still sometimes lack necessary articulation: of course goals, of whom they serve and why, and of how and why the culminating experience fits within its local context.

Next we have "'Sometimes I Forget I'm in an Online Class!' Why Place Matters for Meaningful Student Online Writing Experiences" by Felicita Arzu Carmichael, who argues that space and place matter in the online writing classroom and can often lead students to have meaningful writing experiences. Using the work of Eodice et al., Arzu Carmichael asks online writing instructors to utilize space and place as inventional for writing about the self, as prompts for reflection, and as a framework for thinking through the binaries of "natural/material" and "constructed/metaphorical" in online writing instruction.

Drawing from a range of disciplinary perspectives, Carrie Hall's "'How am I Supposed to Watch a Little Piece of Paper?': Literacy and Learning Under Duress" carefully considers the inequitably distributed attentional difficulties that writing students face when attempting to focus on writing in moments of duress, whether from personal trauma or ambient threat. Using students' own writing as a site for negotiating the tensions of paying attention, Hall develops three strategies for making sure that writing curricula are "curricula capacious enough that students can find processes that work for them": understanding attention, finding footholds, and deep attending.

Finally, Kristin Bennett's "Tracing Ableism's Rhetorical Circulation through an Analysis of Composition Mission Statements" reports on a systematic study of writing program mission statements, noting where attempts to be both inclusive and standardized lead to language that is, instead, exclusive of meaningful difference. Combining research in disability studies with work in technical and professional communication, Bennett identifies where normative programmatic language reproduces and circulates ableist assumptions and then outlines ways of cripping mission statements. Through three specific rhetorical moves–articulating anti-assimilationist multiplicity, validating students' embodied knowledge, and advocating for collaborative interdependence—Bennett reconstructs extant missions statements as models for future practice.

Course Designs

Global Society of Online Literacy Educators (GSOLE) Basic OLI Certification is an instructor-facing two-course certification program designed by Amy Cicchino, Kevin DePew, Jason Snart, and Scott Warnock to help online literacy instructors, tutors, and writing program administrators. The goal is to help writing teachers learn foundational principles, theories, and practices of teaching and tutoring writing for online instruction and apply those where they work (or where they may eventually work). Course one focuses on online literacy education while course two focuses on assignment and activity design for online writing instruction, whether for an online writing course, writing center, or writing-enriched course across campus. Helpfully, their reflection outlines the challenges of rolling out such a sequence and suggests how the move to remote teaching during the COVID-19 pandemic can clarify thinking about "triage" versus "certified" online writing instruction.

The title to Nancy Pine's "ENGL 1100 Contextualized: Designing a FYW Course for Guided Pathways" nearly says it all: this course design provides a locally contextualized, discipline-specific first year writing course for community college students in business and hospitality programs. The course includes "subject matter and the study of rhetorical situations and texts of interest and relevance to students with majors in the pathway," all of which are prepared, designed, and implemented according to Pine's "pedagogy of contextualization" based on transfer, motivation, and program specificity.

Where We Are

We are especially excited about this issue's Where We Are section, which takes up the topic of Teaching Writing in Global Contexts. Scholars from Australia, the Caribbean, Denmark, Hong Kong, India, Latin America, the Middle East, Singapore, and West Africa accepted the invitation to write to us about the teaching, research, and administration of writing in their specific contexts. The result is a kaleidoscopic picture of the histories, values, pedagogies, practices, programs, purposes, and goals of writing programs around the globe. Our only regret is that we didn't have more wonderful contributors or more pages to give them!

Book Reviews

This issue, we have a solid group of individual book reviews–seven to be exact!–and they tackle concepts that are very prevalent in the field right now: literacy in the age of mis/disinformation, strategies for online writing instructors, the anti-ractist writing workshop, lived experiences by non-tenured writing faculty, labor-based grading contracts, empowering community college first year composition instructors, and style and composition studies. The writers provide wonderfully rich summaries and critical responses to each of the books in question.

What, we wonder, would be your word of the year for 2021? And what will the 2022 word of the year be?

Kt and MD
Denver and Boston
December, 2021

Works Consulted

American Dialect Society. "2020 Word of the Year Is 'Covid.'" 2021, americandialect.org/2020-word-of-the-year-is-covid.

Australian National Dictionary. "2021 Word of the Year." *Australian National University*, 17 November 2021, slll.cass.anu.edu.au/centres/andc/news/2021-word-year.

"The Cambridge Dictionary Word of the Year 2020." *About Words: A Blog from Cambridge Dictionary*, 24 November 2020, dictionaryblog.cambridge.org/2020/11/24/cambridge-dictionarys-word-of-the-year-2020/.

"The Collins Word of the Year 2021 Is...NFT." *Collins Dictionary*, collinsdictionary.com/us/woty.

"The Collins Word of the Year 2020." *Collins Language*, 21 December 2020, collinslanguage.com/2020/12/21/collins-word-of-the-year-2020/.

"The Committee's Choice & People's Choice for Word of the Year 2020." *Macquarie Dictionary*, 07 December 2020, macquariedictionary.com.au/resources/view/word/of/the/year/2020.

"Dictionary.com's Word of the Year Is...Allyship." *Dictionary.com*, 6 December 2021, dictionary.com/e/word-of-the-year/.

Froelich, Paula. "Danish Word 'Samfundssind' May Become 2020's New Hottest Term." *New York Post*, 24 October 2021, nypost.com/2020/10/24/danish-word-samfundssind-may-become-2020s-hottest-term/.

Glennon, Jade. "The Cambridge Dictionary Word of the Year for 2021 is . . . Perseverance." *World of Better Learning*, Cambridge University, 17 November 2021, cambridge.org/elt/blog/2021/11/17/cambridge-dictionary-word-year-2021/.

Huffington, Arianna. "The Word of the Year Is 'Resilience.'" *Thrive Global*, 04 December 2022, thriveglobal.com/stories/arianna-huffington-resilience-word-of-the-year-2020/.

"Merriam-Webster's Word of the Year 2021." *Merriam-Webster*, merriam-webster.com/words-at-play/word-of-the-year/vaccine.

"Merriam-Webster's Word of the Year 2020." *Merriam-Webster*, merriam-webster.com/words-at-play/word-of-the-year-2020-pandemic.

"Word of the Year 2021." *Macquarie Dictionary*, 29 November 2021, macquariedictionary.com.au/resources/view/word/of/the/year/.

"Word of the Year 2021: Vax." *Oxford Languages*, languages.oup.com/word-of-the-year/2021/.

"Word of the Year 2020" *Oxford Languages*, languages.oup.com/word-of-the-year/2020/.

At a Glance

Teaching, Writing, Gaming

Richard Colby, Matthew S. S. Johnson, and Rebekah Shultz Colby

Teaching, Writing, GAMING

Games are rhetorical. In games, we read, write, and speak; we listen; we choose; we collaborate; we learn. Writers designing games learn new approaches to rhetorical and literate expression. If teachers consider the classroom or writing *as a game*, new teaching and learning possibilities emerge, ones that enable playfulness and pleasure, problem-solving and decision-making, thus emphasizing rhetorical, embodied experiences. Exploring *around games* reveals the complicated social, political, and economic domains in which games exist. Games are multimodal, rule-based systems to be created, explored, and analyzed; and in which practical writing strategies can be learned, and ethical subjectivities examined. Games represent worlds that criticize and celebrate our own, even while they reflect the cultures and industries that enabled their creation. While the scholarship of games-based pedagogy-writing-rhetoric continually evolves (rapidly!) there's a wealth of interactions between gaming and teaching available to explore. And it can be rather a lot of fun.

AROUND GAMES

WRITING

Paratext: gamers compose texts using words, sounds and videos in gaming forums and on streaming and social media platforms, in the form of reviews, walkthroughs, guides, mods, and fanfiction.

Representation of games: games appear in other media, in politics, in arguments, in the news ... in ways ripe for rhetorical analysis.

TEACHING

Rhetorical analysis: investigating games as persuasive, traditionally and procedurally.

Art: games are multimodal, artistic artifacts used to express identity, emotion, and culture.

Metagame: games only operate in constructed, political spaces that enable them in the first place. In their "messy circles," the "ideological desire to distance leisure from labor, play from production, or games from life breaks down" (Boluk and Lemieux 15). (Contrast with "magic circle.")

Ecosystems: game spaces as "organic frameworks" that "feature both users and system agents (including non-player characters, the environments in which the actions take place, and the rules)" (Eyman 246).

AS A GAME

WRITING

Serio-ludic rhetoric: writing projects that "combined playful with serious purposes and expression" (Rouzie 1), "pleasurable and sophisticated" (9).

Magic circle: emphasizing *play*, games exist in a "magic circle" separate from reality, as "temporary worlds within the ordinary world, dedicated to the performance of an act apart" (Huizinga 10). Playing in a magic circle can help students to *explore* writing, to envision themselves in the role of a writer, an author, an expert. (Contrast with "metagame.")

TEACHING

Gamification: teaching writing through concepts of roleplaying and building identities, choices and optional pathways (hopefully *not* through badges).

Emergent pedagogy: stemming from emergent gaming (Juul 76), students are free to try various strategies while teachers adapt their approaches to accommodate.

Social change: examining the potential of games to represent, promote, even initiate social change.

Richard Colby, Matthew S. S. Johnson, & Rebekah Shultz Colby

CHOOSE YOUR PATH, ADVENTURER. WILL YOU ...

GAME OVER

1) ... gamify merely by adopting badges and points?
2) ... teach **AROUND GAMES**, **IN GAMES**, and **AS A GAME**?

IN GAMES

WRITING

Literacy: "explor[ing] the complexly rendered relationship between computer gaming environments and literate activity (Selfe & Hawisher 1) and assessing the influence of gaming on literacies.

How to play: by itself, how to play a game requires learning — which can also be part of the fun. Navigating interfaces, manipulating controls, issuing commands, interpreting data.

Procedural rhetoric: the "practice of using processes persuasively" (Bogost 28), persuasion facilitated through rule and system design.

Multimodality: writers use codes and algorithms in addition visual, aural, tactile, and/or textual elements when composing.

Ergodic literature: games are texts and narratives that require choices and consequences, creating "inaccessible strategies and paths not taken" (Aarseth 3).

TEACHING

Iterative design: playtesting, prototyping, evaluating, and refining (Salen & Zimmerman 11) multiple iterations of texts.

Design collaborations: reading games reveal real – and virtual – world activity systems to writers.

Semiotic domains: games as experiential learning, collaboration, problem solving, and design spaces (Gee 45-46).

Aarseth, Espen J. *Cybertext: Perspectives on Ergodic Literature* (1997)

Bogost, Ian. *Persuasive Games: The Expressive Power of Videogames* (2007)

Boluk, Stephanie & Patrick Lemieux. *Metagaming: Playing, Competing, Spectating, Cheating, Trading, Making, and Breaking Videogames* (2017)

Colby, Richard, Matthew S. S. Johnson, & Rebekah Shultz Colby (eds.). *Rhetoric/Composition/Play: Reshaping Theory and Practice of Writing* (2013)

Colby, Richard, Matthew S. S. Johnson, & Rebekah Shultz Colby (eds.). *The Ethics of Playing, Researching, and Teaching Games in the Writing Classroom* (2021)

Gee, James Paul. *What Video Games Have to Teach Us about Learning and Literacy* (2003)

Huizinga, Johan. *homo ludens: A Study of the Play Element in Culture* (1950)

Juul, Jesper. *half-real: Video Games between Real Rules and Fictional Worlds* (2005)

Rouzie, Albert. *At Play in the Fields of Writing: A Serio-Ludic Rhetoric* (2005)

Salen, Katie & Eric Zimmerman. *Rules of Play: Game Design Fundamentals* (2004)

Selfe, Cynthia L. and Gail E. Hawisher. *Gaming Lives in the Twenty-First Century: Literate Connections* (2007)

Articles

Are We Overlooking (and Underselling) the Writing Capstone Course?

Timothy Ballingall and Brad Lucas

> Rhetoric and composition has made immeasurable strides in the design of undergraduate writing major programs, but the discipline lacks a clear picture of the culminating capstone course that serves as an end point for the writing major. This article reports on a content analysis of 54 writing capstone syllabi from 44 different institutions, highlighting course descriptions, course outcomes, and assigned textbooks. These findings demonstrate the need to move conversations about the capstone beyond our local program concerns. Toward that end, we offer several recommendations for capstone course design and implementation.

Introduction

The vast majority of undergraduate writing majors requires a capstone course. In 2008, Deborah Balzhiser and Susan McLeod created a map of commonalities across 68 programs with a writing major. They found that 90 percent of majors had some sort of capstone experience, defined variously by a specific capstone course, an internship, or a seminar with a portfolio. Among those programs with professional/rhetorical writing majors, students completed a project designed for career preparation or a practicum (420). In 2017, the National Census on Writing found that respondents from 246 institutions reported their institutions having a writing major (Gladstein and Fralix). Given that respondents from 79 schools reported their "institution require[s] ALL students [to] complete a senior thesis or other writing-intensive capstone experience," we can certainly speculate that a large proportion of the over-200 writing majors includes a capstone course of some kind.

Despite the capstone course's prevalence in writing curricula, we have an unclear picture of the options for what a writing capstone can be and the variety of approaches to the course. Indeed, while the past two decades have shown a remarkable increase in scholarship regarding programs for writing majors generally (Alexander et al.; Everett and Hanganu-Bresch; Giberson and Moriarty; Shamoon et al.), including special issues of this journal in 2007 and 2015, the capstone course has received scant scholarly attention. Moreover, there appears to be great program-to-program variability in how the course is designed and presented. With a clearer picture of the aggregate approaches to the capstone, we believe the discipline can work toward identifying frameworks and practices for our undergraduate majors, while accounting for local contexts and meeting student learning outcomes (one of the charges of the CCCC Committee on the Major in Writing and Rhetoric). To that end, we present below the results of a content analysis of syllabi from writing capstone courses around the country, focusing in particular on course descriptions, course objectives, and assigned readings. These results indicate possible options for moving conversations about the capstone beyond our individual departments. For example, our study of 54 syllabi from 44 institutions found a range of 32 different textbooks across subspecialties (see Appendix A). This range of content for capstone readings suggests the continued relevance of Balzhiser and McLeod's concern about the undergraduate writing major over a decade ago: that "we have little consensus about what a writing major should look like" (420). One way to develop our shared understanding of the writing major may be through considering how the writing major should culminate in the capstone. This descriptive study of program materials is a starting point for developing a clearer picture of the capstone courses for writing majors.

Literature Review and Exigence

The past two decades have shown a remarkable increase in scholarship regarding programs for writing majors. Since Kathleen Blake Yancey invoked the writing major in her 2004 CCCC Chair's address, we have seen the formation of the Committee on the Major in Rhetoric and Composition, special journal issues (*Composition Studies* 2007, 2015), and edited collections on the major (Alexander et al.; Everett and Hanganu-Bresch[1]; Giberson and Moriarty[2]; Shamoon et al.[3]). Despite its presence since the 1970s, the capstone course has been an underdeveloped component of this conversation, though several contemporary scholars do acknowledge its significance. Most recently, Laurie E. Gries has argued that advanced composition courses, including the capstone course, are good venues to "better educate students in the *techne* of social activism" (330). Pointing to the uptick in student activism nationally, Gries encourages writing programs to give students the opportunity to "invent, design, and implement social activist campaigns that respond to shared matters of concern and seek to assemble local bodies into collective action" (332-33). The majority of discussion about the capstone, however, has focused on the course's function within a curriculum. For example, Dan Royer and Ellen Schendel have discussed the central role the capstone plays in the Grand Valley State program, and Judith Kearns and Brian Turner documented an unsuccessful capstone course at The University of Winnipeg.

Only recently has there been some attention to the capstone as reflecting the discipline, notably in Lisa Melonçon and Joanna Schreiber's 2015 study of capstones in technical and professional writing programs. More commonly, the capstone makes a cameo appearance as part of the vertical curriculum (Jamieson) or as an ambiguously defined course among many options (Baker and Henning 164; Bradley et al. 172; Brooks et al. 40; DelliCarpini 34; Everett and Hanganu-Bresch 126, 138, 169; Lowe and Macauley 86; McLeod 288; Peeples et al. 75; Shamoon, et al.; Sylvia et al. 186).

The capstone course has always had a presence in scholarship on the major; however, it has been muted and oblique. The capstone's assumed purpose is culmination—to pull together everything in the curriculum in one climactic final course—but how the capstone came to have this purpose has not been clearly articulated in our scholarship. Nor has there been a broader effort to study how rhetoric and composition as a discipline envisions or delivers the capstone course. The capstone clearly has a place in the writing major, but clarifying the capstone experience and accounting for the diverse visions for it remain unanswered challenges.

A lack of scholarly discussion about what the capstone is, or ought to be, is not completely unique to our field. Yet some researchers in other disciplines have begun assessing their approach to the capstone. Much of the discipline-specific capstone research remains atomized, often based on case studies at a single institution rather than surveys across multiple institutions,[4] and it appears that only the field of engineering has published a book-length treatise on the capstone.[5] However, in the past decade, research on capstone courses in general and across multiple institutions has been the subject of a number of reports (Padgett and Kilgo; Schermer and Gray) and a 2013 special issue of *Peer Review* (a journal focused on higher education).

Robert C. Hauhart and Jon E. Grahe's *Designing and Teaching Undergraduate Capstone Courses* (2015) provides the most recent comprehensive review of research and scholarship on the undergraduate capstone course. Hauhart and Grahe identify the course's role in the undergraduate curriculum, its characteristics, and common impediments, and they set forth guidelines and best practices for educators. Estimating that capstone courses are offered in 81 percent of higher education institutions in the United States, Hauhart and Grahe loosely define the course thusly: "As the culminating experience for students' undergraduate careers, the capstone is intended to tie together previous courses in theory, method, and substantive knowledge within most disciplines" (42). In addition to tying everything together, Hauhart and Grahe continue, "Capstone courses also provide students with a final opportunity to demonstrate their mastery of important skills before they graduate" (x). We agree that the most robust capstones seem to be the ones that balance integration of disciplinary knowledge and demonstration of mastered skills. We do not believe all the features and goals identified by Hauhart and Grahe should be considered the gold standard for capstones, irrespective of discipline; however, they do offer a persuasive set of criteria to consider whether writing capstone courses are culminating learning experiences or "a sort of ... half-gesture, a not fully articulated after-thought" (104). We used Hauhart and Grahe's criteria to inform the coding framework of this descriptive study.

Methods

We set out to lay an empirical groundwork for future considerations of what the writing capstone ought to be, include, and do. To that end, we decided to assemble a composite picture of the contemporary writing capstone course based on available course syllabi.[6] During the initial phase of our work, we requested a list of "writing major" programs from Sandra Jamieson (Chair, CCCC Committee on the Major in Writing and Rhetoric), generated a contact list from the 141 programs identified by CCCC, and visited institutional websites to verify, or identify, a point of contact recommended by, and active, in CCCC.[7] After identifying 133 institutions with a writing major, we emailed the contacts to request materials. After two rounds of queries, we collected 54 capstone syllabi from 44 institutions (see Appendix B).[8] We conducted a content analysis of these syllabi using a coding scheme informed by the features identified as typical by Hauhart and Grahe (see Table 1). Discussion of assignments and projects is outside the scope of this article to maintain our focus on the broader features of the course: course descriptions, course outcomes, and assigned major readings.

Table 1: Findings

Programs	% of Total Syllabi	N Syllabi	N Institutions
Writing Major	61	33	27
Emphasis, track, concentration, or option	31.5	17	15
Certificate programs	7.5	4	2

Program Types	% of Total Syllabi	N Syllabi	N Institutions
Professional/Technical Writing (PTW)	29.6	16	15
Rhetoric & Writing (RW)	26	14	12

	%	N	N
Rhetoric & Writing (RW) and Professional/Technical Writing (PTW)	16.7	9	6
Creative Writing (CW)	11.1	6	5
Creative Writing (CW) and Professional/Technical Writing (PTW)	7.4	4	2
General Writing	3.7	2	2
Literature and Writing	3.7	2	1
Creative Writing (CW) and Literature	1.8	1	1

Course Types	% of Total Syllabi	N Syllabi	N Institutions
Culminating Capstone (per H&G)	57	31	24
Senior seminars	17	9	7
Portfolio workshops	13	7	7
Creative writing workshops	9	5	4
Thesis	2	1	1
Internship or a thesis	2	1	1

Stated Purposes	% of Total Syllabi	N Syllabi	N Institutions
Career Preparation	24.1	13	13
Graduate School	20.4	11	9
Career Preparation and Graduate School	20.4	11	11
Graduate School and Publication	11.1	6	3
Unclear	11	6	5
Other	9.3	5	2
Publication	3.7	2	1

Findings

Capstone courses vary widely by department, instructor, and even multiple class sections with the same instructor. Thus, we note quantities of both syllabi and their origin institutions. We do not venture into claims about how a given department teaches the writing capstone. Rather, the syllabi provided to us suggest how the course is presented, taught, and valued in conjunction with particular writing curricula; these inferences, in turn, provide useful insight into how the writing capstone is approached across the country and in different institutional contexts.

Geographically, for example, the institutions in our sample are concentrated in the Northeast and lacking in the Southwest, but most of the United States is represented (see Appendix B for the full list). Approximately two-thirds of the institutions in our study are public and one-third is private (see Table 2). Specifically, our data set includes 32 syllabi from 28 public institutions; of these public-institution syllabi, 16 are from 15 state or state-related institutions, 9 from as many research institutions, 3 from as many public land-grant universities, 3 from a public liberal arts university, and 1 from a community college.[9] In addition, 22 syllabi are from 16 private institutions. Of these, 16 syllabi are from 11 liberal arts universities and colleges, 4 are from 3 religiously affiliated intuitions, and 2 are from as many research universities. Combining public and private institutions, our data set includes 17 syllabi from 11 liberal arts institutions and 10 from as many research institutions. The syllabi are dated from 2011 to Spring 2018 with the majority (38 of the 48 dated syllabi) falling between 2016 and 2018.

Table 2: Institution Types

Institution Type	N	Percentage
Public	28	64
State or State-related	15	34
Research	9	20
Land-grant	3	7
Liberal Arts	3	7
Community College	1	2
Private	16	36
Liberal Arts	11	25
Religious	3	7
Research	2	5

These capstones function within and across a variety of degree plans. The vast majority of syllabi, 91 percent, are intended for courses to be taken exclusively by writing students, as opposed to capstones designed for all English majors (regardless of focus area) working individually in their respective fields. Not surprisingly, 61 percent of syllabi cap off a writing major, and 31.5 percent are part of an emphasis, track, concentration, or option (plus four syllabi come from two certificate programs). Concerning the sub-specialties within writing majors, we categorized the syllabi in three groups—Rhetoric & Writing (RW), Professional/Technical Writing (PTW), and Creative Writing (CW)—although we identified a small number as General Writing, Literature and Writing, and Literature and Creative Writing. Most of the syllabi emphasized PTW (30 percent), RW (26 percent), and a combined focus on RW and PTW (17 percent).[10] Less common capstones include CW, a dual focus on PTW and CW, General Writing, Literature and Writing, and Literature and CW.

Most syllabi we studied clearly demarcated their "course descriptions" from their "learning outcomes," the former as the initial paragraph(s) below the catalog information, the latter appearing as a bullet list below the course description; however, these lists sometimes included additional description of the course or of assignments, and the above paragraph(s) sometimes contained learning outcomes. We therefore coded based on the presence/absence of descriptions and outcomes no matter where they appeared in the documents.

Analysis

Ultimately, we document here what many of us had surmised over the past decade based on conversations with colleagues and the emerging scholarship on the writing major: these courses appear to meet the needs of their respective programs, sending newly minted writing majors off to the workforce or graduate school. Programs appear to offer a mostly culminating learning experience that combines elements of traditional capstone courses, professional internships, extensive research projects, and student portfolios. A majority of the courses—57 percent—match many of the features for which we were looking (see Table 2). Based on our reading of these documents, many capstones, however, only approximate what Hauhart and Grahe would call a *true capstone* course, such as senior-level courses dedicated to longer pieces of writing (e.g., creative writing workshops) or more advanced content (e.g., special-topic seminars). In total, 17 percent of syllabi are senior seminars, 13 percent are portfolio workshops, 9 percent are creative writing workshops, 2 percent require a thesis, and 2 percent can be either an internship or a thesis. While the discipline appears to be generally accomplishing its curricular goals through the capstone course, we should consider whether we are missing key opportunities to highlight the course as a culminating learning experience. Stated purposes, goals, and descriptions as well as course learning outcomes could be more clearly articulated, and skills development might be overemphasized. Rather than just echoing the learning outcomes from introductory courses (e.g., "Demonstrate skill in revising, editing, designing, and critical thinking"), capstone syllabi could instead take a broader view of curriculum (e.g., "integrate the skills and knowledge acquired throughout the program of study into a portfolio of diverse texts for sharing and showcasing to the university community and beyond"). After all, the inclusion of integrative learning is really what distinguishes the capstone course from others. In addition, we should consider other opportunities around required readings. While our descriptive study reflects the diversity of writing capstones and majors, we hope that the range of options prompts future consideration of, and deliberation about, what readings will support integrative learning.

Course Descriptions

The syllabus is an important, if not the most important, text that students are given for understanding the capstone course. It needs to clearly articulate to students the purpose and components of the capstone (Hauhart and Grahe 193-94). After all, Anis S. Bawarshi and Mary Jo Reiff refer to the syllabus as a "meta-genre," setting the parameters for all other texts produced in and for a course (94, 99). It is worth emphasizing that we should dedicate extensive time and energy into getting the language just right in this meta-genre to best represent the course to our multiple audiences—students, colleagues, and administrators. Course descriptions, often presented as a paragraph or two on the first page of the syllabus, are an opportunity to engage readers and clearly explain the purposes, goals, and approach of the course and to reinforce audience understanding of the capstone's role in the curriculum.[11]

We found that preparation for life post-graduation is the most commonly stated purpose for these syllabi, the specifics of which depend largely on sub-specialty. Twenty-four percent of syllabi clearly aim to prepare students for entering the workforce, 20 percent prepare students to apply to graduate programs, and 20 percent prepare students for entering the workforce and/or applying to graduate school (depending on the future plans and goals of individual students). The future-oriented purposes in 64 percent of the syllabi, then, pertain to career preparation and/or graduate school. A syllabus from Boise State, for example, asks students to "[p]roduce a professional writing portfolio to show potential employers or gain admission to graduate school." Portfolios in the PTW capstone at John Carrol are "expected to demonstrate … readiness to transition from college to the workplace and/or to gradate school." Each of these programs require students to look to their futures and attempt to prepare them for the next steps ahead.

Not surprisingly, there is a strong correlation between professional development and Professional/Technical Writing (PTW): 77 percent of the career-preparation syllabi are PTW, whereas none of the graduate-school syllabi are PTW-only capstones. Generally, capstones in Rhetoric & Writing (RW) and RW-PTW swayed more toward graduate-school preparation or offered a balanced focus between the workforce and graduate school. Eighty-eight percent of the syllabi that aim to prepare students for the workforce, graduate school, or both are PTW, RW, and RW- PTW. In contrast, we observed that capstones intended to prepare students for potential publication in some way (in conjunction with either career prep or grad school) were more likely to be Creative Writing (CW) capstones. For example, the CW capstone at Eastern Mennonite asks students to "devote their time and talents to creating a coherent collection of work (or single longer work) appropriate for graduate application and publication in literary or professional venues."

The more compelling, comprehensive course descriptions, however, clearly introduce the capstone as a culminating experience during which students reflect on their past learning with a vision of their post-graduation future. For example, a syllabus from Montana State introduces the writing capstone like this:

> "Senior Seminar." "Capstone." "Research Seminar." Whatever you like to call it, it's the place where you Put It All Together (it *all* being whatever you've been learning along the way), where you demonstrate your ability to Write Big Things…, where we make sure you have the tools and habits to make your way in the world as A Writer…, and where you demonstrate what your years in the major have let you learn and produce, via a professional online portfolio.

This description, in our opinion, effectively frames the course. It engages the student and articulates a clear set of past- ("what you've been learning along the way") and future-oriented ("to make your way in the world as A Writer") purposes for the course.

As effective as such examples may be, we found that only 48 percent of the syllabi collected announce themselves or strongly present themselves as culminating learning experiences, despite the prevailing wisdom that culmination is the defining characteristic of the capstone course. While some course catalogs on program websites refer to the course as the culmination of the curriculum, many of the syllabi do not do so explicitly. One consequence of a professional-development understanding of the capstone is the risk that the course could be regarded by students (and perhaps even faculty) as just a portfolio workshop on the students' way out the door. Articulating through the course description how the capstone course is intended to be more than a professional development after-thought is one way capstone instructors can avoid undercutting the broader takeaways of the course.

Course Outcomes

Course learning outcomes, much like the syllabus itself, are also a kind of meta-genre providing "the shared vocabulary for assigning, producing, reflecting on, and assessing student writing" (Bawarshi and Reiff 94). Enumerating the specific demonstrable skills and knowledge that students will develop in capstone courses communicates to students what they will be able to do and know in completing the course. Our analysis of collected syllabi reminds us that a bulleted list does not a set of learning outcomes make; many of the learning outcomes listed are actually descriptions of assignments (e.g., "Launch a credible professional portfolio in an online space"). Similarly, just because a course description includes culminating language does not automatically mean that culmination is being assessed. Learning outcomes—when they are included—reveal upfront to students how a program defines *culminating*, how exactly the capstone provides coherence and justification for the rest of the curriculum.

While less than half of all syllabi collected present their courses as culminating learning experiences, less than half of *those* list, or otherwise identify, the integration of disciplinary knowledge as a learning outcome.[12] Put another way, only 22 percent of the collected syllabi appear to define *culminating* as integrative. Many higher-education researchers identify the capstone as a key opportunity for integrative learning: as Jillian Kinzie affirms, "From their inception . . . capstones were intended to foster integration" (29). Moreover, the Association of American Colleges and Universities' Integrative Learning V.A.L.U.E. Rubric defines integrative learning as "an understanding and a disposition that a student builds across the curriculum and co-curriculum, from making simple connections among ideas and experiences to synthesizing and transferring learning to new, complex situations within and beyond the campus" ("Integrative"). The values of integrative learning certainly align with our existing discussion of capstones, but based on our sample, those values may perhaps play out more in the classroom than in the written documents that support it.

Rebecca S. Nowacek similarly discusses integrative learning in *Agents of Integration: Understanding Transfer as a Rhetorical Act*, identifying it as "a broad range of connections between classes and curricular activities" and subsuming integrative learning under the broader concept of transfer (2). The ideal type of integration is "successful integration," which describes "those instances in which students consciously see a connection and successfully sell it to their audience" (41). Successful integration of learning and knowledge occurs when a student is consciously aware of, and has the discursive tools to articulate, a connection between contexts—and can effectively convey this connection to an audience as such. Such an achievement reflects a rhetorical act of metacognition. In the context of a capstone course, students could be explicitly asked to practice "successful integration" in any number of discursive formations: by making connections and insights across the writing curriculum and articulating those connections for their instructor in assignments such as a semester-long project and reflective essays.

Successful (or integrative) learning in the capstone can and should play a role, but we found that only one in four syllabi we examined articulated an integrative learning outcome. Substantive learning outcomes include those from a Ball State syllabus, which asked students to "reflect upon their development as readers, writers and critical thinkers and to summarize and synthesize the skills they have learned through their education as English majors." In a Montana State capstone, students' work on a semester-length project, complete extensive readings, and pursue professional development in order to "convince you and me that you have done your work in this major, and that it has done its work in you." Writing students in a Washington State capstone probe the digital transformation of English, "explor[ing] how the skills and approaches that English majors have learned studying literature, rhetoric, and creative writing can engage the complexities and opportunities of digital technologies." And writing majors in a University of Central Florida course "reflect on disciplinary identity, possible career trajectories, and transferrable strategies for writing in their lives." These learning outcomes show that integrative learning can be presented in various ways: by reflecting on previous coursework as well as synthesizing and applying curricular knowledge to new contexts, situations, and topics in greater depth than in other courses.

While there is value in including the development of key skills for writing majors as a capstone outcome alongside synthesizing the knowledge gained from other courses, we are wary of the overwhelming emphasis on skills via the quantity of skills outcomes. The most commonly stated learning outcomes we found were the development of various cognitive and rhetorical skills (e.g., critical thinking, writing, revising, speaking, presenting). Compared to the 22 percent that list integration of disciplinary knowledge as an outcome, 54 percent list at least one learning outcome that can be described as skills development. The skills outcome appears most frequently in syllabi for PTW, RW, and RW-PTW capstones, although CW, General Writing, and hybrid Literature/Writing capstones also listed skills-development outcomes. For example, the learning outcomes on one syllabus include the following:

Demonstrate skill in revising, editing, designing, and critical thinking; Demonstrate skill in textual analysis; Conduct academic research using primary and secondary sources; Collaborate with others … Apply stylistic and rhetorical analysis … Significantly revise a text [for a] … new argument.

Many of these outcomes echo those of intermediate, if not introductory, composition courses, which makes sense because writers should be continually honing these skills. These outcomes do *implicitly* ask students to practice metacognition but there should also be reflective, integrative language regarding what the mastery of these skills means—the kind of successful integration characteristic of a capstone course. Undergraduate majors at the end of their studies should continue to develop as lifelong learners, but an emphasis on skills acquisition should be presented alongside an equal emphasis on the conscious knowledge of their integration. Without a push for metacognition, emphasizing further skills development alone reinforces the perception of the capstone as *just another course* and misses the opportunity for integrating the learning that comprises the degree.

Readings

Despite the natural emphasis in a capstone course on assignments and semester-long projects, many capstone courses have "common reading lists" (Hauhart and Grahe 53). In our sample, a majority of syllabi—76 percent—list required readings, such as a stylebook or textbook and/or scholarly and popular-press articles. The majority of the textbooks we found are either general writing-related textbooks or RW-related textbooks. Among these readings, there is little consensus on what should be required reading, reflecting the diversity of writing capstones and majors, though some textbooks appear multiple times. For example, textbooks that appear on two or more syllabi include *Portfolio Keeping: A Guide for Students* by Nedra Reynolds and Elizabeth Davis (3rd edition), and Rich Rice (2nd edition); *On Writing: A Memoir of the Craft* by Stephen King; *The Non-Designer's Design Book* by Robin Williams; Aristotle's *Poetics*; and the *MLA Handbook for Writers of Research Papers*. We include the full list of titles in Appendix A to illustrate the breadth of titles in different areas.

Reviewing the readings in this sample reveals opportunities to think strategically about the capstone's place in the writing curriculum. While we would be loath to prescribe a canon of capstone texts, we are encouraged to see the emergence of works designed specifically for our undergraduate writing majors and hope to see similar energies devoted to further textbooks, readers, and open-access resources. For example, while not assigned as reading in any of the syllabi collected, we are heartened by the publication of textbooks designed for undergraduate writing research, such as Lynée Lewis Gaillet and Michelle F. Eble's *Primary Research and Writing: People, Places, and Spaces* (2016) and Joyce Kinkead's *Researching Writing: An Introduction to Research Methods* (2016), the latter explicitly identifying its usefulness for students "undertaking capstone or thesis projects that focus on writing" (xvii). As Kinkead explains, "Capstone experiences in the baccalaureate may include a culminating portfolio, honors thesis, research grant, conference proposal, design project, or exhibition. The goal is for the student writer to move from general academic writing to career-driven tasks" (96). Marshaling our disciplinary resources toward a clearer understanding of the informed approaches to the capstone experience may help us move the academic writing major into a clearer curricular space for careers after graduation, whatever they might be, and the diverse publics for which they might write (Ervin).

Conclusions and Recommendations

As we suspected at the outset, the writing capstone largely appears designed to meet the needs of both writing majors (the students) and the writing major (the curricula). For the most part, our snapshot of the course does not reveal "a sort of . . . half-gesture, a not fully articulated after-thought" (Hauhart and Grahe 104). Based on a holistic assessment of the course descriptions, learning outcomes, and readings, the writing capstone is, primarily, a qualitatively different course from the rest of the curriculum, neither just another course nor a professional-development after-thought.

Despite the general trend toward capstones being truly culminating, we see opportunities to solidify the strengths and innovations in capstone course design and identify areas for improvement. Based on our understanding of capstone research and our analysis of writing major capstones across the country, we think programs aspiring to align their capstone courses with common disciplinary practices might consider the following recommendations.

- Writing-program administrators and capstone instructors should invest ample time, energy, and deliberation in the design of capstone syllabi for all stakeholders in the course.
- Syllabi should foreground and clarify the goals, purposes, learning outcomes, and roles the capstone course plays as a culminating experience for students and all that entails.
- The capstone course should be articulated within the program design of the major, clarifying the aims and outcomes of the degree they are completing.

- The context of the course should be more broadly situated in the field(s) it serves, whether RW, PTW, or CW.

The course readings and assignments should be framed within these contexts for students to orient their thinking beyond the singular course experience and reinforce the culminating aspirations of the capstone. While these features are undoubtedly present in capstone courses beyond the syllabus document, we believe that the focus on syllabi can be a touchstone for program-level and larger disciplinary discussions about the major, making our tacit understanding of the capstone visible for all stakeholders. Along the way, we need to ensure that the capstone is not the sole venue for connections across the major: "If we want students who vary in abilities, backgrounds, identities, and dispositions to make meaningful connections between ideas in the major, the opportunity for that connection-making can't be delayed until the capstone course" (Hall et al.).

We can certainly continue to design capstone courses based on how they have been designed in the past or how colleagues at neighboring institutions design theirs, but we should also work toward developing a clearer set of common-practice resources for the writing capstone course while simultaneously embracing the work of other disciplines—those that have begun this work already (e.g., sociology, psychology, communication, education)—to inform the way we envision and implement our culminating course. We should account for the distinctions not just regarding whether an internship should "count" as a capstone course (Balzhiser and McLeod 428),[13] but to what extent the writing capstone should adhere to, or depart from, the features identified by Hauhart and Grahe. The question becomes: How can the writing capstone retain our principles and best practices while we also, taking stock of research on the capstone across the disciplines, seize opportunities to better present, articulate, design, teach, and theorize this course's place in the writing major and the discipline? Moving forward, we believe writing faculty should continue to question—intentionally, reflexively, and collaboratively—how we present these culminating experiences for our majors through asking questions such as:

- What are the goals of the capstone?
- How does the curriculum prepare students to undertake the capstone course?
- Who will teach it?
- How much autonomy will each instructor be permitted?
- Will it be a single course or a sequence?
- Who will be eligible to take it?
- How will the readings support the learning outcomes and goals?
- How often will it be revisited for potential redesign?

- How will we research the capstone's current effectiveness and lasting impact for alumni?[14]
- Will current writing majors have the opportunity to contribute to course design?

Future research needs to examine the capstone assignments and semester-long projects in greater detail because, especially for research-based capstones, such projects are often the most important deliverable and the central focus of the course. Indeed, the inherent difficulty of discussing the capstone course is that it is designed to facilitate individualized, student-selected projects. In the same way that T.J. Geiger II differentiates between the writing major as curriculum and writing majors as students (108), we value the distinction between the writing capstone course and the writing capstone projects created by students. We envision future work that considers the student side of the equation: reviewing student artifacts created in these capstone classes and interviewing them about their experiences. Familiar with the truisms of distinguishing product from process—apparatus from practice—we entered this discussion realizing that an examination of syllabi could appear at cross purposes for understanding the writing capstone as it actually plays out in the lives of our students. However, as always, we must be mindful of the parameters we set for, and present to, our students. We need to ensure that the syllabus enables students the flexibility to pursue rewarding, interesting, and important lines of inquiry while also providing productive pathways to guide their creativity, critical thought, and rhetorical adaptability.

Notes

1. *Minefield of Dreams: Triumphs and Travails of Independent Writing Programs* (2016) offers more recent glimpses into capstone courses as examples or touchstones for local programmatic concerns—unfortunately without broader discussion of the role of the capstone itself (see Royer and Schendel; MacDonald et al.; Rhoades et al.; Thaiss et al.; and Kearns and Turner).

2. More than half of the contributors to *What We Are Becoming* (2010) mention capstone courses, with some instances appearing in the context of program designs (see Brooks et al.; Lowe and Macauley; Baker and Henning; Courtney et al.). . . . Presciently, Susan H. McLeod concludes in the afterword, "Once we have begun to discuss outcomes, we can then discuss what the gateway course to the major should be . . . and what the capstone course or experience should be" (288).

3. In their pioneering framework for an advanced writing curriculum in *Coming of Age: The Advanced Writing Curriculum* (2000), Shamoon et al. posit a configuration of courses that "provide writing students with a historical and theoretical awareness of writing as a discipline; that prepare students for careers as writers; and that prepare them for using writing as a means of participating in the public sphere" (xv). In doing so, they implicate capstone experiences rooted variously in theory, practice,

research, and career preparation. In their contributions to the collection, H. Brooke Hessler discusses a capstone course in which writing majors "collaborate with community members to identify and fulfill opportunities for contributing to constructive communication practices" (Hessler); Libby Miles describes her publishing capstone course for a professional and creative writing emphasis within an English major (CD, para. 5); and Kathleen McCormick and Donald C. Jones describe a capstone that integrates reading and writing based on composition theory, literacy, and cultural studies.

4. For exceptions in communication, see Rosenberry and Vicker, and in religious studies, see Upson-Saia.

5. See Hoffman, for example.

6. Gries has already begun making the case for ways the writing capstone course can serve larger rhetorical, civic goals for students.

7. We used the CCCC list as opposed to the NSW list because it contains a complete list (i.e., no anonymous responses).

8. Two capstones were eliminated from our total because they were actually literary studies or communication studies syllabi. When multiple syllabi were provided as part of a multi-semester capstone sequence, we counted each as one syllabus/course.

9. All but one institution in our study is a four-year college or university. The outlier—Northern Virginia Community College—may be one of only a few community colleges that offer a writing capstone, which suggests that the role of the capstone course in two-year writing programs should be explored in future scholarship on writing-major curricula. We included NVCC in our study, despite its outlier status, because our aim was to document current practices across all institutions (to the extent that we could collect writing-capstone syllabi volunteered from across the country).

10. Some capstones emphasized one field of writing studies while being in a degree plan in another field.

11. Just as it is important to clearly explain for students that the capstone is a culminating learning experience, it is important that syllabi (if applicable) explain that the student deliverables in the capstone are used for programmatic/departmental assessment because it can help give students a clear sense of the larger purpose of the course. Despite this, only four syllabi from three institutions explicitly state that the capstone is used for assessment purposes. Of course, we suspect that more than two of these capstone courses are indeed used for internal assessment.

12. One syllabus required integrated learning for a minor assignment but was not overall a culmination of the curriculum.

13. Balzhiser and McLeod noted "some debate" among the members of the CCCC Committee on the Major in Rhetoric and Composition about whether the for-credit internship "counts" as a capstone (428).

14. See Weisser and Grobman's survey work with writing majors, which led to changes in their capstone course design (55). They write, "To better understand the ways in which their undergraduate programs shaped and influenced those alumni and how those alumni might re-shape and influence our programs, it is important to speak with them directly, through interviews, surveys, and questionnaires" (41).

Works Cited

Alexander, Kara, et al. "Approaching the (Re)Design of Writing Majors: Contexts of Research, Forms of Inquiry, and Recommendations for Faculty." *Composition Studies*, vol. 47, no. 1, pp. 16-37.

Baker, Lori, and Teresa Henning. "Writing Program Development and Disciplinary Integrity: What's Rhetoric Got to Do with It?" *What We Are Becoming: Developments in Undergraduate Writing Majors*, edited by Greg A. Giberson and Thomas A. Moriarty, Utah State UP, 2010, pp. 153-76.

Balzhiser, Deborah, and Susan H. McLeod. "The Undergraduate Writing Major: What Is It? What Should It Be?" *College Composition and Communication*, vol. 61, no. 3, 2010, pp. 415-33.

Bawarshi, Anis S., and Mary Jo Reiff. *Genre: An Introduction to History, Theory, Research, and Pedagogy*. Parlor Press and the WAC Clearinghouse, 2010.

Bradley, Erin, et al. "Coauthoring the Curriculum: Student Voices and the Writing Major." *Composition Studies*, vol. 43, no. 2, 2015, pp. 172-76.

Brooks, Randy, Peiling Zhao, and Carmella Braniger. "Redefining the Undergraduate English Writing Major: An Integrated Approach at a Small Comprehensive University." *What We Are Becoming: Developments in Undergraduate Writing Majors*, edited by Greg A. Giberson and Thomas A. Moriarty, Utah State UP, 2010, pp. 32-49

Committee on the Major in Rhetoric and Composition. "Writing Majors at a Glance." Conference on College Composition and Communication, NCTE, 2009.

Courtney, Jennifer, Deb Martin, and Diane Penrod. "The Writing Arts Major: A Work in Process." *What We Are Becoming: Developments in Undergraduate Writing Majors*, edited by Greg A. Giberson and Thomas A. Moriarty, Utah State UP, 2010, pp. 243-59.

DelliCarpini, Dominic. "Re-Writing the Humanities: The Writing Major's Effect upon Undergraduate Studies in English Departments." *Composition Studies*, vol. 35, no. 1, 2007, pp. 15-36.

Ervin, Elizabeth. "English 496: Senior Seminar in Writing." *Composition Studies*, vol. 26, no. 1, 1998, pp. 37-57.

Everett, Justin, and Cristina Hanganu-Bresch. *A Minefield of Dreams: Triumphs and Travails of Independent Writing Programs*. The WAC Clearinghouse, 2017.

Gaillet, Lynée Lewis, and Michelle Eble. *Primary Research and Writing: People, Places, and Spaces*. Routledge, 2015.

Geiger II, T.J. "An Intimate Discipline? Writing Studies, Undergraduate Majors, and Relational Labor." *Composition Studies*, vol. 43, no. 2, 2015, pp. 92-112.

Giberson, Greg A., and Thomas A. Moriarty, editors. *What We Are Becoming: Developments in Undergraduate Writing Majors*. Utah State University Press, 2010.

Gladstein, Jill, and Brandon Fralix. "2017 Four-Year Institution Survey." The National Census of Writing, 2017, writingcensus.swarthmore.edu/survey/4/year/2017.

Gries, Laurie E. "Writing to Assemble Publics: Making Writing Activate, Making Writing Matter." *College Composition and Communication*, vol. 70, no. 3, 2019, pp. 327-55.

Grobman, Laurie, and Joyce Kinkead, eds. *Undergraduate Research in English Studies*, NCTE, 2010.

Hall, R. Mark, Mikael Romo, and Elizabeth Wardle. "Teaching and Learning Threshold Concepts in a Writing Major: Liminality, Dispositions, and Program Design." *Composition Forum*, vol. 38, 2018, compositionforum.com/issue/38/threshold.php.

Hauhart, Robert C., and Jon E. Grahe. *Designing and Teaching Undergraduate Capstone Courses*. Jossey-Bass, 2015.

Hessler, H. Brooke. "Constructive Communication: Community-Engagement Writing." *Coming of Age: The Advanced Writing Curriculum*, edited by Shamoon et al., Heinemann Boynton/Cook, 2000. CD-ROM.

Hoffman, Harvey F. *The Engineering Capstone Course: Fundamentals for Students and Instructors*. Springer, 2014.

"Integrative and Applied Learning VALUE Rubric." Association of American Colleges and Universities, aacu.org/value/rubrics/integrative-learning.

Jamieson, Sandra. "The Vertical Writing Curriculum: The Necessary Core of Liberal Arts Education." *Composition(s) in the New Liberal Arts*, edited by Joanna Castner Post and James A. Inman, Hampton Press, 2009, pp. 159-84.

Kearns, Judith, and Brian Turner. "An Outsider's Perspective: Curriculum Design and Strategies for Sustainability in a Canadian IWP." *A Minefield of Dreams: Triumphs and Travails of Independent Writing Programs*, edited by Justin Everett and Christina Hanganu-Bresch, The WAC Clearinghouse, 2017, pp. 43-62.

Kinzie, Jillian. "Taking Stock of Capstones and Integrative Learning." *Peer Review*, vol. 15, no. 4, 2013, pp. 27-30.

Lowe, Kelly, and William Macauley. "'Between the Idea and the Reality . . . Falls the Shadow': The Promise and Peril of a Small College Writing Major." *What We Are Becoming: Developments in Undergraduate Writing Majors*, edited by Greg A. Giberson and Thomas A. Moriarty, Utah State UP, 2010, pp. 81-97.

MacDonald, W. Brock, Margaret Procter, and Andrea L. Williams. "Integrating Writing into the Disciplines: Risks and Rewards of an Alternative Independent Writing Program." *A Minefield of Dreams: Triumphs and Travails of Independent Writing Programs*, edited by Justin Everett and Christina Hanganu-Bresch, The WAC Clearinghouse, 2017, pp. 111-32.

McCormick, Kathleen, and Donald C. Jones. "Developing a Professional and Technical Writing Major That Integrates Composition Theory, Literacy Theory, and Cultural Studies." *Coming of Age: The Advanced Writing Curriculum*, edited by Shamoon et al., Heinemann Boynton/Cook, 2000. CD-ROM.

McCullen, Maurice L. "Looking Backwards: Advanced Composition to Freshman English." *Freshman English News*, vol. 4, no. 2, 1975, pp. 1-2.

McLeod, Susan H. "Afterword." *What We Are Becoming: Developments in Undergraduate Writing Majors*, edited by Greg A. Giberson and Thomas A. Moriarty, Utah State UP, 2010, pp. 287-89.

Melonçon, Lisa, and Joanna Schreiber. "Advocating for Sustainability: A Report on and Critique of the Undergraduate Capstone Course." *Technical Communication Quarterly*, vol. 27, no. 4, pp. 322-35.

Miles, Libby. "Working in the Publishing Industries." *Coming of Age: The Advanced Writing Curriculum*, edited by Shamoon et al., Heinemann Boynton/Cook, 2000. CD-ROM.

Padgett, Ryan D., and Cindy A. Kilgo. *2011 National Survey of Senior Capstone Experiences: Institutional- Level Data on the Culminating Experience*. Columbia: National Resource Center for the First Year Experience and Students in Transition, University of South Carolina, 2012.

Peeples, Timothy, Paula Rosinski, and Michael Strickland. "Chronos and Kairos, Strategies and Tactics: The Case of Constructing Elon University's Professional Writing and Rhetoric Concentration." *Composition Studies*, vol. 35, no. 1, 2007, pp. 57-76.

Rhoades, Georgia, Kim Gunter, and Elizabeth Carroll. "Still Trying to Break Our Bonds: Contingent Faculty, Independence, and Rhetorics from Below and Above." *A Minefield of Dreams: Triumphs and Travails of Independent Writing Programs*, edited by Justin Everett and Christina Hanganu-Bresch, The WAC Clearinghouse, 2017, pp. 133-48.

Rosenberry, Jack, and Lauren A. Vicker. "Capstone Courses in Mass Communication Programs." *Journalism and Mass Communication Educator*, vol. 61, no. 3, 2006, pp. 267-83.

Royer, Dan, and Ellen Schendel. "Coming into Being: The Writing Department at Grand Valley State University in its 13th Year." *A Minefield of Dreams: Triumphs and Travails of Independent Writing Programs*, edited by Justin Everett and Christina Hanganu-Bresch, The WAC Clearinghouse, 2017, pp. 23-42.

Schermer, Timothy, and Simon Gray. *The Senior Capstone: Transformative Experiences in the Liberal Arts*. Teagle Foundation, 2012.

Shamoon, Linda K., et al., editors. *Coming of Age: The Advanced Writing Curriculum*. Heinemann Boynton/Cook, 2000.

Sylvia, Cami, and Michael J. Michaud. "Looking into Writing." *Composition Studies*, vol. 43, no. 2, 2015, pp. 186-89.

Thaiss, Chris, et al. "Part of the Fabric of the University: From First Year through Graduate School and Across the Disciplines." *A Minefield of Dreams: Triumphs and Travails of Independent Writing Programs*, edited by Justin Everett and Christina Hanganu-Bresch, The WAC Clearinghouse, 2017, pp. 149-76.

Upson-Saia, Kristi. "The Capstone Experience for the Religious Studies Major." *Teaching Theology and Religion*, vol. 16, no. 1, 2013, pp. 3-17.

Weisser, Christian, and Laurie Grobman. "Undergraduate Writing Majors and the Rhetoric of Professionalism." *Composition Studies*, vol. 40, no. 1, 2012, pp. 39-59.

Appendix A: Capstone Textbooks Arranged by Subspecialty

General Writing

- *Portfolio Keeping: A Guide for Students* by Nedra Reynolds and Rich Rice
- *Acts of Revision: A Guide for Writers* by Wendy Bishop and Hans Ostrom
- *Crafting a Life in Essay, Story, Poem* by Donald M. Murray
- *Understanding Style: Practical Ways to Improve Your Writing* by Joe Glaser
- *Spunk & Bite: A Writer's Guide to Bold, Contemporary Style* by Arthur Plotnik
- *Around the Writer's Block: Using Brain Science to Solve Writer's Resistance* by Rosanne Bane
- *How to Write a B.A. Thesis* by Charles Lipson
- *Rewriting: How to Do Things with Texts* by Joseph Harris
- *Team Writing: A Guide to Working in Groups* by Joanna Wolfe

Rhetoric and Writing (RW)

- *On Writing: A Memoir of the Craft* by Stephen King
- *Poetics* by Aristotle
- *Professional and Public Writing* by Linda S. Coleman and Robert W. Funk
- *Rhetoric: A User's Guide* by John Ramage
- *The History and Theory of Rhetoric* by James A. Herrick
- *The Rhetorical Tradition* by Patricia Bizzell and Bruce Herzberg
- *Still Life with Rhetoric: A New Materialist Approach for Visual Rhetorics* by Laurie E. Gries
- *Rhetorical Criticism: Exploration and Practice* by Sonja K. Foss
- *What Writing Does and How it Does it* by Charles Bazerman and Paul Prior
- *Becoming a Writing Researcher* by Ann Blakeslee and Cathy Fleischer
- *Macroanalysis: Digital Methods and Literary History* by Matthew L. Jockers
- *Rhetoric and the Digital Humanities* by Jim Ridolfo and William Hart-Davidson
- *The Only Grant-Writing Book You'll Ever Need* by Ellen Karsh and Arlen Sue Fox

Professional/Technical Writing (PTW)

- *The Non-Designer's Design Book* by Robin Williams
- *Writing a Professional Life: Stories of Technical Communicators On and Off the Job* by G.J. Savage and D.L. Sullivan
- *Document Design: A Guide for Technical Communicators* by Miles Kimball and Ann R. Hawkins
- *The Non-Designer's Web Book* by Robin Williams and John Tollett
- *Professional Writing and Rhetoric* by Tim Peeples
- *Portfolios for Technical and Professional Communicators* by Herb Smith and Kim Haimes Korn
- *Practical Strategies for Technical Communication* by Mike Markel

Creative Writing (CW)

- *Creative Writer's Handbook* by Jason and Lefcowitz
- *On Writing* by Stephen King (listed twice to reflect use in RW and CW capstones)
- *A Writer's Journey* by Christopher Vogler

Appendix B: Institutions Included in Study

1. Ball State U
2. Boise State U
3. Briar Cliff U
4. Clemson U
5. DePaul U
6. Eastern Mennonite U
7. Eastern Michigan U
8. Eastern Oregon U
9. Georgia State U
10. Grand Valley State U
11. Ithaca College
12. James Madison U
13. John Carrol U
14. Kutztown U of Pennsylvania
15. Metropolitan State U-Denver
16. Michigan State U
17. Mississippi College
18. Missouri State U
19. Montana State U
20. Northern Virginia Community College
21. Northwestern College

22. Oakland U
23. Oral Roberts U
24. Penn State Berks
25. Sacred Heart U
26. Southwest Minnesota State U
27. St. Ambrose U
28. St. Edwards U
29. St. John Fisher College
30. State U of New York at Cortland
31. SUNY Postsdam
32. Syracuse U
33. U of Central Florida
34. U of Idaho
35. U of Minnesota Duluth
36. U of Mount Union
37. U of South Florida
38. U of Wisconsin-La Crosse
39. U of Wisconsin-Stout
40. Washington State U
41. West Chester U of Pennsylvania
42. Western Kentucky U
43. Worcester Polytechnic Institute
44. York College of Pennsylvania

"Sometimes I Forget I'm in an Online Class!" Why Place Matters for Meaningful Student Online Writing Experiences

Felicita Arzu Carmichael

This essay argues that "place" and "space" are a critical conceptual framework in the online writing classroom and leads students to have meaningful writing experiences. Drawing on what Eodice et al. describe as "personal connection" for writing students, the author invites online writing instructors to pay attention to how the concepts of "place" and "space"—as both natural/material and constructed/metaphorical—might inform our disciplinary understanding of online writing instruction.

Introduction

A few years ago I taught my first fully online writing course. Early in the course, students participated in an activity where I asked them to share their experiences with and expectations of being in an online course. Specifically, I was interested in learning from students what factors contribute to them feeling a sense of belonging to an online course and whether the work they engaged in was meaningful to them. To this end, one of my students posted "sometimes I forget I'm in an online class!" The student went on to share that because there is no physical meeting space, they are not engaged in online courses, especially if they miss reminders for when assignments are due. This student experience seems representative of Mauk's call for the field to pay attention to the "emerging spatial crises in academia" and the effects of this "apparent placelessness" on students (370). Initially, I could not fathom how anyone could forget being enrolled in any course, even if there were no physical meeting room. But then I realized that this student perhaps did not feel a sense of belonging to that particular online course, a sense of belonging which is often attributed to bodies being present in some material space. I also questioned the relationship between a sense of belonging and students' writing experiences. In other words, the student's comment suggests a connection among experience, meaningfulness, and place, which clearly influenced how and if they participated in online courses. This likely connection made me question my own conceptualization of what it means to teach and participate in an online course and whether my course content and pedagogy fostered for students a sense of belonging and meaningful writing experiences.

Fast forward some years later, and I continue to rethink my approaches to online writing instruction (OWI) and the factors that contribute to how my students experience the course.[1] This has become especially complex with the global pandemic shifting most writing instruction to online spaces, a move which heightened my awareness of students' sense of belonging and their constant experiences with technological systems that might problematically suggest a false sense of neutrality. For many students, they were neither prepared for nor oriented toward online learning; yet here we all are. Recognizing that many of my students are already "unsituated in academic space" because "academic space is not an integral part of their intellectual geography" (Mauk 369), I imagine that many students have struggled with thinking of our online class as a classroom, a complex location in and of itself. Instead, and perhaps especially because our class meets primarily asynchronously, I grew concerned that students might perceive the class as simply submitting assignments as opposed to a space where they are immersed in an online writing experience that promotes belongingness and meaningful writing with technologies that produce effects. My institution relies on Moodle as its learning management system (LMS) for teaching and learning, and Moodle is described as a "digital classroom space" (Moodle Policy). This idea of the LMS as a "digital classroom space" is important to how teachers then conceptualize the classroom because it informs how we teach and how our students engage with and in those spaces. Yi-Fu Tuan reminds us that "Space and place are basic components of the lived world; we take them for granted" (3). Of course space and place do not cease to exist when we teach and learn online. In fact, when students learn online, the physical and virtual spaces they simultaneously inhabit become even more impactful toward their writing experiences.

Despite these complexities, I believe that in online classes, we do take place and space for granted. Tuan asserts that we all have a "range of experience of knowledge" (6) when it comes to place. For example, my experiences designing the online class, including the places I inhabit when doing this work and determining which features of the LMS I believe will best support my students in achieving course goals, would be significantly different from my students' experiences engaging in the same course. As Tuan argues, "Experience can be direct and intimate, or it can be indirect and conceptual, mediated by symbols" (6). Even my own experiences with the digital classroom space is mediated by the instructional designers' choices, choices that then mold my and my students' sense of place in the class. Of course, the technology and the experiences of students interacting with these technologies are not mutually exclusive. In fact, my conceptualization of OWI does not exist outside of the technologies and interfaces my students and I rely on. In other words, considering the effects of the materiality of these technologies on my teaching is important because it invites me to be accountable to my students for the inequalities exacerbated by the digital tools with which I ask them to engage.

As writing instruction increasingly gravitates toward virtual spaces due to the global pandemic, OWI warrants a critical consideration of how place and space impact students' writing experience. I argue that place and space form a critical conceptual framework allowing students to engage in "meaningful writing" (Eodice et al., *Meaningful*). Eodice et al. assert that "meaningful writing" occurs when students are invited to (1) tap into the power of personal connection; (2) immerse themselves in what they are thinking, writing, and researching; (3) experience what they are writing as applicable and relevant to the real world; and (4) imagine their future selves. I posit that valuing students' meaning making processes means paying critical attention to the places where this work happens and the technologies with which they engage. Thus to create meaningful writing experiences for my students, I draw specifically on what Eodice et al. describe as "personal connection." This approach to OWI invites students to study how they understand their environments and themselves as writers within it.

There is a need for the field of rhetoric and composition studies to further consider the variety of ways in which scholars might pay attention to how the concepts of "place" and "space"—as both natural/material and constructed/metaphorical—might lead students to have meaningful writing experiences and inform our disciplinary understanding of OWI. In the sections that follow, I first present the disciplinary exigence for this project. I then share how place and space as a critical conceptual framework for OWI responds to the exigence. Next, I discuss the effects of this pedagogical approach on creating meaningful writing experiences for students in my writing course. Lastly, I conclude with implications for adopting such a pedagogical approach.

Disciplinary Exigence

Scholarship on online literacy and writing instruction has increased in recent years (Borgman and McArdle; CCCC; Ehmann and Hewet; GSOLE; ; Kynard; Martinez et al.; Nakamura). Even prior to the global pandemic, Seaman et al.'s 2018 study revealed that distance education enrollments continue to rise despite lower enrollments in higher education. While this evidence is not specific to OWI, it is valuable to scholars in rhetoric and composition studies, especially considering that even prior to the global pandemic, "online courses increasingly are a primary means of instruction for many first year composition students" (CCCC). Because OWI is increasing, scholars in the field have called for more theoretical understandings of what it means to teach online. For example, Ehmann and Hewett call for "viable theories of OWI as a philosophy of writing and as a series of strategies for teaching and learning to write in digital settings" (517). Also, the CCCC Committee for Effective Practices in Online Writing Instruction has revealed that there is a "crucial need for a deeper understanding of OWI." Some scholars have also noted the need for OWI to draw on research-based approaches as opposed to relying on checklists without carefully interrogating them (Oswal and Meloncon).

Online writing instruction, like much of the approach to teaching writing face-to-face (f2f), is rooted in the belief that knowledge is socially constructed (Hewett and Ehmann). While social constructivism provided a theoretical foundation for OWI, the CCCC OWI Statement offer suggestions on "how best to teach writing online" (CCCC). CCCC offers specific examples connected to each principle so that instructors are guided as they make choices about their online writing course. And while the best practices provide a strong support for new and returning instructors, I argue that these principles should also be considered in context of the theories or assumptions that ground them. For example, CCCC explains that "OWI provides an opportunity for teaching various populations in a distinctive instructional setting" (5). More than 20 years ago, however, Cynthia Selfe advised us not only to use technology, but also to think about its implications; it behooves us now to think about this "distinctive instructional setting" and the implications of our actions within this setting. While writing instructors are equipped with practices for teaching online, our field seems to assume that instructors have an awareness of the complexities of this "distinctive instructional setting," including the material conditions that instructors and their students bring to these spaces. To take a case in point: though some f2f pedagogical practices might successfully transfer online as suggested by principle 4, relying solely on this migration might not create meaningful teaching and learning experiences, particularly because instructors won't have considered what these practices mean in a new, online context.

In addition, the Global Society of Online Literacy Educators (GSOLE) devised four principles, with principle 1 indicating that "Online literacy instruction should be universally accessible and inclusive." For GSOLE, attention to accessibility and inclusivity means that "The student-user experience should be prioritized when designing online courses, which includes mobile-friendly content, interaction affordances, and economic needs," among other principles. I focus on this principle because of its attention to the students' experience, a principle which corroborates Eodice et al.'s assertion that these qualities should be built into the course from the outset because they lead to meaningful writing experiences for students.

For example, I worked as a writing program coordinator at my former institution, where one of my major responsibilities was to work with the writing program administrator at the beginning of each school year to organize and execute a one-week orientation for new graduate teaching assistants (GTAs). At one of our orientations, I had conversations with new instructors about what it means to teach first year writing at the institution using Canvas as the LMS. Though most of the new GTAs had used an LMS as a student, only one of the thirteen instructors had used an LMS to teach. In one session, one of the new GTAs asked, "So, do I just use Canvas to have students turn in papers?" I was happy to receive this question because I was certain that many other instructors had a similar understanding of Canvas. Typically instructors use an LMS as a technological tool or an online system with standard functions, such as for posting materials and assignments, grading, and creating discussion forums (Witte). However, the LMS can also serve as a material and metaphorical ecology (or as a complex interface) that produces effects. Thinking of an LMS in this way enables students and teachers to experience how inhabiting virtual spaces--as opposed to simply using them --can yield complicated results (Ulmer). That said, the LMS alone does not account for the complexities in students' learning, especially since students are always shifting between material spaces each time they access the LMS. These always shifting spaces, in turn, affect how they are able to participate in the course. Thus, I contend that the field needs a conceptual framework of place and space for OWI because it provides an opportunity for students to draw on what they bring to the online learning experience, so that this experience, and the writing they do, are meaningful. Drawing on the work of Eodice et al., I contend that place and space as a conceptual framework in OWI creates meaningful writing experiences for students.

Place and Space as a Critical Conceptual Framework

In thinking of place and space as a conceptual framework to create among students a sense of belonging and to engage them in meaningful writing, I draw on key interdisciplinary work in feminist theories, critical and cultural geography, and rhetoric and composition. In *Belonging: a Culture of Place*, bell hooks takes up belonging as a culture of place, emphasizing the effects that different geographic locations have on one's "habits of being" and arguing that a sense of belonging is connected to nature and an inherent relationship with land, especially for black people (13). For hooks, there are significant connections between black people's well-being and the well-being of the earth, between "black self-recovery" and a "renewed relationship to the earth" (40). Elsewhere, in *Ecocomposition: Theoretical and Pedagogical Approaches*, Christian R. Weisser and Sidney I. Dobrin likewise rely on an ecological framework but to examine the field of composition studies. They critically challenge how scholars teach and support students in engaging the material world. For Weisser and Dobrin, ecocomposition is about the relationship between written discourse and the environment (physical and constructed) that it encounters. This is the important work that Nedra Reynolds attends to in *Geographies of Writing*, where she argued that our field needs "material literacy practices that engage with the metaphorical—ways to imagine space—without ignoring places and spaces—the actual locations where writers write, learners learn, and workers work" (3). Corroborating the need for scholars to critically engage the relationship between writing and our environment, Gregory L. Ulmer examines how the internet and technological tools challenge our thinking about writing. In *Internet Invention: From Literacy to Electracy*, Ulmer affirms the importance of rethinking our choices about technology so that we can explore what it means to write in electronic spaces. More specifically, Ulmer invites us to critically consider what it means to inhabit virtual places rather than to simply use them. The effects of inhabiting virtual spaces is central to Lisa Nakamura's arguments in "Feeling Good About Feeling Bad," where she argues that technological platforms have caused material harm to people from historically marginalized groups because of the racism and sexism embedded in these systems in the name of technological advancements.

These field-leading interdisciplinary conversations offer exciting and productive opportunities to understand online literacy and writing instruction, and they also demonstrate why place matters to OWI. When we invite students to study writing through place and space as a conceptual lens, they can learn more about themselves as learners and their sense of belonging to material and constructed spaces. Importantly, students can also learn about how digital technologies create harmful material conditions that impact how they engage in such places and spaces. Geographer Doreen Massey recognizes this dynamic relationship between environment and language, noting that place is "open" and "woven together out of ongoing stories" (131). Massey further explains that what is special about place is a kind of "throwntogetherness," which involves the challenge of negotiating a "here-and-now...and a negotiation which must take place within and between both human and nonhuman" (140). This negotiation within and between the human and nonhuman is what students in online writing classrooms should be asked to consider, primarily because they might not be accustomed to thinking of the complexities of online learning--including how their bodies and the places they inhabit shape the work they (can) do. What they then realize is that place matters. Mauk says it perhaps most succinctly: higher education "is based on an intersection of the material and conceptual, of the real and the imagined" and of students' "interpretation or creation of academic space" (368). Recognizing that online learning has material consequences reveals the dynamic coexistence between material and virtual spaces. My experience is that when teachers design online writing classrooms with place and space as a conceptual framework, it affects the kinds of questions they ask and shifts the kinds of expectations they have about student writing. Experience also tells me that when we invite students to develop or enhance their online literacy, they learn how to navigate through and interact with systems that challenge their thinking about the power embedded in these systems. My goal is for my students to do more than write about place. I strive for my students to pay attention to the kinds of writing they are able to do because of the personal connections they have with the virtual and material places and spaces they inhabit. This is one way to support them in ensuring that writing is meaningful.

Applying Place and Space to an Online Writing Course

Some Background

In fall 2019, I earned an excellence in teaching and learning grant from the Center for Excellence in Teaching and Learning (CETL) at my institution. The purpose of the grant was to redesign a first year writing course and identify the effects of place and space as a conceptual lens on student writing. My hypothesis was that place and space as the conceptual lens through which I ground OWI would make students' writing and learning experiences meaningful by inviting them to leverage personal connections. I also hypothesized that the metacognitive practice of studying place and space as foundational course values would help students become more reflective about the virtual and material places in which they are learning and therefore more successful in responding to the rhetorical contexts in both places.

The majority of writing courses at my current institution are listed as "partially online," which means anywhere from 10%-30% of the course is online. My pilot course, however, was hybrid, so 50%-75% of the course was online. There were 15 students enrolled in this course, and 13 of the 15 consented to participating in this study. During the first two weeks, I met with my students every Monday, Wednesday, and Friday to orient them to the course. Starting in the third week, my students and I met f2f only on Mondays. I was physically present in class on Wednesdays for students who preferred to attend class f2f on that day. Throughout the semester, the same 5-8 students attended f2f class on most Wednesdays while the remaining students attended online. After the third week, Friday classes were fully online for all students. This hybrid course was intentionally designed to account for my students' preference in learning modality. I wanted to be mindful of the spaces and places my students would choose to inhabit each week and the role of technology in their personal choices. Through weekly e-learning logs, which I will discuss later, all my students reflected on these choices to engage with the course either f2f or online on Wednesdays and also how the course's conceptual lens and their own material conditions informed those choices.

Place and space as a critical conceptual framework informed the design and teaching of this hybrid course in order to create meaningful writing experiences for my students. To do this, I

1. provided students with readings that oriented them to a variety of ways of conceptualizing place and space;
2. asked students to write about a place and space that had personal meaning to them and;
3. asked students to continuously reflect on the places and spaces of the course that emerged for them as they write.

The course itself was divided into three units that each ask students to draw personal connections to their experiences, relationships, and topics of interests in a variety of material and virtual places and spaces. Unit 1 was titled "Writing about Self and Place." In this unit, students wrote a personal paper that explored a place that had shaped a particular aspect of their identity. Writing about place is inherently personal, which is one of its strengths; this also accords with studies showing that students' writing is meaningful when they can connect it to personal experiences (Eodice et al.). In Unit 2, "Studying Text and Place," students researched and annotated relevant sources in preparation for the final research project, which was a digital writing project in the form of a public service announcement (PSA). This PSA was about a social issue they cared about that was connected to place and space. In the final unit, Unit 3, students created their PSAs informed by their Unit 2 research. Each unit builds on the one before and each draws on OWI social constructivist's roots. Finally, toward the end of the semester, students created an electronic portfolio, where they reflected on the connections among their three projects and discussed possible areas where the work they did might transfer to other sites. Davidson reminds us that e-portfolios "build ethos" for those who "dwell" in virtual spaces; thus, the e-portfolio provides a space for further self-expression and for students to assess their own meaningful writing experiences.

In the section below, I demonstrate how the "Writing about Self and Place" unit, coupled with the e-learning logs my students wrote throughout the semester, helped create meaningful writing experiences for my students that were grounded in place and space as a conceptual framework. I adapted meaningful writing criteria from three aspects of Eodice et al.'s work: that students are able to "make and extend personal connections to their experiences or histories, their social relationships, and/or subjects and topics for writing"

(320). Drawing on Eodice et al., these personal connections were tied to three forms of influence:

1. individual factors, including the ways they connected to their development as writers, their sense of authorship, their vision of future writing or identities, their desire for self-expression, and their individual experiences;
2. social factors, including family, community, and peers; and
3. students' interests in and passion for the subjects of their writing, and their sense of the importance of those topics (326-327).

Writing about Self, Space, and Place

Asking students to write about themselves as learners whose identities are shaped by the places and spaces they inhabit provides an inherent opportunity for students to have personal connection and engage in meaningful writing. To prepare students for this writing assignment, we read and discussed the introduction to Yi-Fu Tuan's *Space and Place: The Perspective of Experience*. Students grappled with the concepts "space" and "place," drawing from their own experiences with the two and complicating it with Tuan's ideas. Students also read excerpts of Nedra Reynolds's *Geographies of Writing*. Reading Reynolds was intended to challenge students' thinking about spatial metaphors, which I anticipated would show up within their writing. Thinking about spatial metaphors also invited students to engage more critically with online literacy. For example, we discussed how virtual classrooms are often described as online "environments" and online "spaces," concepts which are derived from material places (Reynolds)-- a dynamic repeated in this very article. I wanted students to pay attention to how applying these spatial metaphors without paying attention to their material effects might lead to neglecting their connection. Through the readings, I invited students to pay attention to both the possibilities and the limitations of spatial metaphors. Prior to reading Tuan and Reynolds' work, most students shared that they believed the two concepts were interchangeable. However, the readings equipped them with the language they needed to express their understanding of how space and place shaped them. Students agreed that spaces become places when meaning is applied to them. It is this understanding of place as the relationship between experiences and spaces that my assignment sought to explore.

For example, Jean's description and analysis of growing up in multiple places reflect her contested experiences with place and placelessness. Jean had to spend time in two places due to her parent's separation; of that experience, Jean writes:

> My personal favorite [feature of the house] was the princess stickers I put all over my bedroom that my mother was never able to remove. By the time we moved in 2011, the roof was falling apart, and the house was left with an unfinished bathroom and yard that needed more TLC than anyone was willing to give.

Jean's account highlights the social and family influence of meaningful writing criteria. For Jean, one of the homes she grew up in as a child, specifically her bedroom, was the place that had a significant impact on her. Jean's focus on the wall decor along with the connections she made between the physical changes of the house from past to present emphasizes the "social process" that exists between writing and learning (Eodice et al. 331). Jean further writes:

> Living in a town that had less people than the high school I graduated from meant that people didn't have a lot of experience with other ethnicities. In elementary school, we had less than a handful of kids that identified as a minority, myself included.

When Jean moved to her dad's home city, her experiences with place and self-identity became more evident. Through her writing, I was able to see her shift away from what seemed like a feeling of placelessness in the earlier excerpt toward a sense of place, belonging, and struggle. She continues:

> Being in such a culturally rich city made me get in touch with my Mexican heritage. Whenever I am there I always feel that sense of pride and I am more willing to learn about my culture.

What is notable in Jean's response is the inherent role of racial history and dynamics in a sense of belonging and self identity (hooks). In other words, her sense of belonging to a place is not separate from her racial and ethnic heritage. Jean's experiences in the city her father lived drew her closer to her self identity. Her writing was connected to a combination of family and social factors and her own confrontations with cultural and linguistic identities rooted in place. hooks writes that "geography more so than any other factor shaped [her] destiny," and I see this perspective reflected clearly in Jean's response. Moreover, Jean's awareness of her embodied practices in her dad's home city exemplifies the personal connection that Kynard highlights between geography and language. Drawing on the work of critical geographer Kathrine McKittrick's, Kynard reminds us that geographies are always infused with distinct yet multiple knowledges and language systems: "Since space and place are always much more than just vessels that contain peoples and their social relations, geographies represent connective and connected sites of struggle" (334).

Jean's relationship between cultural identity, language, and place is similar to the importance of individual and community influence on place that three other students in the course discussed. One of these students, Kelsey, attributed a sense of place to her religion. Kelsey wrote:

> Where you live is not what makes it a home, but wherever you are with your family. Learning and experiencing life together, is what made that space become a place that you now call home, whether that being a city, a park that you all go to once a year, or your family's favorite ice cream shop. In the same way, Zion no longer is a building but a people, and a feeling.

In writing about place, Kelsey developed a deeper understanding of her connection to her church community and the feelings that emerge when she is a part of her religious community. Eodice et al. reminds us of the importance of allowing students to draw on those experiences that are integral to their communities because "[d]evaluing personal connections can devalue whole communities of people, their experiences, and their knowledge" (336). What is also evident from Kelsey's response is how she transformed a sense of community from a physical material structure to a feeling that coincides with "learning and experiencing" as she describes it. As Dobrin affirms, how we name and understand places is a rhetorical act informed by ideological assumptions (23). These ideological assumptions, I argue, inform how our students then practice the writing we ask them to do based on the places in and about which they choose to write.

There were also instances when students made connections to place and space that initially seemed superficial, but later revealed more in-depth connections. For example, two students drew connections between place and their field of study. Noah wrote the following:

> My first experience with construction and carpentry was at this cottage, helping build an addition to the deck and creating an entire new enclosure on the side of the cottage facing the water. It seems fitting that now my mark is on our beautiful cottage forever just as it has left a permanent mark on me. [...] That first experience with carpentry is what got me interested in my major of mechanical engineering because it made me realize that drawing out plans and then seeing those plans come to life in some space is one of the greatest feelings in the world.

Noah identified a personal connection between place and his identity as a student, including placing himself within the larger mechanical engineering discourse community. As hooks argues, "We are born and have our being in a place of memory. We chart our lives by everything we remember from the mundane moment to the majestic. We know ourselves through the art and act of remembering" (5). Noah's responses above also show a sense of authorship and a personal connection to a vision of future writing or identities. As Eodice et al. indicate, "we often ignore the role students and their identities and experiences play within the larger discourse community of higher education" (323). Noah's own experiences show this and corroborates Eodice et al.'s assertion that students develop agency when they write about subject matter that is of personal and professional interests to them and that they truly care about. People's experiences in the places they care about is what invites a sense of belonging to other places, and it is the ability to make these connections that makes place and space as a conceptual framework important to OWI.

Like Noah, Jasmine also drew connections between experiences in one place informing choices in another, which led to her field of study. Jasmine wrote:

> I had my senior year ripped away from me, having to spend hours in a courtroom…that courtroom became more than a dingy, small room, it became a stage… It was in this courtroom that I realized my voice really did have an effect. It is when I realized how strong of a person I am. In a small, unfamiliar place, I learned to speak up for what I believe in, and what I know is right.

Jasmine is a nursing student, and in her response, she wrote about how important it was for her to advocate for others who might have had difficult experiences similar to hers. Eodice et al. argue that students having the agency to control their writing and construct their learning is valuable; however, this matters less "amidst the challenges of the social and material conditions they face" (33). Jasmine delved into a difficult past experience and drew a connection between that experience and her current professional goals. What this experience reveals is the connection between place and students' "passion for the subjects of their writing, and their sense of the importance of those topics" (Eodice et al. 326-327). This passion and sense of importance also invites us to recognize the embodiedness of writing and the ways in which teaching and learning environments might problematically reinforce a mind/body binary (Perl).

Reflection on Self, Space, and Place

When we shifted to a more hybrid and online teaching and learning modality after the first few weeks of class, my students and I participated in robust discussions about what it means to inhabit virtual spaces. I drew on Ingold's understanding of place as a way of inhabiting the world, which means living "in the open" where life isn't "contained within bounded places" (1796). Ingold makes an important distinction between what it means to "occupy" the world versus what it means to "inhabit" it. An occupied world, for Ingold, "is furnished with already-existing things. But one that is inhabited is woven from the strands of their continual coming-into-being" (1797). Ingold's views of place are apt in conceptualizing place and space as a lens through which to view OWI because our students tend to "occupy" the online space but not "inhabit" it, especially when the online space is seen as co-identical to the course LMS. However, in conversations with my students, we discussed our online class as a process of "coming-into-being" that requires us to recognize that what matters is not only the LMS through and with which they interact, but also their surroundings and how they experience the course, which is always ever changing.

To respond to this idea, students wrote a weekly e-learning log exploring questions such as:

- What places are you inhabiting as you work through this course? What relationship exists between those places and the work you are able to do online?
- What assumptions do you think the technological interface makes about you, the student, about how you learn? How do these assumptions affect how you engage with the course, your classmates and/or the instructor?
- What places do you take for granted? How does writing about place in an online class help you reassess your relationship to those places?
- What roles/responsibilities are you asked to perform and what roles/responsibilities do you choose to perform in the places you inhabit while working in this course? How do those roles shape your writing online?
- As you inhabit our online classroom, what or who seems to be privileged through the design of the interface with which you engage?

The series of questions I propose for students' logs vary, and they function as possibilities--not directives--for students to consider. The goals of the logs are to support students in developing metacognitive awareness (VanKooten) of writing about place and to reflect on their online learning in relation to place. Importantly, the goal is also to promote deep thinking about how the technological platforms students engage with, including social networking as places and spaces, potentially pose harm to students from historically marginalized groups by exacerbating systemic oppression upon them (Nakamura). For example, prior to the global pandemic, most online students were already accessing their courses from home ("Research in Online Literacy Education"). While it is certain that even more students are now learning from home, the ways in which this happens might be even more complex. Many students are also working from home and have relatives to care for, so how they experience place and interact with the writing course has shifted tremendously. They are moving in between places and roles connected to these places; thus, experiencing places as "woven together out of ongoing stories" (Massey 131). Their backgrounds and motivations for engaging in an online writing course speaks to their culture (St.Amant), a foundational part of their engagement in online courses, especially during the COVID-19 pandemic. It is important that those stories are validated and that students see those stories as an integral part of their writing experience (Martinez).

The e-learning logs my students write invite them to grapple with these ways of being. Notably, while students complete the e-learning logs each week, some have spent more time in the f2f classroom on Wednesdays while others chose to engage with the class virtually for the majority of the week. By asking students to reflect weekly on questions related to place and space, I strive to create a sense of belonging among my students and within the course. I also aim to draw on Weisser and Dobrin's identification of the relationship between written discourse and the constructed environment. For example, in response to one of their e-learning logs, Noah noted the following:

> Writing about place in an online environment really creates a unique challenge that I had never experienced before because my writing is not tied down to one physical location. Now I think about each location when I write and it adds another dimension to how I feel in the place, especially when I am not in class.

Noah's description of online writing as posing a "unique challenge" was tied to his recognition that writing online has material consequences shaped by inhabited places. This idea shows the power of reflection because it demonstrates that students can develop a deep sense of responsibility to the course even though they were not physically in class.

What Noah's response also shows is the reciprocal relationship between mind, body, and spaces. Fleckenstein (1999) terms this the "somantic mind: a permeable materiality in which mind and body resolve into a single entity which is (re)formed by the constantly shifting boundaries of discursive and corporeal intertextualities" (286). The "permeable materiality" shaped by "shifting boundaries" of which Fleckenstein writes helps me make sense of the virtual and material spaces where my students' identities are "(re)formed reciprocally" (286) in the online writing course. The concept of the somatic mind recognizes, as Fleckenstein (1999) points out, that students in online courses inhabit at least two places at once, their virtual classroom and their physical site, while keeping in mind that "virtual locations are always layered with multiple physical locations" (163).

Another student, Alex, admitted being skeptical about learning online initially sharing that:

> Online learning was always challenging. Reason being is because I am a procrastinator. And because I am a procrastinator, I would prefer face to face interactions. But through studying place and writing about place, I am motivated to change my relationship with online learning.

Notably, Alex also revealed in a subsequent response that writing about places he cared about made him think about his writing as "not just an assignment I am completing for a grade" but as an assignment that had a broader meaning and purpose. This level of reflection, I argue, allows us to challenge problematic notions of online education. Place and space as a conceptual lens through which students write and reflect about their subjectivities allows the field to challenge the "ideology of normalcy" embedded in online education (Moeller and Jung, par. 2). This occurs when we create the space for students to recognize the material effects associated with online education and the implications of these effects with how they then engage in the online class. In other words, students do not simply acclimate to online learning; they engage in the active work of disrupting the status quo by first deciding when and how to participate in online education and subsequently studying their own internalized attitudes about learning online and its privileges and consequences. In order for students to feel a sense of belonging to an online course and have meaningful writing experiences, they should investigate what it means to be embodied in spaces, particularly online spaces, and what this embodiment reveals about their rhetorical writing practices. This embodiment can also reveal their choices in the kinds of places where writing happens or their various "modes of experience" that emerge as they learn online (Tuan, 3).

Conclusion

Eighteen years ago, Jonathan Mauk asked "What happens to writing pedagogy, and the practices of learning to write, in the absence of traditional university geography?" This question has critical implications today with the majority of our students inhabiting places and spaces that do not primarily include the brick and mortar classroom. Thus, it behooves us to recognize that our students will likewise continue to inhabit virtual spaces even as they make their way back to the physical classroom space. In these times, "a sense of *where*" (Mauk 369) is imperative to the work our students do in the online writing classroom. We can begin by assessing our assumptions of students in online learning spaces and what these assumptions lead us to believe about how our students learn, what they value, and how our teaching impacts these two ideas.

Place and space as a conceptual framework in online literacy and writing instruction recognizes the foundational role that students' lives and experiences play in their learning. When carefully integrated into an online writing course, this conceptual framework helps students craft new relationships to these critical concepts, write and reflect more deeply on the places of their lives, and more purposefully inhabit--instead of just occupy--the spaces in which they learn and write. Additionally, methods for understanding students' meaningful writing (e.g. Eodice et al.) are helpful for identifying how students relate to space and place as along a number of axes, not the least of which is personal connection. All students should have the opportunity to connect their literacy practices to the places they inhabit through personal connection. In other words, students deserve meaningful writing that engages their experiences, beliefs, and aspirations. As scholars in rhetoric and composition studies, we understand the importance of students' experience in OWI; however, it is time for us to direct our attention to ensuring this experience is a meaningful one that is informed by a more critical interpretation of place and space.

Acknowledgment

I thank Oakland University's Center for Excellence in Teaching and Learning for the funding that supported this work. I thank my friend and mentor Kellie Sharp-Hoskins for the rich conversations and invaluable feedback that guided my early thinking about this work. Also, many thanks to Katherine Bridgman and other reviewers of *Composition Studies* for their thoughtful and constructive suggestions on my article. These allowed me to shape it into what it became.

Notes

1. I follow Beth Hewett in defining OWI as "using computer technology to learn writing from a teacher, tutor, or other students and by using it to communicate about that writing, to share writing for learning purposes, and to present writing for course completion purposes" (36).

Works Cited

Borgman, Jessie, and McArdle, Casey (Eds.). "PARS in Practice: More Resources and Strategies for Online Writing Instructors." *The WAC Clearinghouse*. University Press of Colorado, 2021. 10.37514/PRA-B.2021.1145.

Conference on College Composition and Communication. *A Position Statement of Principles and Effective Practices for Online Writing Instruction (OWI)*. 2014. ncte.org/statement/owiprinciples/.

Davidson, Cynthia. "Reconstructing Ethos as Dwelling Place: On the Bridge of Twenty-First Century Writing Practices (ePortfolios and Blogfolios)." *Thinking Globally, Composing Locally: Rethinking Online Writing in the Age of the Global Internet*, edited by Rich Rice, and Kirk St.Amant, University Press of Colorado, 2018, pp. 72-92.

Dobrin, Sidney I. "Writing Takes Place." *Ecocomposition: Theoretical and Pedagogical Approaches*, edited by Christian R. Weisser and Sidney I. Dobrin, SUNY Press, 2001, pp. 11-25.

Ehmann, Christa, and Beth L. Hewett. "OWI Research Considerations." *Foundational Practices of Online Writing Instruction*, edited by Beth L. Hewett and Kevin Eric DePew, WAC Clearinghouse and Parlor Press, 2015, pp. 517-545.

Eodice, Michele, Anne Ellen Geller, and Neal Lerner. "The Power of Personal Connection for Undergraduate Student Writers." *Research in the Teaching of English*. National Council of Teachers of English, vol. 53, no. 4, 2019, pp. 320-39.

Eodice, Michele, Anne Ellen Geller, and Neal Lerner. *The Meaningful Writing Project: Learning, Teaching and Writing in Higher Education*. Utah State University Press, 2016.

Fleckenstein, Kristie S. "Writing Bodies: Somatic Mind in Composition Studies." *College English*, vol. 61, no. 3, 1999, pp. 281-306. DOI: 10.2307/379070

GSOLE. "Online Literacy Instruction Principles and Tenets." *Global Society of Online Literacy Educators*, gsole.org/oliresources/oliprinciples, 2020.

Hewett, Beth L. "Grounding Principles of OWI." *Foundational Practices of Online Writing Instruction*, edited by Beth L. Hewett and Kevin Eric DePew, WAC Clearinghouse and Parlor Press, 2015, pp. 33-92.

Hewett, Beth L., and Christa Ehmann. *Preparing Educators for Online Writing Instruction: Principles and Processes*. National Council of Teachers of English, 2004.

hooks, bell. *Belonging: A Culture of Place*. Routledge, 2009.

Ingold, Tim. "Bindings Against Boundaries: Entanglements of Life in an Open World." *Environment and Planning*, vol. 40, no. 8, 2008, pp. 1796-1810. DOI: 10.1068/a40156

Kynard, Carmen. "'Wanted: Some Black Long Distance [Writers]': Blackboard Flava-Flavin and Other AfroDigital Experiences in the Classroom." *Computers and Composition*, vol. 24, no. 3, 2007, pp. 329-345. DOI: 10.1016/j.compcom.2007.05.008.

Martinez, Aja Y. *Counterstory: The Rhetoric and Writing of Critical Race Theory*. National Council of Teachers of English, 2020.

Martinez, Diane, Mahli Xuan Mechenbier, Beth L. Hewett, Lisa Meloncon, Heidi Skurat Harris, Kirk St.Amant, Adam Phillips, and Marcy Irene Bodnar. "A Report on a US-Based National Survey of Students in Online Writing Courses." *ROLE: Research in Online Literacy Education*, vol. 2, no. 1, 2019. roleolor.org/a-report-on-a-us-based-national-survey-of-students-in-online-writing-courses.html.

Massey, Doreen. *Space, Place and Gender*. John Wiley & Sons, 2013.

Mauk, Johnathon. "Location, Location, Location: The 'Real' (E)states of Being, Writing, and Thinking in Composition." *College English*, vol. 65, no. 4, 2003, pp. 368-388. DOI: 10.2307/3594240.

Moeller, Marie, and Julie Jung. "Sites of Normalcy: Understanding Online Education as Prosthetic Technology." *Disability Studies Quarterly*, vol. 34, no. 4, 2014. dsq-sds.org/article/view/4020/3796.

Oakland University, "Moodle Policy." Google Document, 2020. docs.google.com/document/d/1TOiSV6xgMjhyo4YRiqm0QMXgJWB6NFNu3FmFsigT8h4/edit.

Nakamura, Lisa. "Feeling Good about Feeling Bad: Virtuous Virtual Reality and the Automation of Racial Empathy." *Journal of Visual Culture*, vol. 19, no. 1, 2020, pp. 47-64. DOI: 10.1177/1470412920906259.

Oswal, Sushil K., and Lisa Meloncon. "Saying No to the Checklist: Shifting from an Ideology of Normalcy to an Ideology of Inclusion in Online Writing Instruction." *WPA: Writing Program Administration*, vol. 40, no. 3, 2017, pp. 61-77. tek-ritr.com/wp-content/uploads/2017/09/say_no_to_checklist.pdf.

Perl, Sondra. *Felt Sense: Writing with the Body*. Boynton/Cook Heinemann, 2004.

Reynolds, Nedra. *Geographies of Writing: Inhabiting Places and Encountering Difference*. Southern Illinois University Press, 2007.

Sackey, Donnie Johnson, and Danielle Nicole DeVoss. "Ecology, Ecologies, and Institutions: Eco and Composition." *Ecology, Writing Theory, and New Media*, edited by Sidney I. Dobrin, Routledge, 2011, pp. 203-220.

Seaman, Julia E., I. Elaine Allen, and Jeff Seaman. "Grade Increase: Tracking Distance Education in the United States." *Babson Survey Research Group*, 2018. bayviewanalytics.com/reports/gradeincrease.pdf.

Selfe, Cynthia L. "Technology and Literacy: A Story about the Perils of Not Paying Attention." *College Composition and Communication*, vol. 50, no. 3, 1999, pp. 411-436. DOI: 10.2307/358859.

St.Amant, Kirk. "Afterword: Contending With COVID-19 and Beyond: The 5Cs of Educational Evolution." *Journal of Technical Writing and Communication*, vol. 51, no. 1, 2020, pp. 93-97. DOI: 10.1177/0047281620977157.

Tuan, Yi-Fu. *Space and Place: The Perspective of Experience*. University of Minnesota Press, 1977.

Ulmer, Gregory L. *Internet Invention: From Literacy to Electracy*. Pearson, 2002.

VanKooten, Crystal. "Identifying Components of Meta-Awareness about Composition: Toward a Theory and Methodology for Writing Studies."*Composition Forum*, vol. 33, 2016. files.eric.ed.gov/fulltext/EJ1092005.pdf.

Weisser, Christian R., and Sidney I. Dobrin, eds. *Ecocomposition: Theoretical and Pedagogical Approaches*. SUNY Press, 2012.

Witte, Alison. "'Why Won't Moodle…?': Using Genre Studies to Understand Students' Approaches to Interacting with User-Interfaces." *Computers and Composition*, vol. 49, 2018, pp. 48-60. DOI:10.1016/j.compcom.2018.05.004

"How am I Supposed to Watch a Little Piece of Paper?" Literacy and Learning Under Duress

Carrie Hall

The COVID-19 pandemic has revealed the troubling fact that many students struggle to pay attention to literacy learning while they are in situations of extreme duress. This duress did not begin with pandemic, nor will it end with it. Neither is duress distributed at random; those negatively affected by the nation's prejudices, as a general rule, are under more duress than those who reap the benefits of these systems. To achieve an equitable curriculum, we must teach with the attentional needs of those under duress in mind.

This article explores how writing instructors can develop curricula that work with these needs. It looks at research on learning under duress as well as student work that was written in crisis, building upon the strengths of those under duress (who often, for example, write with a sense of urgency and keen awareness of their immediate surroundings) instead of trying to "cure" what we may perceive as weaknesses. A curriculum that speaks to the strengths of students with these experiences will be vital both during the pandemic and beyond it.[1]

The first time one of my students called a reading "boring" in a class I taught, I asked the whole class, as I often do, what makes a reading boring. I got many of the responses I usually get: students describing being forced to read texts that they felt had nothing to do with them or just wanting to do something else. But then I got a response I had never heard before. Ray, a young man on a football scholarship who had grown up around a great deal of violence, said, "How am I supposed to watch a little piece of paper when I'm worried someone might be coming at me?" This response has stuck with me for a number of reasons: first of all, of course, because of the violence implicit in it and also because of my own naivete: though it's obvious, it had never crossed my mind that it would be difficult, if not impossible, to concentrate on "a little piece of paper" if one had to be hypervigilant of one's surroundings. It also clarified for me the idea of attention as a limited resource, and a resource whose distribution is not just a matter of personal preference or neurological capacity, but which is learned, taught, and demanded by forces which are often out of our control.

In his 1994 address, "The Economics of Attention," rhetorician Richard Lanham claimed: "if one is looking for a glimpse of what literacy will look like in the future, the fighter cockpit is a good place to look" (Lanham). In other words, he predicted that literacy acts would involve the fending off of numerous distractions and require an increasing amount of attentional skill in order for the reader to remain focused on the task at hand.[2] In his address, Lanham suggested that we were facing, "not a population explosion, but a document explosion," which would lead to a new scarcity, the scarcity of "the human attention needed to make sense of information."

I don't think we can look at how an individual inside a fighter cockpit behaves without looking at the factors that placed them in a fighter jet in the first place. In other words, just as the study of economics is much more than the study of how one individual distributes the pennies in their piggy bank, so should the study of the economics of attention be the study of more than how each individual distributes their kernels of attention among the many possible attractors of that attention. And yet, the discussion of literacy and attentional economics is often just that: how does an individual slog through the endless information they are faced with? How does a person parse through all the articles on the internet? My point here is that attention is not a purely physiological or personal impulse, but also a social one; we learn to pay attention (or to act like we're paying attention;) we learn what ways of paying attention are socially acceptable in certain situations and not others. This learning is cultural, not just a personal neurological resource.

I am interested in the politics of paying attention, especially supposed failures of attention like boredom and distraction, as in the anecdote about Ray. I am interested in what kind of work these distractions do; we're always paying attention to something, even if it's not what we're supposed to be paying attention to. In the words of cognitive neuroscientists Dima Amso and Gaia Scerif: "attention processes determine what information is selected for subsequent perception, action, learning and memory, imposing a crucial bottleneck" (606). That is, if attention functions "properly," it slows perception down, helping us make sense of cluttered worlds and cluttered brains. But attention often functions improperly or, rather, sometimes the way attention works doesn't quite match instructors' desires. Ray's attention was functioning just fine to protect himself in the situation in which he grew up, for example, but it was not functioning in the way I wanted it to—to help him focus on the reading.

Under duress, attention functions differently than it might under other, less demanding circumstances. There are strengths to all attentional skills, though the skills that come more easily to us when we are not under duress tend to be valued more highly in academia. When I use the term "duress" here, I am using it in its original etymological sense, that is: "hardness, oppression, constraint" ("Duress, *n.*"). These constraints come with serious attentional demands. This duress–and these demands—are not distributed at random. They follow the cultural biases: those negatively affected by white supremacy, sexism (and corresponding sexual violence), homophobia, transphobia, and so on, as a general rule, are under more strain than those who benefit from these systems.

To achieve an equitable curriculum, we must teach with the attentional needs of those under duress in mind. This article sets out to consider the present and imminent implications of these aforementioned crises for literacy learning in terms of attention and distraction under duress. It also takes as a given the unfortunate fact that violence and duress will not end with these particular crises (as they did not begin with them) and that some students have exposure to more stressors than others and are therefore more taxed attentionally. Most importantly: this article argues that this reality—that duress taxes attention—should be considered when all curricula are designed. Even without a pandemic, experiences that tax attention—like poverty and trauma—disproportionately affect students of color, disabled students, LGBTQIA+ students, and women, due to societal influences like homophobia, poverty, misogyny, transphobia, sexual violence, police brutality, and institutional racism. Therefore, when designing a curriculum, we must ask: how do I design this in a way that does not exclude those actively under duress? How do we build on attentional strengths instead of trying to "cure" what we may perceive as weaknesses?[3]

I argue that we can do this by focusing on a few simple principles, which I outline throughout this article, both by the use of research on attention and also by examples of student writing. These principles are:

1. Understanding attention. Those under duress are often mislabeled as lazy or even belligerent, students who aren't trying to succeed. This is rarely, if ever, the case.
2. Finding footholds. Here, I turn to psychologist Bessel van der Kolk's research on trauma, which suggests students begin with skills that give them a sense of calm competence and from there build toward the more uncomfortable sites of uncertainty in writing.
3. Deep attending. In his 2019 address to the Conference on College Composition and Communication, Asao Inoue talked about "deep attending" when interacting with students. In other words, in order for students to pay attention, they must be paid attention to. We should assume our students are making meaning, though that meaning may not always be immediately clear.

Methods

My research on attention, literacy, and duress began pre-pandemic in a classroom at a large public research university in the Midwest. The class was composed entirely of young men on football scholarships who had been placed on a track that required them to take one basic writing course before they took mainstream freshman composition. (Ray, of the opening anecdote, was one of these scholars.) Of the eighteen students, seventeen were African American. Of these students, three were also mixed race. This was a large proportion in a school that was approximately 8% African American ("Student Diversity Dashboard"). Many players reported coming from situations where violence and poverty were commonplace, and all of the Black players reported having been harassed by police starting from a very young age. I never asked students to disclose any of this information; students volunteered it in their writing. The first semester, the football players had been placed together due to a scheduling anomaly; the class requested to stay together in the second semester, with many students reporting enjoying an environment where they could feel "at home" with one another.

Because of my work with these scholars in the first semester pre-transfer level course, I wanted to concentrate on designing a curriculum and teaching methods for the second semester transfer-level course that included students who have experienced trauma and violence, as well as other forms of duress within a mainstream curriculum, by using principles of Universal Design. I didn't assume all of the students had experienced trauma or violence (though I knew some had), and I didn't want to ask students to reveal more than they wanted to. I also did not want to set the learning experience of those under duress apart from other students. As Margaret Price writes, "Universal design sets as its ideal a learning environment that is accessible to all learning styles, abilities, and personalities" (87). I wanted a curriculum that assumes our classes include students with complex, sometimes troubled lives, and I wanted to design capacious curricula that includes as many students as possible without insisting on disclosure.

The curriculum consisted of three major papers, based largely on students' interests. I also wanted to work toward library research. The assignments were roughly as follows: In essay one, students wrote about a word or phrase that was important to their community. They were asked to express the history and importance of this word to potential outsiders. In essay two, because the students were very interested in music, and because I was able to get an MTV music reviewer as a guest speaker, I asked the students to write a music review, using the music as a jumping-off point to talk about other important cultural issues the songs brought up for them. In essay three, because many of the students expressed an interest in writing about Black history, the assignment (scaffolded from a close reading of a history-rich, and quite difficult, article by essayist Greg Tate) was to write about an historical event of their choosing for a modern-day audience, convincing that audience why this event was important to contemporary life. They were required to research the topic.

I tried to read the players' bodies of work with the openness a literary scholar might read an experimental writer like Jean Toomer or Gertrude Stein. That is to say: if I didn't understand something, I assumed the fault lay, at least in part, with my inexpert reading, so I read it again. Alongside scholarship on literacy, and attention and duress, I read the body of the student's work looking for patterns, repeated topics, places where the language surprised me. I looked for where they were losing attention and to what they paid attention. I searched for sites where it seemed these writers had started building meaning in unexpected places. This is how I began to learn about the strengths of writing through trauma and distress, research which has proven increasingly pertinent during this time of global duress.

Understanding Attention

Before I move on, I would like to situate myself and my own experience. When I first went to college, I was diagnosed with a "developmental trauma disorder," a form of posttraumatic stress brought about by ongoing violence or abuse in early childhood. I wasn't in an environment in which there was constant gunfire (which might explain why, despite my own experience with trauma, I was taken aback when Ray found danger in concentrating on "a little piece of paper," an experience quite different from my own,) but I was in an environment where I was in constant fear and under constant threat of physical abuse.

Developmental trauma is particularly salient for issues of attention because it can cause not only hypervigilance, hyperarousal, and dissociation, but also severe and ongoing difficulty constructing logical and linear narratives. Although I am a white woman with a middle-class upbringing and the privilege that comes along with those identities, I see myself inside the discussion of duress. As Elizabeth Dutro points out in "Writing Wounded: Trauma, Testimony and Critical Witness in Literacy Classrooms," the discussion of trauma can easily become one in which the researcher discusses the student as "other":

> The class-privileged assumptions that ascribe otherness to students and families living in poverty operate from an arm's length perspective, employing "those people" language both literally and figuratively. Such language . . . constructs a distinction of value among human beings creating an "us" and "them" that casts the middle class as the subjects and the poor as objects, thus perpetuating assumptions of deficiency in high-poverty families and communities. (208)

For that reason, I feel it's important to point out that I was once the aggravated student who stormed out and eventually dropped out, who refused certain assignments, and who—when I finally returned to college—pent the first year hunting for classes in which I didn't have to write traditional essays because I found the process profoundly disorienting. Exposition assignments made it viciously clear to me that I couldn't organize my thinking, that I couldn't make sense.

My situation wasn't uncommon, especially for those experiencing duress. An important thing to understand about attention is that distraction is not a simple formula. It doesn't follow a pattern like: something troubling happened, so I'm thinking about that troubling thing instead of my schoolwork. The workings of the brain are complex and surprising. Of course, not everyone functions the same way when confronted with stressors. Some people go into a hyperfocus mode: organizing their homes and taking up new hobbies. Others can't remember a thing; they are scattered, and their house is a mess; they forget appointments or simple recipes that they once could call up from memory. These—and others—are simply different strategies for the brain to cope with new and distressing situations.

According to neuroscientists, when under stress our brains tend to eschew long-term decision making and instead evaluate the threats in our immediate environment. In a recent article on stress during the Coronavirus era, Laura Sanders explains that the prefrontal cortex, which controls executive functions like decision-making and focused attention, is impaired, or perhaps more accurately, "set aside," during times of stress, giving more "primitive structures," like the amygdalae center stage. These structures help us respond quickly to perceived threats. "Helpful if you're being faced with a snake," says Yale neuroscientist Amy Arnsten, "but not helpful if you're being faced with a complex . . . decision" (Sanders).

What's important here for writing teachers is that under stress we become worse at long-term planning but better at noticing our environment and taking rapid-fire action. We become, like Ray, concerned primarily with our surroundings—and the threats or immediate concerns of those surroundings. These aren't decisions we make about what we want to attend to; this is how brains generally function under stress. "In some sense," says Stanford University neuroscientist Anthony Wagner, "we're privileged when we're not stressed, [we are then] able to fully harness our cognitive machinery" (Sanders). While we rarely use one area of the brain or the other exclusively, when under stress, humans often respond largely to immediate environmental cues instead of planning for the future or evaluating our stored knowledge. This makes survival sense but may not fit neatly into some common expectations of writing assignments, which tend to depend upon evaluating stored knowledge and value linear narrative or cause-and-effect logic.

When something seemingly random happens, when outcomes are unpredictable due to a global pandemic, police violence, poverty, abuse or other violence, the logical structure of cause-and-effect is thwarted, cognitively speaking. And for those for whom violence and unpredictability has been the norm, some abstract idea of cause-and-effect may have never made sense at all. This relationship can and does carry on into the classroom. In other words: for writers experiencing duress, or for whom duress is the norm, the relationship between cause-and-effect can be confusing and logic itself can be fraught. One outcome is that the expository form, which tends to rely upon logic and cause-and-effect, can feel highly disorienting. After all, it is hard to make a sensible point in a linear fashion when life doesn't seem to be doing a writer the same favor.

Still, when we are in a state of urgency, we are more aware of our environment, and we are keen observers—a useful writing skill. For example, while it may be difficult to write long passages that rely upon (supposed) logic under extreme duress, details and sensory memories are often more clear in these situations. As psychologist and trauma researcher Bessel van der Kolk writes, "When memories cannot be integrated on a semantic/linguistic level, they tend to be organized in more primitive ways of information processing: as visual images or somatic sensations" ("Trauma and Memory" 102). In other words, most memories are fit into an existing semantic schemata, part of the "story of my life," and once the memory is "placed" there, it isn't accessible as a memory separate from the rest of the story ("Trauma and Memory" 98). Memories of disturbing situations function quite differently. They are often purely sensory, without any semantic explanation attached. A memory of a low-stress situation might register as something like: "I sat on the couch in my neighbor's house with my brother, sweating like it was the middle of summer although it was Christmas Eve," while the memory of a trauma would be feelings of being hot, flashes of the brother's face, flashes of the room and the daunting silence. This latter is exemplified in the following poem written by my student, Jonas, about the moments before his brother's murder:

Where's the money?
Sweat drips from my head like a cold bottle of water in a warm room.
We know where the money is. We know who took it.
But we sit in silence because we don't snitch. Ride or die.
That's the bro code.
The room is quiet and colorful almost like the botanical gardens.
But there is still no answer. There is still no code broken.
You took the fall for me.
My brother.
I write to you about a moment that made us truly family.

If only it was all a lie.

Traumatic memories are often isolated, not fitting into any existing story. When a narrative is constructed of the trauma, often years after the fact, the sensory memories are the basis of the story, and the plot is laced in, as opposed to the other way around. I did not, nor would I ever, ask Jonas to write about his brother. This was a low-stakes assignment in preparation for Essay One—the portrait of a word or phrase. Jonas' phrase was "Ride or Die." His engagement here shows us that professors can design assignments which ask students to write specific scenes and sensory memories as a way to engage and value those who may be skilled in these areas due to duress, or for any number of other reasons.

Finding Footholds

In discussing recovery from trauma, van der Kolk states the importance of "the feeling of being in charge, calm and able to engage in focused efforts to accomplish goals" ("Developmental Trauma Disorder" 408). The Conference on College Composition and Communication "DEMAND for Black Linguistic Justice" frames this concept a bit differently: "Black students," the demand reads, "need the kind of artful language instruction in which they are positioned as the linguistic mavens they are who can teach you a thing or two" (Baker-Bell et al.). The demand reminds us that when students are positioned as experts, they can find strength. Van der Kolk reminds us that this positioning—of having some knowledge and autonomy—brings people a sense of calm. Calm is especially valuable in times of duress but may also help any student having a difficult time finding a foothold in writing. From this place of strength and safety, writers can begin to take risks.

Providing an orienting structure to which students can refer when lost also gives them a possible foothold. Duress is profoundly untethering, and while choice can be empowering, it can also be unnerving if students have no idea of professor expectations, where to begin, or what to do if they are disoriented. One of my favorite examples of providing such a structure comes from the poet Yona Harvey, who I invited to visit the class I taught with the football students. Before she came, Professor Harvey asked the students to write to her telling her who their favorite superhero was. (This exercise was not tied to any particular essay, but to the students' request that they be allowed to write poetry in class. We took a break from our regular curriculum one day for our esteemed guest). Here is Jonas' email to Harvey, which did not stand out to me at the time, though the poem that arose from it draws me back to it for a closer reading:

Barry Allen, also known as the Flash, is a DC comic superhero and is secretly the second character to be called "the Flash." [Flash's] abilities allow him to travel at the speed of light and sometimes beyond the world's limit. I chose this superhero because he relates to my everyday life, as speed and urgency play a huge role in it. Speed is required to play at the highest level in football, and urgency is needed to complete work academically as well as anything in life. Flash has always been my favorite superhero growing up as I was forced to choose a different superhero living in a household of five brothers.

Though I didn't see it at the time, I can now see an undercurrent of his brother's murder throughout: Allow him to travel beyond the world's limit… speed and urgency…urgency… forced to choose…household of five brothers.

Professor Harvey had us read a series of epistolary poems to Superman by Lucille Clifton. The students then used the content of their emails to Professor Harvey and drew from Clifton's poems as models to write poems to their superheroes. They wrote for about ten minutes. This is Jonas' poem:

> It's funny how time seems to Flash,
> One second you're Barry
> The next you're flash.
> You can travel through time,
> but we both can't change
> the past, we both lost
> a part of ourselves
> but decide to keep on
> running.

Jonas reported disliking writing—poetry in particular, though he admitted that he guessed he might be good at it. But while Jonas and the others complained about what they considered to be the rigid structures of essays, they had no such complaints about the structure of this assignment, perhaps in part because there was no penalty for breaking those rules. The assignment simply stood as a structure to consult should the disorientation of trauma or from an unfamiliar writing assignment make them feel too untethered. Whether or not Jonas liked writing this poem, it gave him a foothold from which to own his place in the classroom. And it also gave his classroom writing a life of its own outside the class; Harvey, with Jonas' permission, hung it on her office wall.

Language itself, and especially joy with language, is another firm foothold for many writers. Students' language systems have value. Professors should always acknowledge this, not just in word but in deed. As the "DEMAND for Black Linguistic Justice" says "we cannot claim that Black Lives Matter in our field if Black Language does not matter!" (Baker-Bell et al.). To treat academic language or standard English as the pinnacle of linguistic usage and everything else as a bridge or low-stakes exercise toward that pinnacle not only reinforces white (language) supremacy but also knocks the ground out from under students trying to get a foothold on the page and at the university.

My policy is that students can write with whatever language they choose, as long as they write with care (and they write their own definition of care). My experience is that students thrive when they use language that makes them feel at home. Take the following example from Marshall, who hailed from South Florida. In essay three—the music review—he examined the language of musical group Migos, known for their somewhat inscrutable—and very Southern—lyrical style. (According to Marshall: "People say that the Migos be saying anything and niggas can't understand them.") He was specifically interested in the fact that Migos have power because they not only make a lot of money, but also because they make people learn to speak their language:

> I could see why people be lost with it for real cuh they [Migos] from all the way down south and bringing that bih to the norf is a different way of life. Yes if you are thinking I grew up around this all my life swea it sound normal to me. You can talk this to anyone from the crib and they will know what you talm bout. It is called social identity and everyone has that no matter where they from.

From Marshall, we can see that encouraging students to enjoy being conversationalists, writers, readers, tweeters, poets, orators, trash-talkers, and listeners—in short, as budding masters of language—helps them pay attention to the language they use and the language around them. They can write however they think they will best reach their "audience invoked," whoever that might be, but it doesn't need to be the imagined scholars in Burke's parlor—unless that is the crowd they are trying to invoke (Ede and Lunsford). The choice is the student's. This kind of linguistic freedom is what allows students to see themselves as experts; it therefore opens avenues for a sense of calm confidence that moves past duress and into composition.

Deep Attending

What happens once students have gathered a collection of poems, fragments, and scenes—once they have practice attending and are working toward firm footing? How do we help them approach writing as the search for a coherent whole? First, instructors might use these smaller compositions as points for larger, structured writing tasks, but I also suggest that, for some writers, the fragments may begin to organize themselves into a structure of their own.

When Frederic Jameson criticizes the language poets and other experimental writers, he describes their writing as "schizophrenic," and hypothesizes that if:

> the subject has lost its capacity actively to . . . organize its past and future into coherent experience, it becomes difficult to see how the cultural productions of such a subject could result in anything but "heaps of fragments." (qtd in Ngai 286)

But as Sianne Ngai points out, "anyone with agricultural, office, laundry or postal experience can attest [that] a heap *is* an organization, though perhaps not a particularly organized-looking one" (291). She argues that if we only allow pre-existing concepts of order to count as coherent, we bar ourselves from discovering new processes of linguistic adhesion, organization and meaning-making. Similarly, Aneil Rallin writes, "I hear a voice in my head pestering me, warning me not to lose focus, to stay on track. But I write…knowing that this emphasis on focus, on coherence may be what keeps us from noticing what is around us, may be what prevents us from writing" (625).

Perhaps if a student has written something seemingly incoherent, as is likely in situations of duress, we don't ask them to clean up their mess but instead to make a bigger one. As the saying goes: One envelope on the ground is a mistake; twenty is a pile. The same may be true with paragraphs, scenes, or idea fragments. Perhaps looking for patterns in a student's writing—what they find important, how they use and want to use language—is part of the work of the composition classroom, part of what Inoue calls "deep attending." Inoue suggests we ask our students such questions as "Do I understand you enough? Am I making you suffer? Please help me to read your languaging properly." This, he points out, is a process that combats the white supremacist ideologies that permeate and organize our classrooms. Instead of trying to figure out how a student's writing fits into some pre-ordained structure or framework, we look with the student at the writing they are doing and see what structures and frameworks emerge. I argue that we should read student writers the same way we read experimental writers, putting the onus on ourselves as readers to find meaning in their texts or bodies of work.

An example: Victor wrote in heaps of fragments that I didn't initially understand. In essay three, in which I asked students to write about an historical event important to contemporary audiences, Victor wrote about the movie *Scarface*. Though his essay began with a few sentences describing the history of the Cuban embargo, it was difficult to figure out how his paper related to the prompt. His essay read like an off-the-top-of-his-head synopsis of the movie's plot, as in the following: "Tony starts off in a refugee camp in Florida where him and his right hand man Manny were located." Victor goes on to describe Tony's rise to power: "Manny realizes something is wrong and kills the Columbians. When one tries to escape Tony chases him into the street with pedestrians all around. He doesn't care and guns him down in front of everyone." If we attend more closely, however, we can see that these snippets—as with the paper more generally—concentrate both on gun violence and Tony's dedication to his family. Victor writes: "Tony's little sister and him haven't seen each other in years and he does not know how to handle her being so grown up." Victor never analyzes either of these phenomena, simply choosing to mention them and then move on. Nor does he describe Tony's eventual murder, only his dead body "shown under a statue of a globe saying 'the world is yours.'" Looking back, I see the essay contained what I now know are themes that Victor would write about regularly: family, particularly his sister and his mother, and an exploration of gun violence. While it looked like he was brushing the assignment off, it turns out that he was looking for a foothold to write about an event that was extremely difficult for him to discuss which did, in fact, begin with *Scarface*.

In a conference, I asked him the only question that came to mind: why he'd decided to write about *Scarface*. He answered quietly, but matter-of-factly: "My uncle always told me that when he went out, he wanted to go out like Scarface, and he did. He got gunned down that same way." He then proceeded to tell me the story of his uncle's murder, and then his cousin's murder, and then his brother's murder in calm, excruciating detail. "But my uncle was the first one," he said. There have been times I have simply told students that what they wrote was unacceptable and they needed to start again. I am lucky I didn't do it that day, but instead had the wherewithal to ask Victor the simple question: "Why Scarface?" and then listen to his answer, take Inoue's advice, and attend to Victor's experiences.

It seems to me now that because the event Victor really wanted to write about—a workplace shooting in his family history which had become news, and then part of the history of his hometown—was so difficult for him, he did not know where to begin. He also may have had trouble focusing on the assignment's more logic-driven goals, in light of the difficulty of his situation. I do know that Victor was doing everything he could to get anything down on the page. He reported struggling with logical and linear connections—not only between the assignment and his story, but between the scenes of the story itself. He was trying to pay attention; he was trying to figure out what I wanted him to do. But he also really was trying to write about *Scarface*. It would be easy to call this first paper a failure…or we could attend differently, more deeply, and see it as a foothold.

In a conference, we decided a good starting place would be for Victor to write a scene about the discussion he and his uncle had about *Scarface*. We then decided he could continue to write more scenes that seemed pertinent to the story of his uncle, using the concrete scene skills we had been working on in class. The research portion of the essay would be from newspapers at the time; reading the papers might make a second scene. After he'd written the scenes, he could figure out what order he wanted to put them in. In other words, he would make a heap of fragments.

When it came time that revisions were due, Victor's was missing. The next time I saw him, I told him I needed the essay as soon as possible, but he told me he had be gone due to a memorial for the anniversary of his brother's murder. He told his tutor he had changed his mind; he was going to write about something else, but I could not understand what his new topic was. In the following class, I told Victor he'd have to come meet with me to talk about the new topic. Instead, he announced, "I did it," and shoved the revised paper into my hand. Here is how it began:

> Summers in South Brunswick, New Jersey were always the same for me. Driving through town with windows down, staring at the green grass and trees around. Or riding with a few friends blasting music trying to find our next move in the day. What I remember more than anything is countless days of being outside with the sun beaming off my helmet, the sweat dripping off my jersey, and struggling to find comfort in my cleats because the turf felt like hot cement.

I was struck then, as I am now, by the vividness of these first few lines. Notice, too, the vibrancy and rhythm of the descriptions. Next, he zooms in on a particular day football practice in 6th grade:

> Practice was going smooth and everything seemed to be going great when all of a sudden a loud pitch scream from a distance caught my attention. [My mom] was the person who had screamed. The fields were spray painted onto a regular open grass plain behind the town's middle school. My mom was behind one of the far fields.

The diction here unfolds by the second, like we're with him when he pieces together where the scream is coming from—whom it is coming from—and we dwell with him, for a second, while we listen to this horrible screaming, on the strange detail of spray paint on grass. This reads as the sensory detail of extreme duress that van der Kolk refers to, remembered almost out of time, which feels both distant and present.

The paragraph about *Scarface* follows immediately after he finds his mother:

In July before the start of football that year, my family . . . was having a big cookout with a DJ in New Brunswick at my aunt's house. It started around 3 and all my cousins and family were there. I was sitting with my sister most of the night because I felt too young to hang out with my older cousins and dance with them plus I was shy. With the salsa music blasting there were plenty of my family dancing around the yard. My uncle Tata was grilling, drinking and having fun. Whenever my family members talk, it would never be a normal conversation, they yell and have shouting matches so no one can get a word in. In one group of my uncles they were talking and I can remember my uncle shouting, "when I go out, I wanna go out like Scarface!" Later that day after the cookout I asked my mom what he meant by that and she simply told me its from a movie I'm not allowed to watch, so of course I watched it later that day. Seeing all the violence and drugs involved and seeing how it ended, I couldn't understand why he would joke about going out like him. But it was how my uncle was, he was a tough hard working and passionate man.

Narratively, we have gone from his mother's screams to the shouts, cheerful now but just as loud, of the party. In the paragraph after this description, with no hint of transition, the tone changes. Like a reporter, Victor finally tells us about the murder:

In Bristol, Pennsylvania, a man by the name of Robert Diamond was fired from his job. . . . He was fired because he was accused of being racist and was uncooperative with his coworkers. . . .His plan was to kill his boss, who was black, and anyone else black who came in his way. On August 1, 2008, Robert Diamond drove around for about an hour before pulling up to his old workplace. My uncle was Puerto Rican and seemed to fit the profile. . . . Robert Diamond opened fire from a distance. My uncle was hit a couple times and he stopped the car. My uncle was hurt badly and he punched the car door open. However, for some reason, my uncle did not try to run. He looked his shooter in the eye and began trying to walk towards him. He could not walk for long and collapsed to the pavement. The shooter stood over Angel Guadalupe, and shot him until he was not moving anymore. . . . The shooter planned everything out. Even the shirt he was wearing said "stupidity is not a crime." . . . My uncle was a brave man, and the way he faced his killer in his last moments shows me what kind of man he was. He went out like a man, like he wanted to, he went out like he said, just like Scarface.

My attention is drawn to a number of things about this essay. Of course, I'm prompted to attend to the horror of the story, the racism and senselessness, but my attention is also drawn to the vividness of detail, both remembered and imagined: the cleats on concrete, the dominoes game, the salsa music, the "stupidity is not a crime" t-shirt, Victor's description of his uncle's death as though he were there. We can see the awareness of the environment that those who have experienced trauma often possess. At the same time, we see Victor's difficulty constructing a linear narrative. But there is value in that difficulty.

In fact, what emerges from that struggle is a fragmented but sophisticated structure apt for the telling of this event: summer days in New Jersey, a particular summer day in New Jersey, an unexplained scream, a party with an uncle who "wants to go out like Scarface," news-like reporting of the murder of that uncle dying like Scarface, and, later and omitted from my excerpt here, a scene of Victor bringing food to his mother after school because for months she wouldn't leave her bed. The essay does end wrapped in a bow, with a final pro-death penalty paragraph, arguing for the execution of his uncle's murderer: "I believe that if criminals know they will be put to death before murdering someone else, they will hesitate to do the crime." Otherwise, the jarring jump from scene to scene is both more heartbreaking and makes more emotional sense than a chronologically linear narrative might.

One of the main things to note about Victor's essay, and the process by which he arrived at it, is that we can see the strengths he has as a writer are consistent with the difficulties of attention and memory under duress. Victor doesn't follow a traditional, logical, expository essay structure because his life has not, at least the way he described it to me, moved seamlessly from thesis to point to conclusion. But there is a logic to his writing. The strength of this essay is in the form of the jarring chronology of the events as he experienced them, in the vividness of sometimes unwanted details barreling in at inopportune moments. The narrative chaos, the way the essay jumps around in time, the way screams emerge from seemingly nowhere and then disappear into laughter and salsa music, which then disappears into gunfire: this the way crisis works on human attention.

Conclusion

As writing teachers oriented to deep attention, perhaps we can see that Victor found his foothold in talking about *Scarface,* that he built on that foothold by writing a heap of fragments held together by urgency and vivid detail, that he organized those fragments into an order using a logic of his own. To see this, however, writers need to gather multiple fragments of their writing together to find patterns in the seemingly disconnected low-stakes assignments, journal entries and drafts they do throughout a semester—what themes emerge?

What threads run through the writing they do week after week? As professors, teachers, and writers ourselves, we need to pile more and more fragments onto that heap, "message fragments," in cartoonist and writer Lynda Barry's words, "we may not recognize until we have enough of them to understand. Liking and not liking," she goes on to say, can orient our attention away from what is there (12–13).

In college, I could not avoid writing essays forever, so I had to develop a process that worked for me. I started by scribbling each idea and pertinent quote down on an individual index card and rearranging the cards in piles on the floor until the groups made sense. These groups became paragraphs. Then I wrote, by hand, at least two drafts before I started to type. I still handwrite at least two drafts when I compose. Working this way borders on the ridiculous, but this is the process that works for me. I still need to find ways to organize the noisy thoughts zipping around in my brain. I am not very different from some of my students this way.

Which returns us to the question: how is Ray supposed to look at a little piece of paper when someone might be coming at him? How are our students supposed to look at little computer screens when they are worried about the pandemic or the police? The answer is that there isn't an easy answer. I get my foothold by calming myself with a process full of physical busywork. Jonas gets his foothold through vivid scenes, Marshall through love of language and Victor through telling a story at the periphery of the story he really wants to tell. Everyone has their own way onto the page, and we need curricula capacious enough that students can find processes that work for them, no matter how counterintuitive they may seem to the instructor. The concepts of understanding attention, finding footholds and deep attending are a good start for the study of literacy learning under duress, but they're only a start. There is a great deal of room for research into the relationship between attention and learning—what draws students away from a little piece of paper and what draws students, even under duress, to that paper? These are crucial questions to ask as writing instructors try to figure out how to best serve students during this crisis and beyond it.

Notes

1. All student names have been changed and all student writing has been used with permission and IRB approval. At the beginning of the second semester, I asked students to fill out a form stating whether or not I could use their writing for my research and future publication. Those who agreed to let me use their writing received no benefits, nor did those who refused receive any penalties.

2. Though Lanham went on to write a book by the same name (*The Economics of Attention: Style and Substance in the Age of Information*), he was not the first to discuss

attentional economics. In 1971, economist Herbert A. Simon pointed out that an influx of information created a "poverty of attention" (Simon 40).

3. I have eschewed discussions of ADHD in this article because individual diagnoses are not of particular interest to this discussion. In the words of McDermott et.al in "The Cultural Work of Learning Disabilities," I am less interested in labels and more interested in the "cultural arrangements that make a . . . label relevant" (13).

Works Cited

Amso, Dima, and Gaia Scerif. "The Attentive Brain: Insights from Developmental Cognitive Neuroscience." *Nature Reviews Neuroscience*, vol. 16, no. 10, 2015, pp. 606–19., doi:10.1038/nrn4025.

Baker-Bell, April, et. al. "This Ain't Another Statement! This Is a DEMAND for Black Linguistic Justice!" *Conference on College Composition and Communication*, 3 Aug. 2020, cccc.ncte.org/cccc/demand-for-black-linguistic-justice.

Barry, Lynda. *Syllabus: Notes from an Accidental Professor*. Drawn & Quarterly, 2015.

"Duress, n." *Oxford English Dictionary Online*, Oxford University Press, 2021.

Dutro, Elizabeth. "Writing Wounded: Trauma, Testimony and Critical Witness in Literacy Classrooms." *English Education*, vol. 43, no. 2, 2011, pp. 193–211.

Ede, Lisa, and Andrea Lunsford. "Audience Addressed/Audience Invoked: The Role of Audience in Composition Theory and Pedagogy." *College Composition and Communication*, vol. 35, no. 2, 1984, p. 155.

Inoue, Asao B. "2019 CCCC Chair's Address: How Do We Language so People Stop Killing Each Other, or What Do We Do about White Language Supremacy?" *Arizona State University*, National Council of Teachers of English, 2019, asu.pure.elsevier.com/en/publications/2019-cccc-chairs-address-how-do-we-language-so-people-stop-killin.

Kolk, Bessel A. Van Der. "Trauma and Memory." *Psychiatry and Clinical Neurosciences*, vol. 52, no. S1, 1998, pp. 52–64., doi:10.1046/j.1440-1819.1998.0520s5s97.x.

Kolk, Bessel Van Der. "Clinical and research implications of developmental trauma disorder." *25th ISTSS Annual Meeting-Traumatic Stress Disorders: Toward DSM-V and ICD-11*. 2009.

Lanham , Richard. "'The Economics of Attention.'" The Research Library the Day After Tomorrow. The Research Library the Day After Tomorrow, 22 Nov. 2015, Austin, TX, Association of Research Libraries.

Ngai, Sianne. *Ugly Feelings*. Harvard University Press, 2007.

Price, Margaret. *Mad at School: Rhetorics of Mental Disability and Academic Life*. University of Michigan Press, 2014.

Rallin, Aneil. "'Can I Get a Witness?': Writing with June Jordan." *College Composition and Communication*, vol. 70, no. 4, 2019, pp. 615–30.

Sanders, Laura. "How Coronavirus Stress May Scramble Our Brains." *Science News*, 28 May 2020, www.sciencenews.org/article/coronavirus-covid19-stress-brain.

Simon, Herbert. "Designing Organizations for an Information-Rich World." *Computers, Communications, and the Public Interest*, edited by Martin Greenberger, Johns Hopkins Press, 1971, pp. 37–72.

"Student Diversity Dashboard." *Office for Equity, Diversity, and Inclusion | University of Pittsburgh*, 8 Jan. 2021, www.diversity.pitt.edu/social-justice/student-dashboard.

Tracing Ableism's Rhetorical Circulation through an Analysis of Composition Mission Statements

Kristin C. Bennett

Circulated documents, like mission statements, demarcate normative boundaries related to student and instructor identities, behaviors, and experiences. In attempting to create inclusive documentation, universities frequently use standardizing language. While promoting standardization, however, such documents may prove exclusive by disregarding a range of student and instructor identities and abilities. Grounded in insights from disability studies and technical and professional communication theory, this study models the use of corpus linguistic analysis for analyzing mission statements, thereby providing interdisciplinary methods for writing programs to evaluate the documents they create and circulate. The findings show that by attempting to universalize experience, composition programs may contribute to normalizing structures that circulate ableism. These findings help programs recognize the discursive impact that mission statements may have by illustrating how ableism may move across even seemingly neutral spaces. In turn, the article calls for composition studies to consider critical documentation practices that prioritize disability and offers data-driven guidelines for revising mission statements.

Introduction

Universities frequently turn to universal standards to promote inclusion and transcend student and faculty difference. However, the field of technical and professional communication (TPC) argues that when relying upon "normative commonplaces," institutions may, in fact, dictate "rigid ideals" that contribute to the ongoing exclusion of disabled individuals by confusing inclusion with normative assimilation (Konrad 135).[1] When using standardizing language across their documentation practices, university professionals do not account for uniquely embodied differences like those represented by disability. Furthermore, such practices may contribute to the circulation of ableism, which positions particular individuals as disabled, or "lacking" when they do not meet standard embodied norms (Cherney 8). Standardized documentation practices may thus communicate conditional notions of inclusion that contribute to ableism's movement across university spaces by endorsing individual alignment with the status quo.

To understand the circulation of ableism, one must first understand neoliberalism, which denotes "a set of economic principles and cultural politics that positions the free market as a guide for all human action" (Stenberg 4-6). Striving for "profit, control, and efficiency," neoliberal standards frame certain bodyminds and behaviors as more productive and, consequently, more able than others (Giroux 434).[2] Neoliberalism normalizes such productive, ableist standards by endorsing them as natural and encouraging individuals to align with them. When university professionals rely on seemingly neutral standards of productivity across classroom and departmental documentation practices, they may thus be circulating ableist ideals.

As the field of TPC has recognized, institutional documentation practices directly impact individual understandings of identity by framing certain behaviors, values, and standards as normal (Slack et al. 28). Specifically, technical and professional communicators have identified how reliance on seemingly neutral, universal norms across institutional documentation practices may exclude disabled identities. As mission statement documents articulate departmental values and behavioral standards, it is critical that composition programs and independent writing departments better understand if and how such documents may disregard disabled bodyminds and contribute to institutional ableism.

Responding to Tara Wood et al.'s 2014 call to integrate disability as "central" to composition, this article recommends an epistemic shift to composition documentation practices that resist ableist rhetoric by prioritizing disabled individuals at the forefront of design processes (147-148). To trace how ableism may move through documents, I turn to an understanding of neoliberal ableist rhetoric as circulatory. Because neoliberalism impacts daily life, tracing it requires the recognition that "rhetoric circulates through our everyday, situated activities" (Chaput 20). Ableism is a rhetoric that functions at the level of the everyday, as institutional norms frequently assume able bodyminds. Thus, an understanding of ableism as rhetorical circulation allows us to trace how standardized documents may exclude disabled individuals.

To demonstrate how ableist rhetoric may circulate across documents, I use critical discourse analysis and examine mission statements from thirty-two Research-1 institutions (see Appendix A) through WordSmith Tools, a corpus linguistic analysis program. I analyze frequency, concordances, and collocations to evaluate the discursive construction of student and faculty identities across mission statements. Based on these findings, I offer guidelines for composition instructors and writing program administrators to trace the circulation of ableist rhetoric across their programmatic and departmental documents. Drawing from disability studies (DS) and TPC, these guidelines encourage compositionists to resist ableist documentation impulses.

The Ableism of Neoliberal Documentation

In their discussion of the ideological impacts of mission statements on institutional spaces, John M. Swales and Priscilla S. Rogers explain that mission statements directly influence "the plethora of regulations, instructions, and procedures" in an institution and may act as "carriers of culture, ethos, and ideology" in programs and departments (226). Megan Schoen recognizes these ideological implications and proposes that mission statements reflect a "critical ground of investigation" for composition as they "communicate the core identity of the university as a whole" and demonstrate that "writing programs [function] as part of a rhetorical ecology—a constellation of people, programs, initiatives, opportunities, constraints, and cultures that emerge and interact within a specific university context" (38). In addition, mission statements denote a significant site of analysis because they are often featured on public-facing websites. Compositionists, then, should examine who is and is not anticipated by the norms such documents uphold and should attend to mission statement documentation practices to determine how they discursively influence the identities and experiences of students and faculty. Although scholars have recognized that mission statements may influence individual experiences, the field has not fully analyzed how these documents may contribute to the circulation of neoliberal, ableist rhetoric. This article thus extends the existing conversation by examining these influences.

Integral to neoliberal rhetoric is a reliance on seemingly inclusive, neutral language (Welch 547). Disregarding unique embodiments, neoliberal standardization generally privileges the most dominant or "unmarked ...white, male, cisgender, heterosexual, able-bodied, and middle-class bodies—that appear neutral" (Hamraie, n.p.). Neoliberalism's standardizing influence, as the following analysis will show, plays out in how program documents often neglect writing's embodied, intersectional nature. In the context of departmental mission statements, students frequently are referred to as a standard group and held to common expectations. As Robert McRuer writes, composition's heteronormative, ableist standards reflect "a corporate model of efficiency and flexibility" that often prioritizes "order and efficiency" while "forgetting ... the composing bodies that experience it" (148-152). As neoliberal logics frequently disregard disparity in students' academic opportunities and economic resources, they frequently promote ableist assumptions. Consequently, when drawing from neoliberal ideals, university mission statements may, unknowingly, contribute to ableism by positioning some bodyminds as more efficient, or able, than others.

DS provides an avenue for understanding the relational impact that mission statements can have on disabled bodyminds. By situating disability as a personally embodied and sociopolitically "relational" experience, those in DS recognize disability as existing in the relationship between an individual body and a specific context (Garland-Thompson, "Misfits" 600). Those in DS understand disabled conditions as involving a complex relationality between bodies, space, and social discourse (Dolmage, *Disability* 19-20). Whereas the able or normal identity is understood as "neutral" because the environment is seamlessly constructed for it, the disabled identity cannot "conform with [the] architectural, attitudinal, educational, occupational, and legal conventions" of that same environment (Garland-Thomson, *Extraordinary* 8, 46).

At the heart of neoliberalism is ableism, or the belief in "an idealized norm that defines what it means to be human" and assumes "that those who do not fit that norm are disabled … [and] lacking" (Cherney 8). Integral to neoliberal productivity, each idealized norm becomes naturalized as human through its circulation across "a convergence of networks of association" (Campbell 17-20) that designate which qualities may further "the common good" within institutional structures (Cherney 17). Relying on what Michel Foucault refers to as the "power of homogeneity," neoliberalism regulates populations on the everyday level through discursive technologies—such as documentation practices--that locate, measure, and fix individuals against prescribed standards (184). Such technologies influence individuals' "thinking and acting" by evaluating them against standard, productive norms (Chaput 4). Through ableist assumptions, then, neoliberal standardization disenfranchises particular bodyminds.

The Circulation of Neoliberal Ableism

Since neoliberal rhetoric functions in "everyday, situated activities"; or, in institutions housing those activities (Chaput 20); or, and in bodies that engage in those activities (Dolmage, *Academic* 9), so, too, does ableism. To examine the influence of neoliberal rhetoric across institutions, Catherine Chaput encourages a shift from understandings of rhetoric as "an isolated instance or… series of instances" to one of "a circulation of exchanges, the whole of which govern individual and collective decisions" (8). I follow Chaput's theory of rhetorical circulation to examine how mission statements may contribute to ableism's circulation when they align student and instructor identities with the neoliberal status quo.

To explore this, I analyzed the mission statements of thirty-two Research-1 (R-1) universities. R-1 composition programs serve a significant number of students and largely influence national trends in composition. Referring to the 2018 "Carnegie R1 and R2 Research Classifications: Doctoral Universities" list, I visited the website of each of the 131 R-1 universities' Writing Programs, First Year Writing (FYW) Programs, or English Departments (when FYW was housed there). From these sites, I collected mission statements from December

2020-January 2021. To ensure that the analyzed documents were mission statements, I chose the thirty-two documents that used the term "mission" either in their labeling of the statement or in statement language (see Appendix A). If labeled mission statements included visions and goals, I also analyzed those. Though other universities had documents that likely served as mission statements, I did not include them in my analysis if programs did not specifically refer to them as such. Importantly, this analysis was not intended to critique individual programs or to generalize about all R-1 composition programs, but instead to demonstrate the connection between the standardized language used in many university mission statements and neoliberal, ableist assumptions.

To identify ableist rhetoric, I used critical discourse analysis. Acting as an "identity kit," discourse guides one's "words, acts, values, beliefs, attitudes, and social identities" so that one may be recognized by others (Gee 526). By establishing a normative baseline of ability as natural, neoliberal discourse designates and regulates certain behaviors as more valued, able, and ideal than others. I utilized critical discourse analysis (CDA) "to analyze discourse practices … and to investigate how meaning is created in context" across these university mission statements (Bloor and Bloor 13). CDA traces the relationship between discourse and identity by examining discourse's role in reinforcing social norms and correlating power relations (20). CDA thus allowed me to identify how the language used across mission statements may position certain identities and behaviors as more productively valuable than others and may consequently circulate ableist assumptions that contribute to disability's exclusion across departmental spaces.

To critically analyze the circulation of ableist discourse, I used WordSmith Tools, a corpus linguistic analysis program. Although such programs do not replace traditional rhetorical analysis, they do highlight linguistic trends through frequency, collocational, and concordance data. Frequency reflects the most frequently used words in a corpus and offers "a sociological profile of a given word or phrase enabling greater understanding of its use in particular contexts" (Baker 47). By studying word frequency, my analysis underscores the discursive significance of the linguistic patterns across the study's corpus. I also conducted collocational and concordance analyses to understand the sociopolitical implications of the language in these documents. Concordances are the occurrences of a particular word in context. Collocations are words that frequently "occu[r] next to each other" and reveal significance between word associations (Baker 71-96). In examining concordances and collocations, I gained insight into the discursive framing of student and faculty identities within the mission statements. This method also allowed me to look systematically at the mission statements' grammatical constructions and to assess their role in potentially circulating ableism.

Analyzing Mission: Frequency, Concordance, Collocation

In this section, I provide an overview of the findings yielded from my corpus linguistic analysis, organized by word. A brief discussion precedes a summary table of corresponding data.

Frequently Occurring Words

Using WordSmith Tools, I first determined the most frequently occurring words in my corpus. Of the 375 total words (occurring five or more times), I've featured forty of the most frequent in Table 1 below. This list includes the first forty words (occurring twenty-six times or more), excluding function words (which were unrelated in my study). I attended specifically to two groups of word frequencies:

1. To better understand the impact of mission statements on identity, I attended carefully to the frequency of the words "faculty" (40) and "students" (168).
2. I also examined the most frequently occurring pronouns--"we" (107), "they" (39), and personal pronouns "our" (123) and "their" (74)--because pronouns may denote power differences and influence experiences of belonging (Bloor 21).

Table 1: List of 40 of the 375 most frequently occurring words in the corpus

Word	Frequency	Texts
WRITING	247	31
STUDENTS	168	31
OUR	123	23
WE	107	20
ENGLISH	99	20
DEPARTMENT	74	20
THEIR	74	22
COURSES	72	21
RESEARCH	61	25
THROUGH	60	21

Word	Frequency	Texts
PROGRAM	56	15
MISSION	53	26
LITERATURE	52	17
CREATIVE	47	14
UNIVERSITY	46	20
COMPOSITION	43	15
RHETORIC	43	16
ABOUT	42	21
PROFESSIONAL	41	21
FACULTY	40	15
THEY	39	14
FIRST	38	13
TEACHING	38	23
CULTURAL	37	16
FROM	35	21
GRADUATE	35	14
ALL	33	13
WORK	33	14
CRITICAL	31	17
LEARNING	31	12
YEAR	31	11
ACADEMIC	30	18
COMMUNITY	29	13

Word	Frequency	Texts
COMMUNICATION	28	11
DEVELOP	28	12
KNOWLEDGE	28	16
UNDERGRADUATE	28	15
SKILLS	27	15
WORLD	27	15
LANGUAGE	26	16

Faculty

Having identified key terms, I then examined the concordances and collocates for the word "faculty" (40) which was often paired with "members" (6), as in the phrase "faculty members" (refer to Table 2). Collocates "in" (9), "of" (15), "program" (5), and "department" (4) also frequently co-occurred with faculty. Collectively, these constructions position faculty as insider "members" who exist "in" their "programs" and "departments." In addition, a lack of reference to faculty bodyminds and the co-occurrence of faculty with "the" (19) suggest that mission statements presume that faculty "members" reflect standard, universal embodiments.

Based on this collocate analysis, I examined the grammatical constructions across the concordances. "Faculty" was equally positioned as an active subject in sentence-level constructions (21) and as a direct object (19). However, when positioned as a subject, "faculty" were framed as productive contributors to the department, demonstrated by their association with active verbs like "support," "coordinate," and "contribute." Specifically, one mission statement notes, "Faculty members contribute to … creative activity in the humanities to advance knowledge and serve the public good." This statement positions faculty as collectively facilitating the advancement of the university and the larger public. Likewise, among the active verbs associated with faculty were "teach" and "integrate," indicating that faculty are responsible for educating and thus integrating others. Specifically, faculty were most frequently associated with the direct object of "students" (3), demonstrating that students were most often the assumed recipients of faculty efforts. This suggests that when mission statements rely on standardizing language, they may reinforce goals of capitalist productivity that situate particular forms of faculty engagement as more valuable than others. Likewise, such constructions frame learning as a process in which faculty align students with existing norms. This language does not attend to students' agency in determining their own knowledge-making experiences.

Table 2: "Faculty" Summary Table

Most Frequent Collocates of Faculty	Frequency of Faculty in Subject/Object Position	Examples of Associated Active Verbs when Faculty Is Positioned as Subject	Examples of Associated Direct Objects when Faculty Is Positioned as Subject
The (19) In (9) Of (15) Students (12) Members (6) Program (5) Time (5) Our (5) Its (4) Department (4) Writing (4)	Subject Position: (21) Object Position: (19)	Publish (2) Coordinate (1) Contribute (1) Engage (1) Include (1) Integrate (1) Represent (1) Support (1) Teach (1) Participate (1) Produce (1)	Research (3) Students (3)

Students

To better understand how mission statements may use standardizing language in representing students, I examined collocates and concordances of "students" (refer to Table 3), the second most frequent word across my corpus (168). The collocate analysis indicated that "students" were frequently associated with words like "of" (46), "in" (46), and "our" (30). Though "our" was associated with "students" (30) and might suggest insider status--as it did with faculty--it was positioned to the left of "students," as in "our students," in 26 of 30 appearances. This frames students as belonging to another entity, whether the faculty, program, department, or university. However, "students" were also associated with "their" (20), which, contrastingly, situates them as outsiders.

To gain additional insight into the discursive construction of "students," I examined the grammatical constructions across the word's concordance. Of its 168 instances, "students" appeared as direct objects (136) rather than active subjects (32) predominantly across the corpus (refer to Table 3). Furthermore, when "students" appeared as active, they were associated with verbs like "will" (5), "need" (4), and "develop" (4). This suggests that when standardized language is used to designate agency to "students" in mission statements, such agency is often limited to prescribed expectations in relation to tasks that students are told they "will" do or "need" to do. This is corroborated by the frequent positioning of "students" as an indirect object (136) that others "help" (15), "teach" (9), and "prepare" (8).

Positioning "students" predominantly as indirect objects, the language used by mission statements in my corpus credits students' actions to the efforts of others. Specifically, one mission notes that their "department is dedicated to . . . inculcating in them [students] the ability to think critically and communicate effectively in their professional and personal lives." Here, students are positioned as objects rather than agents, being taught how to communicate effectively. Equating student behavior with that of the department, this statement's neutral language does not account for a range of students' thinking and communication styles; instead, its language frames students' thought processes and communication practices as behaviors shaped by standardized departmental efforts. Likewise, despite the association of "students" with the words "become" and "develop," students' bodyminds are never mentioned in the missions. Instead, through assumptions of standard bodies engaged in productive action, these statements reinforce specific forms of student engagement as indicative of "progress" and therefore appropriate for the classroom. These mission statements thus occlude the value of students' unique experiences, knowledges, and thought processes in shaping classroom and departmental practices.

Table 3: "Students" Summary Table

Most Frequent Collocates	Frequency of "Students" in Subject/ Object Position	Examples of Associated Active Verbs When "Students" Are Positioned as Subjects	Examples of Associated Direct Objects When "Students" Are Positioned as Subjects	Examples of Received Actions When "Students" Are Positioned as Objects	Examples of Indirect Actions When "Students" Are Positioned as Objects
The (58) Of (46) In (46) Writing (31) Our (30) Their (20) With (19) We (16) Develop (14) Courses (13) Faculty (12) Help (10)	Subject Position: 32 Object position: 136	Will (5) Need (4) Develop (4) Learn (2) Apply (1) Perform (1) Engage (1)	Research (2) Experience (2) Study (2) Scholarship (1) Lives (1) Knowledge (1)	Help(s), helping (15) Teach/ teaching (9) Prepare(s) (8) Provide/ providing (7) Encourage (5) Offer(s) (5)	Read (7) Write (7) Develop (6) Learn (5) Become (4) Practice (4) Gain (3) Understand (3)

We

"We" was the most frequently occurring pronoun in the corpus (107), and I analyzed its appearances to better understand the role of pronouns in constructing student and faculty identities (refer to Table 4). "We" was heavily associated with "students" (16), which consistently occurred somewhere to the right of "we." This suggests that "we" and "students" are framed by the mission statement language as separate entities. Through sentence-level analysis of the concordances, I found "department" (58) and "faculty" (20) to be the only identifiable referents of "we," excluding students from this group. In addition, "we" was frequently associated with verbs like those co-occurring with faculty, such as "offer" (8), "encourage" (4), "help" (3) and "provide" (3). For example, one mission statement notes, "We provide cutting-edge training in writing for first year students." This suggests that mission statement language positions "we" as active agents whose efforts enable the "training" and subsequent development of "students."

Table 4: "We" Summary Table

Most Frequent Collocates of "We"	Referents of "We"	Frequent Actions Associated with "We"	Frequent Direct Objects Associated with "We"
The (48) Of (34) In (26) Our (20) Students (16) Believe (14) Offer (9) Writing (7) Have (6)	Faculty (20) Department (58) Unclear (29) Students (0)	Believe (14) Offer (8) Encourage (4) Aim (3) Help (3) Provide (3) Produce (3) Prepare (3) Seek (3)	Students (15) Writing (7) World (4) Courses (3)

Our

I next examined the concordances and collocates of the possessive pronoun "our," as the term often was used across the mission statements (123). While "students" (30) was a frequent collocate of "our," it was mostly positioned as a direct object (24), indicating that students belong *to* "us," or faculty, rather than *with* them. "Courses/ classes" (14) was also a common direct object of "our," suggesting that "our" reflects the perspective of faculty or departments. One program explains that "Because … texts in their infinite variety take as their subjects our fellow humans, our histories, and our cultures, we aim in effect to equip our students both to read the world, and write the future." In this statement, students are positioned as objects rather than agents, who are "equipped" by educators to read and write. By standardizing all "histories" and "cultures" as "ours," this statement also problematically equates a range of histories and cultures, including those frequently underrepresented in classroom or popular discourse. In the absence of a specific referent, constructions of "our" confuse classroom experiences with those of all.

The use of "our" across the corpus likewise demonstrates the term's capacity to demarcate normative, ableist boundaries. Phrases like "our own" (5) suggest that independent action and ownership is valued by this collective group. Likewise, "our" was frequently associated with "work" (4) and "research" (4), which suggests that "our" group is united through their productive commitments. In addition, through the relationship of "our" with direct objects like "place" (3) and "community" (3), "our" presumes that all of "us" are part of one, singular community. For example, one mission statement notes, "Our commitment is to enrich the intellectual and cultural life of our campus, our community, and the individuals who compose them." This presumes that to be a part of "us," one must identify with prescribed understandings of "intellect," "culture," and "community." While words like "our" may seem inclusive, their tendency to draw universal assumptions may lead to the exclusion of populations like disabled individuals who reflect non-normative experiences. As I highlight later in the discussion of these findings, such language may thus contribute to the erasure of embodied differences within classroom and institutional contexts by encouraging individuals to assimilate with standard, normative structures.

Table 5: "Our" Summary Table

Frequent Collocates of "Our"	Referents of "Our"	Frequent Direct Objects of "Our"
To (40) Of (40) In (36) The (36) Students (30) We (20) Writing (18) Courses (14) Mission (10)	Department: 79 Faculty: 20 Unclear: 24	Students (24) Courses/classes (14) Mission (6) Faculty (5) Own (5) Program (5) Research (4) Work (4) Department (4) Work (4) Place (3) Actions (3) Community (3)

They

Given the insider/outsider dynamics emerging from the data, I next examined the concordances and collocates of "they" (39) to see how the word compared and contrasted with "we." Upon analysis of the "they" concordance, I found that the most common referent of "they" was "students" (30). Like "students," "they" was associated with indirect action verbs like "can" (8), "need" (5), and "learn" (4), and indicating that "they" are similarly framed by missions as passive outsiders learning to engage in prescribed ways. Likewise, by associating "they" with words like "can," such statements presume that "they" are universally able. The mission statements thus do not account for the generative value of students' embodied differences in shaping their individual learning experiences and the broader knowledge-making practices within university classrooms.

Table 6: "They" Summary Table

Most Frequent Collocates of "They"	Referents of "They"	Frequent Actions Associated with "They"	Frequent Direct Objects Associated with "They"
In (13) Of (11) Can (8) Writing (7) Write (5) Need (5) Learn (4) Our (4)	Students (30) Faculty (2) Other (7)	Need (5) Learn (4) Initiate (2) Complete (2) Understand (1) Practice (1) Constitute (1) Discern (1) Teach (1) Use (1)	Research (2) Perspective (1) Listening (1) Voices (1) Conditions (1) Connections (1)

Their

I then examined the collocates and concordances of "their" (74) as this word also frequently occurred across the corpus. As previously demonstrated by "they," findings indicated that "students" was a frequent collocate (20) of "their," occurring predominantly to its left side (19). Through a close analysis of the "their" concordance, I found that "students" (59) was predominantly positioned as the referent of "their," while "faculty" (7) was far less frequently associated with "their." Like the other pronouns, "their" was often used to denote in and out-group boundaries, specifically when positioned in contrast to "our." Like "our," "their" reflected an assumption of ableist independence through its association with "own" (8). Likewise, "their" "writing," (5), "lives" (4), "communities" (4), and "thinking" (4) are presumed by mission statement language to be universal. For example, one mission statement notes, "We emphasize writing skills, critical thinking, and creativity as a means of preparing students for the increasing demands on their literacy in the workplace and in their communities." While this statement uses standardizing language applicable across contexts, it does not account for the fact that writing classrooms offer a specific, limited understanding of literacy that may or may not fully prepare students to engage across diverse cultural and professional contexts. Likewise, this statement does not consider how productive, rational understandings of literacy may invalidate certain thought processes or behaviors that do not align with standard logics. Finally, such generalizing statements do not consider the complex ways in which certain bodyminds may experience political inequities in certain professional and cultural contexts when their literacies and knowledge-making practices do not align with expected norms. By not addressing students' embodied differences, these statements miss the opportunity to articulate how their programs and courses validate the personal and political literacy experiences of a range of student identities.

Table 7: "Their" Summary Table

Frequent Collocates of "Their"	Referents of "Their"	Frequent Direct Objects of "Their"
In (26) Of (22) Students (20) Writing (10) Lives (9) Own (8) Develop (8)	Students (59) Faculty (7) Other (8)	Own (8) Writing (5) Lives (4) Communities (4) Thinking (4) Goals (3)

What We Learn: Assimilation, Disembodiment, and Productivity.

Through an analysis of word frequency, concordance, and collocation, three themes emerge from the language in this mission statement corpus. Each of these, in turn, leads to subsequent insights about how to recraft mission statements to avoid neoliberal, ableist assumptions and language.

Assimilation

The language of the mission statements in my corpus generally demarcates boundaries between students and the broader academic community. Faculty are positioned as a standard group, united as "members" through their ongoing "commitment" to their departments and students. Faculty were positioned frequently as both subjects and objects in mission statements: their agency seems grounded in their alignment with department expectations. Across the mission statement documents, "faculty" are often charged with "teach[ing]" students prescribed, insider behaviors (Table 2). The use of pronouns in the mission statements further indicated this dynamic, with "we" and "our" typically designating faculty and "they" and "their" indicating students (Tables 4-7). Specifically, "our" faculty and departments, united by collective "actions" and "community" (Table 5), are charged with acclimating students to the university and preparing them for the workforce. The frequent positioning of "students" as the indirect objects of faculty and departmental efforts further illustrates this trend (Table 3). Collectively, these mission statements hold both faculty and students accountable to normative standards.

By attempting to transcend student and faculty differences to promote inclusion, such standard language actually excludes. This standardization of student experience is most apparent in discussions of "students" as "develop[ing]," "learn[ing]," "becom[ing]" and "practic[ing]" in universal ways (Table 3). Through such discourse, these mission statements standardize experience by dictating appropriate behavioral norms. These findings demonstrate that neoliberalism-- the forces of profit, control, and efficiency--inflects how these missions encourage student and faculty assimilation with normative expectations (Mitchell and Snyder 8). Although many of the missions note values of diversity, CDA of the documents suggest that such values are occluded by language that encourages alignment with the status quo. Rather than including disabled bodyminds as they are, such normalizing discourses rhetorically circulate ableism and contribute to disability's erasure. Consequently, by presuming that classroom content and practices will align with students' individual knowledges, experiences, and behaviors, the standard language reflected by this mission statement corpus may indirectly communicate that knowledges and experiences beyond standard universals are invalid and unwelcome within classroom spaces.

Disembodiment

The standard language in the corpus's mission statements also disregards uniquely embodied experiences, thus reinforcing the homogeneity of imagined student and faculty bodies. Framed as belonging to an "our" or "we," individual faculty difference is erased by references to collective "work," "actions," and "community" (Table 5). Student embodiment is similarly overlooked, as students are assumed to "develop" uniformly (Table 3). Such framing situates disabled individuals in precarious positions, as they reflect bodyminds that challenge idealized norms. Specifically, normative understandings of rhetorical engagement often reflect communication and behavioral practices associated with able bodyminds. These rhetorical standards, in turn, guide norms related to social interaction and human citizenship. Historically, the non-normative engagement of disabled individuals has been framed not only as "rhetorically suspect" but also as less than human (Yergeau 3, 6). In standardizing engagement, these mission statements simultaneously dictate the bounds of social experience. Furthermore, student engagement is frequently divorced from the body through the continuous positioning of students as objects rather than embodied agents across the documents (Table 3). Engaged in processes of "develop[ing]," "learn[ing]" and "becom[ing]," student actions are credited to the efforts of faculty and departments. In drawing from standardized, neoliberal language, these collective mission statements do not account for the embodied nature of the writing process and the unique knowledges that students bring with them into the classroom. In addition, by presenting all students' rhetorical experiences as equal, such statements do not account for the ways in which students' intersectionally embodied differences, such as ability, race, class, sexuality, and culture, may impact their rhetorical capacities when engaging with specific audiences in certain contexts. Such constructions thus disregard the highly political nature of the writing process.

Productivity

The ableist implications of standardizing language are similarly reflected through the corpus's focus on productive independence. "Faculty" and "we" are discursively framed as active agents across the mission statements (Table 2 and 4), engaged in efforts of "publish[ing]," "coordinat[ing]," "contribut[ing]," and "produc[ing]." To participate successfully within the department and university, such language communicates that faculty must align with standard notions of productivity. In addition, both "faculty" and "we" are expected to contribute to the progress of "students," indicated by the frequency of words like "support," "teach," "offer," and "help" used across the mission statements.

Students, in turn, are positioned as direct objects, passively receiving faculty efforts and "learn[ing]," "develop[ing]" and "becom[ing]" universally productive (Table 3 and 6). In addition, through frequent discussions related to what "student(s)" "will," "can," and "need" to do, the standardized language of this mission statement corpus suggests that certain behaviors are normative, perhaps even necessary for full participation (Table 3 and 6). The mission statements do not anticipate difference, complication, or failure. The language in these mission statements also does not consider the unequal distribution of resources across student populations and the varying degrees of labor required of them.

Focused on standard, independent students, these mission statements forget the "inequities" and "economic realities" that privilege some students over others (Dolmage, *Academic* 107). Emphasizing efficient individual progress, the neoliberal language in these statements contributes to ableism's circulation by excluding disabled individuals, such as those with autism or mental illness, whose rhetorical actions may appear involuntary, unproductive, or dependent when measured against neoliberal standards (Yergeau 9-10).

Framework for (Re)constructing Mission Statements

CDA analysis of these mission statements reveals that they may unknowingly circulate ableism across universities through their reliance on neoliberal standards that prioritize profit, control, and efficiency in ways that exclude or invalidate disabled experiences. When drawing from such neoliberal language, universities may impede their department's efforts towards equitable inclusion by endorsing disembodied, apolitical understandings of writing education. I thus recommend that writing programs and compositionists "crip" their documentation practices. To "crip" means to be "non-compliant" and "anti-assimilationist" by upholding disability as "a desirable part of the world" (Hamraie and Fritsch 2). By "cripping" documentation strategies, we can resist the assimilative impulses reflected across these findings and consider disability not as a problem to be resolved but as a generative source of institutional transformation (Dolmage, *Disability* 96). To "crip" documentation practices, I recommend that compositionists consider insights from TPC, which recognizes how documents "construc[t] reality and determin[e] what—and more relevantly, who—counts as normal" (Browning and Cagle 443) because they endorse particular "identities, social practices, ideological positions, discursive statements [and] social groups" (Slack et al. 28) within institutional spaces.

To resist potentially ableist documentation strategies, I offer three general guidelines that contextualize this study in relation to TPC: articulating anti-assimilationist multiplicity, validating students' embodied agency, and advocating for collaborative interdependence. This section outlines each guideline and models that strategy through revisions to analyzed mission statements. I offer these revisions in recognition of their limitations as distanced from each program's initial intentions but with the hope that they will be useful through local contextualization.

Articulating Anti-assimilationist Multiplicity

As TPC articulates, reliance on "normative commonplaces" may result in documents that confuse inclusion with normative assimilation by overlooking individuals' uniquely embodied experiences and needs (Konrad 135).

When mission statements endorse behaviors and expectations associated with dominant, neoliberal standards of productivity and efficiency, they may, indirectly, communicate to readers a need for alignment with such standards. By attending to how disabled students experience academic spaces differently, we can better understand and challenge "professional discourses ... [that may] reinforce normalcy and marginalize the embodied knowledge" of disabled individuals" (Palmeri 50). I thus recommend that composers of mission statements identify and resist neoliberalism's normalizing tendencies by anticipating a range of student and faculty bodyminds in their language practices in order to produce more equitable documents. To do so, I offer the following guidelines:

1. Avoid Norm-Prescribing Language

The mission statements in this corpus prioritize able embodiments through linguistic assumptions related to productive success. This is illustrated in the repetition of "can" and "will" across the statements and the presence of ableist language like "see," "vision," and "voices." Such language disregards other forms of engagement that may not align with ableist standards, such as those demonstrated by deaf or blind students. By interrogating normalcy, we can identify and disrupt ableism in institutional spaces (Moeller and Jung, n.p.). I thus recommend that mission statements avoid norm-prescribing language. To demonstrate the impact of this shift, I offer a revision of text from my corpus:

> Original Text: "Students **need to** become more globally aware and better equipped to **navigate nimbly** a broader and ... rapidly shifting world."
>
> Revision: In these courses, **students may** become more globally aware and better equipped to navigate writing amidst rapidly shifting **cultural and global dynamics.**

This revision removes ableist language like "nimbly," and it resituates the writing process from reflecting a series of necessary mandates to a process that students may engage in across dynamic contexts. Composers of mission statements may thus resist neoliberal goals of normative assimilation by avoiding language that assumes students and faculty of able bodyminds and statements that frame certain behaviors as imperative. Through such methods, compositionists can begin to move away from neoliberal articulations that understand access as an assimilation with ableist norms and instead articulate access as a frictional opportunity to both critique and move beyond established structures (Hamraie and Fritsch 10).

2. Cultivate Multiplicity

Similarly, this study indicates that mission statements often promote equal access to the same, standard knowledge. Thus, these statements "hol[d] bodies and texts to normative ideals" by offering "alternative ways into the same thing" (Boyle and Rivers 31, 37). This may enforce homogeneity while negating alternative forms of engagement. Consequently, I recommend the generation of multiple forms of engagement and end goals attuned to diverse embodiments. To indicate how this shift might be accomplished, I offer the following revision to corpus text:

> Original Text: The "department is dedicated **to enlightening** students about the world and **inculcating in them** the ability to think critically and communicate effectively in their professional and personal lives."
>
> Revision: The department **supports student and faculty efforts to** think critically and communicate effectively in their professional and personal lives by **drawing from a diverse multiplicity** of personal, professional, academic, social, and political **perspectives**.

This revision situates students' experiences as integral to classroom knowledge construction. Rather than a skill "inculcated" in students by a department, critical thinking is here reframed as a process that requires students' active engagement with a complex range of perspectives. This revision challenges neoliberal standardization and cultivates multiplicity by anticipating a range of intersectional knowledges and prioritizing students' lived experiences as integral to classroom learning. Such revisions may also foster what Casey Boyle and Nathaniel Rivers refer to as "multiple ontologies," or multiple ways of being. Challenging accessible initiatives that offer individuals various routes to standardized constructions, Boyle and Rivers call for an idea of access that promotes multiplicity through accommodations that expand, deepen, and potentially challenge dominant structures (37). The revisions offered here thus not only resist assimilation with neoliberal standards but ultimately challenge such standards by multiplying rhetorical possibilities.

Validating Students' Embodied Knowledge

Standardized mission statements may obscure the needs of unique embodiments by universalizing student and faculty experiences. One possible reason is that composers of such documents often assume an audience of "unproblematic and disembodied" users and do not anticipate the unique needs of diverse bodyminds (Melonçon 69). In addition, like all embodiments, disability is experienced dynamically by individuals "depending on the time of day, specific physical environment, and condition of their body at any particular moment" (Oswal and Melonçon 275). By assuming an audience of consistent, disembodied ability, composers of mission statements may fail to anticipate the flexible resources that disabled individuals may need (Wendell 39). To pursue more complexly embodied understandings of users, I recommend the following:

1. Value Embodied Difference

Mission statements should prioritize embodied difference through attention to intersectionality, or how personal experiences of "privilege or oppression" are mutually and complexly informed by embodied identity categories like disability, race, gender, and sexuality (Berne et al. 227). I would suggest that mission statements avoid "mechanistic" understandings of audience and instead attend to the complex and uniquely situated nature of human experience (Gutsell and Hulgin 92). To demonstrate considerations for intersectional context, I offer the following revision of text from my corpus:

> Original Text: **"We** emphasize writing **skills,** critical thinking, and creativity **as a means of preparing students** for the increasing demands on **their literacy** in the workplace and in **their communities."**
>
> Revision: **Students draw upon class content and their individual and collective intersectional experiences to** develop the writing skills, critical thinking capacities, and creative thought-processes to negotiate literacy demands in **diverse** workplaces and communities.

While the original version positions "we" as the active agent and students as passive recipients of "skills," the revision frames students as agents who draw upon their intersectional experiences as valid sources of knowledge to develop writing, critical thinking, and creative capacities. This allows all students, including disabled students, to understand literacy as a complexly contextual, intersectional, and frictional "negotiation" and to recognize the value of diverse knowledges in navigating professional and public contexts. It likewise expands notions of critical thinking beyond rational standards by positioning it as influenced by personal experiences. Mission statements that draw from intersectional understandings of individual embodiment can both foster more dynamic understandings of embodiment and resist the universal standardization that often encourages disability's erasure (Berne et al. 227).

2. Promote Student Agency

Mission statements in the corpus frequently positioned students as passive recipients of faculty and departmental efforts. Such constructions deny students the capacity to influence classroom knowledge and writing structures. Instead, I recommend that mission statements anticipate and "value…diverse embodied experiential knowledges" as integral to writing processes, specifically in relation to populations who may be historically marginalized (Smyser-Fauble 88). I thus recommend that programmatic and departmental documents position students as active agents in mission statements, so that it is clear how students influence classroom epistemologies and practices. To exemplify how missions might be reconstructed to consider student agency, I revise text from my corpus below:

> Original Text: "**We provide** cutting-edge training in writing for first-year students."
>
> Revision: **Students** individually and collectively develop writing skills and co-construct knowledge by integrating classroom content with their **diverse literacy experiences.**

This revision denotes not only a change in language but likewise an epistemic shift from an understanding of writing as skills passed down from faculty to students to a process that asks students to co-construct knowledge by integrating classroom learning with their own literacy experiences. Through this revision, writing is represented as a collective, dynamic experience, rather than a set of skills to be passed on. Missions can actively displace dominant, neoliberal norms by centering the embodied experiences of a range of students, including disabled students, in document design. Such a redesign promotes the DS value of universal design, or design for as many individuals as possible, by situating students of diverse bodyminds, including disabled students, as co-constructors of classroom knowledge in relation to literacy and writing (Dolmage, *Academic* 127-129; Hitt 54-55).

Advocating for Collaborative Interdependence

Collectively, the missions disregard students' ranging abilities through phrases like "students can" and "students will." Such statements promote able ideals by advocating for a productive independence that disregards students who may engage with class materials in unanticipated ways or with access to resources others do not have. I thus recommend a shift to statements encouraging collective interdependence that demonstrate how "relational circuits between bodies, environments, and tools" influence individual autonomy (Hamraie and Fritsch 12). To show how documentation strategies might consider collective interdependence, I offer the following recommendations:

1. Remove Insider/Outsider Markers

The use of pronouns across the mission statements establishes boundaries of belonging that promote a particular status quo. I thus recommend that composers of mission statements specifically avoid the use of insider pronouns such as "our," us," and "we." Likewise, rather than positioning students as passive recipients of faculty efforts, classroom agency should be communicated as collectively negotiated between and among faculty and students. To demonstrate these tactics, I offer a revision of selected text from my corpus:

> Original Text: "Because [literary] texts in their infinite variety take as **their** subjects **our** fellow humans, **our** histories, and **our** cultures, **we** aim in effect to equip **our** students both to read the world and write the future."
>
> Revision: Because [literary] texts engage **diverse** histories, cultures, and personal perspectives, students and faculty **collectively examine** course texts by **dialoguing across their different histories, cultures, and positionalities** to both read the world and write the future.

By removing "our," and "we" and by framing textual examination as driven by difference, this revision anticipates students' and faculty's varying positionalities rather than encouraging individuals to assimilate with prescribed standards. Likewise, by understanding the collective nature of this process, this revision prioritizes DS's goals of interdependence, which resists neoliberalism's individualizing impulses through collective efforts to support differently abled individuals as they are (Berne et al. 227-228).

2. Promote Collaboration

Phrases like "every student," present across the corpus, position learning as an individualized process of meeting standard expectations, which may erase differences like disability. I therefore recommend the prioritization of difference through constructions that anticipate and draw upon a myriad of dynamic experiences. As TPC articulates, disability should inspire large-scale environmental change across institutional contexts (Konrad 138; Palmeri 57). To illustrate considerations for disability, I offer a revision of text from my corpus:

> Original Text: "FYW aims to **develop each student's** capacity to understand and adapt to new writing situations."

Revision: In FYW courses, **students and faculty collectively work** to critically understand and adapt to new writing situations.

Rather than positioning "students" as objectively "developed" by FYW, this revision frames students and faculty as collaborators. Likewise, this statement articulates "understanding" as a process that requires collective, critical effort rather than a static, individualized activity. As part of fostering collaboration and promoting student agency, writing programs and departments might even incorporate student feedback in the review and revision of materials (Smyser-Fauble 87). Such tactics challenge neoliberal goals of independence by positioning learning as an interdependent process between students and faculty. They likewise support universal design by directly involving students in the ongoing redesign of classroom spaces and the documents, like mission statements, that organize behavior within them (Dolmage 127-129; Hitt 54-55).

Conclusion

A CDA study of a corpus of R1 mission statements provided, here, the raw material for considering how composition programs and departments position themselves and their students relative to each other; to neoliberalism's aims of profit, control, and efficiency; and to ableism's language practices with respect to assimilation, embodiment, and productivity. This positioning fuels the rhetorical circulation of standardizing language that may have exclusionary effects, particularly upon disabled individuals. There are, however, strategies for thinking about institutional documentation that steer away from both neoliberalism and ableism's pitfalls: validating students' embodied knowledge, articulating anti-assimilationist multiplicity, and advocating for collaborative interdependence. These guidelines reflect a starting point for thinking resistance; they can, and should, be developed further for departments' unique needs. In offering these guidelines, I recognize constraint: many programs and departments construct mission statements in response to the assessment practices of institutional structures or accrediting organizations. While such practices aim to ensure that students receive consistent educational experiences, this article illustrates that such standard goals may contribute to the circulation of an ableist rhetoric that marginalizes disabled individuals. Future research therefore might examine these impacts and pursue non-assimilative forms of assessment. Methodologically speaking, future research might push past the limits of CDA and analyze the embodied impacts that mission statements can have on students and faculty. As neoliberal standardization continues to permeate higher education, it is vital that compositionists acknowledge and assess its impacts on documentation practices.

By cripping mission statements and other documents through considerations for DS and TPC, compositionists may celebrate difference and expand documentation beyond ableism's violently neutral bounds.

Notes

1. I use disability-first language (i.e., disabled individuals) rather than person-first language (i.e., individuals with disabilities) to prioritize disability as a desirable aspect of one's lived experience. Person-first language rmay einforce ableist assumptions that one is a person despite one's disability and disregards the political nature of disability (Cherney 23-25).

2. Margaret Price's term "bodyminds" demonstrates the connection and mutual influence between the body and mind.

Acknowledgments

I gratefully acknowledge the *Composition Studies* reviewers and editors whose generous feedback helped to improve the quality of this piece. I also express sincere appreciation to Dr. Maureen Daly Goggin, Dr. Elenore Long, Dr. Shirley Rose, and Dr. Mark Hannah for their guidance and support as I developed this project.

Works Cited

Baker, Paul. *Using Corpora in Discourse Analysis*. Continuum, 2007.

Berne, Patricia et al. "Ten Principles of Disability Justice." *The Feminist Press,* vol. 1, no. 2, 2018, pp. 227-30. https://doi.org/10.1353/wsq.2018.0003

Bloor, Meriel and Thomas Bloor. *The Practice of Critical Discourse Analysis: An Introduction*. Hodder Arnold, 2007.

Boyle, Casey and Nathaniel Rivers. "A Version of Access," *Technical Communication Quarterly*, vol. 25, no. 1, 2016, pp. 29-47. https://doi.org/10.1080/10572252.2016.1113702

Browning, Ella R. and Cagle, Lauren E. "Teaching a 'Critical Accessibility Case Study': Developing Disability Studies Curricula for the Technical Communication Classroom." *Journal of Technical Writing and Communication*, vol. 47, no. 4, 2017, pp. 440-63. DOI: 10.1177/0047281616646750.

Campbell, Fiona Kumari. *Contours of Ableism: The Production of Disability and Abledness*. Palgrave Macmillan, 2009.

"Carnegie R1 and R2 Research Classifications, Doctoral Universities." 2018. https://cehd.gmu.edu/assets/docs/faculty/tenurepromotion/institutions-research-categories.pdf

Chaput, Catherine. "Rhetorical Circulation in Late Capitalism: Neoliberalism and the Overdetermination of Affective Energy." *Philosophy and Rhetoric*, vol. 43, no. 1, 2010, pp. 1-25. https://doi.org/10.1353/par.0.0047

Cherney, James. *Ablest Rhetoric*. Penn State University Press, 2019.

Dolmage, Jay. *Academic Ableism: Disability and Higher Education*. University of Michigan Press, 2017.

—. *Disability Rhetoric*. Syracuse University Press, 2014.

Foucault, Michel. *Discipline and Punish: The Birth of the Prison*. Translated by Alan Sheridan. Vintage Books, 1979.

Garland-Thomson, Rosemarie. *Extraordinary Bodies: Figuring Disability in American Culture and Literature*. Columbia University Press, 1997.

—. "Misfits: A Feminist Materialist Disability Concept." *Hypatia*, vol. 25, no. 3, 2011, pp.591-609. https://doi.org/10.1111/j.1527-2001.2011.01206.x

Gee, James Paul. "Literacy, Discourse, and Linguistics: Introduction and What is Literacy?" *Literacy: A Critical Sourcebook*, edited by Ellen Cushman, Eugene R. Kintgen, Barry M. Kroll, Mike Rose, Bedford/St. Martin's, 2001, pp. 525-44.

Giroux, Henry A. "Neoliberalism, Corporate Culture, and the Promise of Higher Education: The University as a Democratic Public Sphere." *Harvard Educational Review*, vol. 72, no. 4, 2002, pp. 425-63. https://doiorg.ezproxy1.lib.asu.edu/10.17763/haer.72.4.0515nr62324n71p1

Gutsell, Margaret and Kathleen Hulgin. "Supercrips Don't Fly: Technical Communication to Support Ordinary Lives of People with Disabilities." *Rhetorical Accessibility: At the Intersection of Technical Communication and Disability Studies*, edited by Lisa Melonçon, Baywood Publishing Company, Inc., 2013, pp. 83-94.

Hamraie, Aimi. "Designing Collective Access: A Feminist Disability Theory of Universal Design." *Disability Studies Quarterly*, vol. 33, no. 4, 2013. http://dsq-sds.org/article/view/3871.

Hamraie, Aimi and Kelly Fritsch. "Crip Technoscience Manifesto." *Catalyst: Feminism, Theory, Technoscience*, vol. 5, no. 1, 2019, pp. 1-33. https://journals-sagepub-com.ezproxy1.lib.asu.edu/doi/pdf/10.1177/2329490617752577

Hitt, Alison. "Foregrounding Accessibility Through (Inclusive) Universal Design in Professional Communication Curricula." *Business and Professional Communication Quarterly*, vol. 8, no. 1, 2018, pp. 52-65. DOI: 10.1177/23299490617739884.

Konrad, Annika. "Reimagining Work: Normative Commonplaces and Their Effects on Accessibility in Workplaces." *Business and Professional Communication Quarterly*, vol. 81, no. 1, 2018, pp. 123-41. DOI: 10.1177/232949061772577

McRuer, Robert. *Crip Theory*. New York University Press, 2006.

Melonçon, Lisa. "Toward a Theory of Technological Embodiment." *Rhetorical Accessibility: At the Intersection of Technical Communication and Disability Studies*, edited by Lisa Melonçon. Baywood Publishing Company, Inc., 2013, pp. 67-82.

Mitchell, David T. and Sharon L. Snyder. *The Biopolitics of Disability: Neoliberalism, Ablenationalism, and Peripheral Embodiment*. University of Michigan Press, 2015.

Moeller, Marie and Julie Jung. "Sites of Normalcy: Understanding Online Education as Prosthetic Technology." *Disability Studies Quarterly*, vol. 34, no. 4, 2014. https://dsq-sds.org/article/view/4020/3796

Oswal, Sushil K. and Lisa Melonçon. "Saying No to the Checklist: Shifting from an Ideology of Normalcy to an Ideology of Inclusion in Online Writing Instruction." *WPA: Writing Program Administration*, vol. 40, no. 3, 2017, pp. 61-77.

Palmeri, Jason. "Disability Studies, Cultural Analysis, and the Critical Practice of Technical Communication Pedagogy." *Technical Communication Quarterly*, vol. 15, no. 1, 2006. https://doi.org/10.1207/s15427625tcq1501_5

Price, Margaret. "The Bodymind Problem and the Possibility of Pain." *Hypatia*, 2014, pp. 1-17.

Schoen, Megan. "Your Mission, Should You Choose to Accept It: A Survey on Writing Programs and Institutional Mission." *Writing Program Administration*, vol. 42, no. 2, 2019, pp. 37-57.

Slack, Jennifer Daryl et al. "The Technical Communicator as Author: Meaning, Power, Authority. *Journal of Business and Technical Communication,* vol. 7, no. 1, 1993, pp.12-36. https://doi.org/10.1177/1050651993007001002

Smyser-Fauble, Barbi. "The University Required Accommodations Statement: What Accommodation' Teaches Technical Communication Students and Educators." *Key Theoretical Frameworks: Teaching Technical Communication in the Twenty-first Century,* edited by Angela M. Haas and Michelle F. Eble, Utah State University Press, 2018, pp. 68-92.

Stenberg, Shari J. *Repurposing Composition: Feminist Interventions for a Neoliberal Age.* Utah State University Press, 2015.

Swales, John M. and Priscilla S. Rogers. "Discourse and the projection of corporate culture: The Mission Statement." *Discourse and Society*, vol. 6, no. 2, 1995, pp. 223-42.

Welch, Nancy. "La Langue de Coton: How Neoliberal Language Pulls the Wool over Faculty Governance." *Pedagogy*, vol. 11, no. 3, 2011, pp. 545-53. DOI 10.1215/15314200-1302759.

Wendell, Susan. *The Rejected Body: Feminist Philosophical Reflections on Disability.* Routledge, 1996.

Wood, Tara et al. "Where We Are: Disability and Accessibility: Moving Beyond Disability 2.0 in Composition Studies." *Composition Studies*, vol. 42, no. 2, 2014, pp. 147–50.

Yergeau, M. Remi. *Authoring Autism: On Rhetoric and Neurological Queerness.* Duke University Press, 2018.

Appendix A: List of Mission Statements

1. Arizona State University-Tempe, Writing Programs
2. Colorado State University-Fort Collins, Composition Program
3. Cornell University, Knight Writing Institute
4. Emory University, First Year Writing Program
5. Iowa State University, Department of English
6. Kansas State University, English Department
7. Michigan State University, First-Year Writing Program
8. New Jersey Institute of Technology, Department of Humanities
9. Northeastern University, Department of English
10. Syracuse University, Writing Program
11. Texas Tech University, Department of English

12. Tulane University of Louisiana, Department of English
13. The University of Alabama, Department of English
14. University of Arizona, Foundations Writing Program
15. University of Arkansas, Rhetoric and Composition
16. University of California-Los Angeles, Writing Programs
17. University of Central Florida, Department of Writing and Rhetoric
18. University of Colorado-Boulder, Program for Writing and Rhetoric
19. University of Florida, University Writing Program
20. University of Hawai'i-Monoa, Department of English
21. University of Louisville, English Department
22. University of Michigan-Ann Arbor, English Department
23. University of Minnesota-Twin Cities, Center for Writing
24. University of Missouri-Columbia, Campus Writing Program
25. University of Nebraska-Lincoln, Department of English
26. University of New Mexico-Main Campus, Department of English
27. University of North Texas, First-Year Writing
28. University of South Florida-Main Campus, Department of English
29. The University of Texas at Arlington, Department of English
30. The University of Texas at El Paso, Department of English
31. University of Washington-Seattle Campus, Department of English
32. University of Wisconsin-Milwaukee, English Department

Course Design

Global Efforts to Professionalize Online Literacy Instructors: GSOLE's Basic OLI Certification

Amy Cicchino, Kevin DePew, Jason Snart, and Scott Warnock

The Global Society of Online Literacy Educators (GSOLE), an organization that we describe more fully below, was founded in 2016 as "an international organization connecting those who teach reading, alphabetic writing, and multimodal composition as digital literacies in online educational settings" (GSOLE Website). Rather than this course design describing a student-facing course, the course design that follows describes GSOLE's Basic Online Literacy Instruction (OLI) Certification courses for *instructors* within our discipline (our Basic OLI Certification). Because the course is instructor-facing, and we recognize these instructors are our colleagues, we have chosen to use the word participant to name them (instead of calling them *students*, even those they hold the student role in the courses).

Course Description

GSOLE's Basic OLI Certification is open to GSOLE members and is designed to help online literacy instructors, tutors, and writing program administrators learn foundational principles, theories, and practices of teaching and tutoring writing online and apply those to the contexts in which they work or anticipate working. The certification consists of two courses that span an academic year. Both courses guide participants, who come to the experience with various levels of online teaching and/or tutoring experience, toward meeting the pedagogical and curricular standards established by experts of online literacy education as articulated by GSOLE.

Participants experience both courses within a learning pod, made up of one instructor-mentor and up to five participants. The first course introduces participants to online literacy education, to key concepts and theories (e.g., accessibility and inclusivity; asynchronous, synchronous, hybrid, online, and hyflex course design; and writing pedagogy) and to GSOLE's Online Literacy Instruction (OLI) Principles and Tenets (https://gsole.org/oliresources/olip-rinciples). As well, participants explore how the principles connect to the local contexts in which they work and the ways that digital technologies do and can affect writing pedagogies. The second course focuses on assignment and activity design for online writing instruction (OWI), whether that instruction takes place within a writing course, writing center, or writing-enriched course across campus. Participants also develop strategies for assessing online learning experiences and justifying pedagogical approaches using OLI and OWI research.

Rather than participants working through a set of course objectives taken as a whole, this certification is designed around objective-specific modules. Each module includes the following:

1. Two to four essential readings with additional optional readings provided
2. A reading discussion prompt
3. An opportunity to engage in synchronous (e.g., video conferencing or phone) and/or asynchronous discussions within learning pods
4. The creation of an artifact chosen from a menu of options or created by the participants based on their professional goals and local context

Each artifact provides evidence of skills, experiences, and knowledge gleaned from that module. These artifacts are also placed in an ePortfolio along with a short personal reflection. At the end of the first course, participants draw upon their developing knowledge to produce a personal, evolving theory of OLI that communicates their OLI identity, approach to OLI, rationale for this approach, and examples from their practice. The theory of OLI should be informed by GSOLE's Principles and Tenets and readings from the first course. At the end of the second course, participants refine their theory of OLI and add it to their ePortfolio.

During the two courses, participants have multiple opportunities to receive feedback on their ePortfolio from their instructor-mentor, the two program administrators for the certification, and peers. At the end of the certification process, participants submit their ePortfolio for review for a pass/fail assessment by a GSOLE Certification Board of Evaluators, a board of GSOLE members who review the ePortfolio outside of the context of the course.

Context

GSOLE initially had a different name to fit a very different identity: ISOLE, with the "I" standing for "Institute." The original conception of the organization, which essentially came from Beth Hewett, was a professional organization that would validate the teaching practices of online writing teachers (later literacy came to replace writing). As far back as October 2015, Hewett envisioned that the first goal of such an organization would be a "Certification in Online Writing and Reading Instruction" (Hewett, pers. comm.). Those involved with the early conversations about ISOLE focused on the idea that online writing/literacy instruction required discipline-specific professional training and development. While, of course, all fields have their own nuances and require (or at least should require) their own focused training, the GSOLE founders believed that the kind of strategy-driven pedagogy of online writing/literacy courses is substantially different from the generally presentation-driven pedagogy that is the focus of certifications provided by organizations like Quality Matters. Informed by disciplinary knowledge and values, participants move through the certification dialogically with peers and instructor-mentors so as to socially construct knowledge about OLI and link it to local practice—a design that is vastly different from static, self-paced professional development that often involves participants working through materials or modules in isolation.

The idea was that GSOLE would provide a meaningful, high-quality credential at multiple levels of OLI beginning with a Basic Certification and then moving into more specific topics in OLI, like OLI in international contexts, OLI across the curriculum, and fostering community in OLI courses. However, many issues—explained in greater detail below—made starting the certification design process a challenge.

- Personnel. The organization was first non-existent: just a thought then fledgling. In the beginning, a small number of people made up GSOLE, and they were heavily involved with getting the organization running. There were not enough hours for them to be instructors, course designers, and program administrators. Questions surrounding who would design and teach the certification loomed large.
- Money. Certification also hit a snag because of a fundamental inequity in higher education. Certainly, an organization like this was going to need money to operate, and the concept was very much a business model, with certifications supporting the organization. However, those most in need of certification were often contingent faculty and graduate students for whom paying for the certification would be most difficult. It was a catch-22 that derailed the process for several years.
- Platform. How would the course be taught? On what platform? As much as we might criticize Blackboard and similar learning management systems (LMSs), they do many things instructors and participants need in familiar ways, and these are often the platforms instructors would be using in their teaching. There are free platforms, but they can be glitchy or underpowered. If we used an institution's LMS, we would have to negotiate ownership of GSOLE's course material with that institution, which could make it difficult to control other decisions, especially the price point.

- How would the certification matter and to whom? A certification, of course, is meaningless unless others value it. Certainly, with only a few dozen members at its start, GSOLE did not have the kind of traction that would enable it to be highly regarded if it appeared on a job candidate's CV. We needed to figure out how to communicate the value of the certification to those outside of GSOLE and the discipline.
- Ownership of materials. Especially considering the low-budget-by-necessity initial efforts, the question of who owned certification materials was tricky: Could individual instructors take materials with them? Would the materials belong to GSOLE—a prospect that nobody overtly liked but that raised the problem of re-creating courses?
- Administration. Again, the idea of volunteerism loomed large. Would an army of volunteers simply run the entire certification process?

Because of these challenges, there were several false starts in trying to get a certification course up and running, and we decided to move away from the certification once GSOLE launched. Hewett had made agreements with one institutional department to develop the institute; however, upper administrators were not interested in this initiative. Furthermore, the organization was involved with other initiatives, such as developing conferences, a journal, and webinars; GSOLE has been quite successful—a topic for another publication—so much so that certification was pushed to the side. But, as we realized the enormous impact a literacy-concentrated pedagogical training structure could have, a GSOLE Certification Committee formed in recommitment to the certification in 2019. The curriculum for the certification was finalized in spring 2020 (just as the COVID-19 pandemic began) and a condensed micropilot was launched in the summer of 2020. The first full cohort was enrolled during the 2020–2021 academic year.

Theoretical Rationale

Longstanding calls for online literacy instructor professionalization have emphasized the need for preparation to be discipline-specific and theoretically informed (CCCC; GSOLE; Hewett and Bourelle; Hewett and Warnock). After all, effective OLI demands more than moving face-to-face learning materials online. Scholars in OLI recommend professionalization for online instructors include learning about different instructional modalities (Mick and Middlebrook; Snart), understanding how delivery formats and modalities can impact student learning (Boyd; Harris et al.), designing and justifying accessible OLI curriculum that leverages the affordances of the online space

(Cargile Cook; DePew; Nielsen; Oswal and Meloncon; Rodrigo), enhancing teaching practices to confront student retention issues that often surface in online learning (Borgman and Dockter; Harris and McCloud), and considering how OLI theory can be linked to local practice.

While many institutions offer training on using the technologies that mediate online education (namely, the LMS), few have access to the expertise and resources necessary to deliver the training described above (Hewett and Hallman Martini). These constraints are further complicated by the reality that online instruction is often taken on by contingent or part-time faculty, who may or may not be local to the institution at which they are teaching (Bedford; Mechenbier). For all these reasons, designing and delivering this much-needed professional development can be a challenge for institutions. General technology and LMS training do not necessarily help instructors design discipline-specific assignments and learning activities.

The need for discipline-specific online professional development only intensified when COVID-19 drove institutions across the world to online, or emergency remote, instruction with little time or resources to prepare faculty. GSOLE saw a capacity to fill this need and deliver theoretically rich, praxis-focused professional development. Building upon Hewett's vision, the GSOLE Certification Committee understood two principles about the certification's design:

1. GSOLE would not be using the certification to tell participants what practices they needed to adopt. The committee deliberately wanted to distinguish itself from other non-discipline-specific professional development opportunities, especially some popular programs that focus on online instruction generally that teach rules for online instruction but that neglect disciplinary specificity and local contexts
2. The certification had to balance and bridge theory and practice. Graduate pedagogy courses provided an aspirational model for striking such a balance.

The GSOLE Principles and Tenets became the core of the curriculum, and the certification was designed to guide participants in applying these principles and tenets to their local contexts. Readings from OLI scholars who practice in a variety of contexts—writing centers, WAC programs, first year composition programs, K-12 classrooms, and international contexts—are linked to each principle. Voices from antiracist writing pedagogy, culturally responsive teaching, disability studies, and multimodality are also present as resources that participants should put in conversation with OLI scholarship and GSOLE's Principles and Tenets. The curriculum centers this work alongside the development of an OLI identity culminating in the creation of an ePortfolio housing a coherent OLI identity, theory, and artifacts, which serve as evidence of OLI learning. To help participants do this work, learning pods (one instructor-mentor and five participants) engage participants with OLI experts and peers. Ultimately, participants exit the certification with artifacts that they can immediately put into practice and an ePortfolio that they can use to communicate their OLI expertise to others.

Critical Reflection

In this critical reflection, we first consider the feedback from our first cohorts of participants from summer 2020 and the 2020–2021 academic year, which significantly guides us in revising the certification for future years. Then, we move into the tensions and needs instructor-mentors, program administrators, and GSOLE leadership have raised during the first year of the certification. We conclude with our plans for revision and our reflections on the value of the GSOLE Basic OLI Certification.

Participant Voices

As part of preparing this course design, we informally interviewed five GSOLE OLI Certification course participants who were in the midst of certification or completed the micro-pilot in the summer of 2020 in efforts to collect programmatic feedback. We wanted to know what motivated them to take the certification and how they were using or planned to use its credential. Interviews were conducted via Zoom, usually with one or two participants per session. Sessions ran about 30 minutes to an hour (a more formal, IRB-approved study is currently underway).

From the interviews we conducted, we gained interesting insights. For many, the initial impulse to pursue the certification was a practical desire to know more about OLI theories and concepts. One participant indicated that pursuing the certification connected to his natural inclination to lifelong learning. However, even participants who expressed an innate desire to learn more about pedagogy also identified a specific motivation: to gain greater insight and a more solid theoretical footing in OLI. One participant, a writing center administrator, said, "I wanted to explore the best practices to make sure that we were offering the best online services that we could and that what we were doing aligned with the literature and best practices of the OLI field." Another "was really interested [in] what's available that's coming out of writing studies as a discipline to help people teach writing online."

Perhaps not surprising is the degree to which the COVID-19 pandemic's effect on education writ large compelled many to focus on OLI in ways they had not done so previously. What was already a concern was made unavoidably acute by a global health crisis. Many participants said "timing" played a key role in their interest in the certification, both as instructors and those in administrative capacities. As one interviewee asked, vis-a-vis their role as a writing program administrator during summer 2020, "What's the first year writing program going to look like being taught remotely?" Another interviewee said that as their institutional role shifted from faculty to an administrative/full-time staff position, they became acutely aware of the need to establish a solid foundation in OLI as they took on train-the-teacher positions with greater peer oversight: "A huge part of my job now is to assess…and work with faculty who teach…writing in the disciplines and capstone courses."

Another pattern that emerged was that while participants felt they already had some degree of technical training in general online teaching, and indicated that their respective institutions offered professional development for online teaching, a lot of that training was technical, not theoretical (i.e., focusing more on how to use the technology). It was about what buttons to click to make the LMS do certain things. While helpful for working efficiently in an LMS, such training, many observed, was often decontextualized from pedagogy and missed the nuance that characterized teaching in particular disciplines. One interviewee noted: "…everything [in the general training] was really about like, how do we test? How do we assess students?" There was little discussion about "writing process" or "peer review," clearly central to OLI. Another commented that even when training turned to pedagogy, it felt like, "We were like 'Yeah, I'm not going to be using a quiz in my class. That's just not how I teach'—so it felt really kind of disconnected from my discipline." Even participants with substantial existing online learning professional training (like Quality Matters certification, for example) remarked how beneficial the teaching focus on the demands, challenges, and opportunities of online *literacy* instruction is (as opposed to a technical focus).

Two other aspects that drew people to the GSOLE Certification are worth noting. The first is that many, though not all, participants were already connected in some way with GSOLE, either as existing members or, more often, as presenters at one of the GSOLE annual online conferences. So, when GSOLE began to advertise its certification course—via general listservs (like WPA) and to its existing membership—many people who chose to sign up already had some affiliation with and knowledge of GSOLE. That level of familiarity helped make the certification seem less intimidating. Second, a distinguishing feature of the GSOLE certification, in fact, is its high-touch, interactive nature, very unlike what one interviewee described their previous general professional development to be: largely checklist driven and "very quantifiable." Along these lines, participants commented on the qualifications of those who were facilitating the certification, not just the level of engagement course participants had with facilitators (and each other). Participants felt as though they were getting an almost individualized graduate class experience, but, as one participant said: "It really helped that it was $75 and not, you know, like $2,000." So, we should not overlook the basic cost—or let's say value—of the GSOLE certification, especially in comparison with other general online instruction professional development.[1] A number of certification course participants report being able to garner departmental or institutional support to cover costs (often not as likely when the price tag is $1,000 or more). One interviewee mentioned they were able "to get the dean to pay for it, which was kind of amazing because they weren't paying for anything at that time."

With regards to how certification course participants are using the certification, there were a range of responses. Of course, there is the practical application of knowledge gained from readings, peer-to-peer interaction, and participant-to-facilitator interaction. One participant noted that the course "has helped to give me a lot of language, especially around areas of access and inclusivity and especially at the intersection(s) of access and technology." While they may have been aware of and actively attending to broad concerns like equity and access, they had not, prior to the certification, had a concrete vocabulary or a disciplinary framework to ground those concerns. For some, especially those in administrative roles, having that strong basis for talking about access and technology has, as one interviewee noted, "given me some resources to kind of begin those conversations [about access, equity, and technology] on campus."

Yet another interviewee working in an administrative tutoring center capacity, noted,

> I used what I learned as part of the certification right away: I designed a new tutor training module for online tutoring. I was able to adjust my own online tutoring practices and also share new tips and suggestions with the peer tutors, and I took what I learned about accessibility in an online environment and used it to improve the online resources we had available for students.

Again, the application to local concerns was immediate and particularly impactful in regard to accessibility. One interviewee summed up a common refrain quite well: "I felt less like I was just trying things out and more like I was able to use the knowledge gained from the course materials, instructors, and my peers to formulate something really solid."

In addition to practical application, we wanted to know if course participants were able to leverage the actual certification as a credential in some professional setting. One interviewee was frank in their observation that during a recent tenure review, the certification was nice to have but "I don't know how much weight that [it had] ...they were glad I was doing it, but it didn't really add any weight or anything." However, a full-time, non-tenure track participant mentioned, "I am ... proud to note that my department chair cited my ongoing efforts to complete the GSOLE Certification course in my reappointment letter to the dean. This effort, among others, she cited as evidence that I 'exceed expectations in teaching' for the department." Others, however, reported quite the opposite. For example, one interviewee directly applied the certification course knowledge to teaching work in the remote/online classroom and as part of writing center administration. For that participant, the certification is "a formal program that allows me to actually, intentionally reflect on the things I'm doing ... it also provides me with a theory, a theoretical basis, for other things I'm doing [not only] as a writing Center administrator, but also as an instructor in the writing classroom." This interviewee continued to say, however:

> I also just interviewed not too long ago for a job, and they were very interested in my certification program...they asked me specific questions about [it]...my response was very much informed by the conversations we've had in the program...The certification program helped me to articulate a theoretical, but also very practical... response to the questions that they had. It made me come across as someone who knew what [I] was about as far as online teaching was concerned..I can actually point to concrete differences that the certification program has made for me.

In addition to the practice-based knowledge that can make participants' immediate teaching and/or day-to-day administrative work better, the certification course further offers a broader framework within which to consider OLI and a vocabulary to articulate important ideas to others. It is in this sense of framing and vocabulary building that many participants found the certification so profound: it did not just allow them to become, individually, more effective, it gave them the tools to begin or strengthen conversations, processes, protocols that would make entire departments and programs more effective. Also, for at least a few of our GSOLE certification course participants, the certification is a professional credential that they have leveraged directly in professional settings like job interviews.

Successful course participants receive a digital badge created using the digital badging system called Badgr. While the badge might not be immediately recognized by an employer, it is an excellent conversation starter for someone who wants to discuss their background and expertise in OLI. Importantly, when the badge is awarded, the participant's ePortfolio link is included, so a conversation that is initiated by the badge can easily move into discussion and examination of the concrete products of GSOLE certification. With these benefits in mind, however, we still have several critical considerations driving curricular revisions in year two, which we discuss in further detail below.

Challenges to Delivering Faculty Development Online

The challenges we faced delivering the certification courses mirrored challenges that often arise in online learning environments. And, of course, many of these challenges were exacerbated by the COVID-19 pandemic, which made it difficult to determine whether challenges were caused by the personal hardships and general strain created by the pandemic or features of course design. While our participants are not students, they are online learners. For some, this was the first online course they were taking. Initially, participants in the year-long cohort struggled to acclimate to Google Classroom (the LMS). We had been hesitant to use Google Classroom at first, but our summer micro-pilot participants generally liked it and told us in an exit discussion that it functioned well across different devices. Based on their feedback, we continued with it—aware of the constraints. However, the pilot cohort that followed struggled to adjust to an LMS that looked very different from their institutional systems.

A main limitation of Google Classroom is its lack of a traditional discussion-board space, making it difficult for asynchronous peer-to-peer interaction outside of the Class Stream (an announcements thread on the homepage). This puts a lot of pressure on the other opportunities for engagement. Learning pods were instructed to offer a synchronous and/or asynchronous meeting time every three weeks (one for each of the ten modules). Additionally, the two program administrators shared opportunities for the entire cohort to come together for synchronous workshops with all participants receiving access to the recordings (facilitated by instructor-mentors or GSOLE members). Without exception, every participant wanted more opportunities for synchronous engagement.

Logistically, working around full schedules and multiple time zones to meet this desire was challenging. Equally important, as OLI experts, we wanted participants to gain experience in asynchronous community building. OLI research recommends that online literacy instructors can design synchronous and asynchronous opportunities for learning (CCCC; Mick and Middlebrook). While some students might learn better in a synchronous format, synchronous meetings are not always possible when teaching online. We continue to consider how to balance synchronous opportunities for engagement with opportunities to practice asynchronous community-building.

Several weeks into the semester, we learned that some of the open-access publication websites we linked to for readings and assignments were blocked in a few African and European countries. Quickly, we had to create downloadable versions of these materials for participants and forward our concerns to journal editors. Two such publications were GSOLE's own *Research in Online Literacy Education* and the *Online Literacies Open Resource,* with restricted viewing relating to broader Weebly access issues. This challenge of establishing international access is considerable, as restrictions can emerge from platform providers or local or national internet restrictions. However, GSOLE, as a growing international organization, recognizes the need for globalized conversations in OLI. Consideration of how national context (which includes material things like internet speed and reliability) affects access is essential to developing international professional development, like the Basic OLI Certification (Rice and St.Amant).

Other online faculty development challenges were deeply tied to labor. We estimated the certification to be roughly equivalent to a graduate-level course and expected participants to spend between three to four hours each week engaging with readings, meeting in learning pods, and completing artifacts. However, participants were active writing instructors who had demanding teaching and/or administrative loads, and some participants held contingent positions across multiple institutions. Some participants had difficulty finding the time necessary to engage in the deep learning we had hoped to foster throughout the course. On top of the general stress of finding time, our participants were experiencing a pandemic, job insecurity, and the additional stress of having to care for family members and children. Unsurprisingly, attrition rates were high. Thirteen of the 37 individuals enrolled successfully completed the certification—meaning nearly two-thirds of our participants did not complete the certification.

While participant persistence issues were, to some degree, related to the unique circumstances of 2020, they highlighted a larger issue of access and inclusion. Even the most altruistic considerations of accessibility do not always work with the actual target audiences. This, of course, is an argument for user-centered design and usability testing. COVID-19 has intensified challenges that have always existed for some members of our academic community: susceptibility and fear of illness, caretaking responsibilities, job insecurity, assuming responsibilities for struggling colleagues, stress, and trauma. Therefore, we must reflect on attrition rates from the first cohort and ask how we can balance the amount of effort we believe is critical for meaningful OLI faculty development with the need to design and deliver faculty development in ways that are accessible and manageable for full-time professionals.

Instructor and Administrative Labor and Scaling

We were aware that a professional organization like GSOLE could more easily create OLI faculty development than any individual institution. First, as mentioned above, local institutions often locate faculty development outside of disciplinary contexts within offices like teaching and learning centers. Second, few local institutions have robust enough online programs to house multiple OLI experts within the same department, which means the labor for developing and sustaining faculty development programs in online instruction often falls to a few individuals. GSOLE's community allowed us to tap into a pool of OLI experts who could serve as instructor-mentors and program administrators.

Aspirationally, GSOLE would like the certification to evolve into a sustainable program. To reach this goal, we must figure out how to compensate instructor-mentors and program administrators equitably while still maintaining an affordable certification program. In this first year, instructor-mentors were paid $500 to lead a learning pod of five participants throughout the year—not nearly enough to compensate them for their time, labor, and expertise. Yet, we are hesitant to raise enrollment for the certification beyond the $75. Several members of the pilot participants were contingent faculty across multiple institutions and others were graduate students—two often-exploited populations. As the participants stated above, some participants from these populations were able to get institutional funding because of the current price point.

Our justification for the initial cost of certification enrollment was to keep costs low enough that the certification could be obtainable to individuals without access to institutional professional development funds. However, GSOLE is currently losing money so that it can compensate instructor-mentors $100 per participant (with neither program administrator being compensated). In reflection, we know that $500 is not appropriate compensation for the time instructor-mentors spend giving feedback, hosting learning pod meetings, and sustaining one-on-one mentorship across the academic year. In future years, we must determine how we can charge enough to sustain the program and equitably compensate those whose labor drives the program, all while keeping the certification from becoming so expensive that it can only be accessed by full-time and tenured/tenure-track faculty. One potential option we are exploring is tiered registration costs with registrants paying a fee that is directly relational to their self-reported salary.

The Value of the Certification

We wanted the certification to provide participants with theoretical knowledge and online practices grounded in research so that the certification's value would be in its deep connection to the participant's connection to community knowledge of praxis, and demonstration of application. The certificate curriculum was designed to promote praxis and the ability for participants to be able to communicate their OLI knowledge to those outside of GSOLE and the discipline. Every learning objective, reading, and artifact drives participants towards the creation of an ePortfolio. As a method of assessment, ePortfolios support integrative learning and the development of a coherent learner identity (Yancey). By placing the ePortfolio as the main output of the certification, we wanted participants to develop an OLI identity and use their developing expertise to connect their instructional practices back to theory and research, communicating that connection to others. Therefore, we emphasize that ePortfolios have utility across a variety of contexts: within the learning context of a certification, in the evaluation and review process at many institutions, and during the hiring process on the job market.

Curricular Revisions

After piloting this course with participants, we have identified several areas for meaningful revision across course design and delivery. These changes, we hope, respond to participant feedback while forwarding the tenets and principles GSOLE upholds for OLI.

Course Design

We will revise the timing, LMS, and course materials. As mentioned above, participants struggled to balance the responsibilities of the course with their professional and personal commitments. We understand this is a reality of delivering online professional development that overlaps with the academic year. However, we do not feel like a condensed version of the certification program would be as valuable. First, a shortened window will make it more difficult for participants to develop connections to others within the OLI community and develop an OLI identity. Participants need opportunities for ongoing interactive engagement and time to do that work. Second, for the participants, learning about online instruction as one practices online instruction creates a productive synergy between what they are learning as certification course participants and what they are practicing as online literacy instructors. Moreover, there is no interval of time that is outside of the academic calendar for all potential participants, who work according to various institutional calendars at institutions across the globe. For these reasons, we have decided to expand the timing for the certification by stretching each module from three weeks to a month. The expanded timeline will, we hope, allow for more flexibility in pacing for participants.

We will also be leaving the Google Classroom LMS in search of an open access LMS that has a more familiar interface for participants, who are using systems like Blackboard, Canvas, and D2L at their local institutions. We will continue to prioritize the need for the LMS to be accessible to participants using assistive technologies, learning from smartphone devices, and accessing course materials from international contexts. As individuals well-versed in online learning, we understand that no technology or LMS is perfect. Yet, we are open to considering new LMS platforms because we understand the impact a technological barrier can have on learning and engagement. In leaving Google Classroom, we are choosing to prioritize the participant learning experience and more equitable access.

Because any curriculum should be regularly revisited and revised, we will also continue to update the readings and assignments for the certification. This past year, especially, has sparked important conversations related to OLI—conversations that we want to be represented within the certification materials. In addition to publications specific to OLI practice (e.g., Borgman and McArdle; Linder and Hayes), emerging scholarly conversations reflecting advances in writing instruction, student engagement, equity in learning, and writing across contexts will also be shared with participants and placed in conversation with online teaching practices (e.g., Kinloch et al.). While we do not expect the certification curriculum to ever be in stasis, updating materials to reflect research-based OLI pedagogy informed by COVID-19 is crucial.

Course Delivery

Aside from these course design revisions, we will also make changes to how the course is delivered to create a more consistent experience for participants. In this first year, pilot participants heard from three major certification voices:

1. instructor-mentors who led learning pods and gave feedback on artifact assignments,
2. other instructor-mentors who opened modules with introductory videos,
3. program administrators who shared regular announcements regarding whole-cohort events and reminders, reached out to participants as a form of intervention, and answered general questions regarding the certification process.

Participants told us that they often felt overwhelmed by the different voices representing the certification and that these voices lacked a coherent teacher presence. To create more consistency, we would like to streamline who talks to participants, narrowing that communication down to the instructor-mentor who is leading their learning pod and a general GSOLE account that can be used by multiple certification leaders to send updates, reminders, and introductory videos, as needed.

As the certification progressed throughout the 2020–2021 academic year, participants asked for more opportunities for whole-cohort, synchronous events. In response, in the spring semester, the certification team provided numerous opportunities for participants to join optional synchronous tutorials about OLI technologies, developing their ePortfolio, and OLI instruction and practice. For comparison, the fall semester had four such opportunities, while the spring semester had eight. Though participants appreciated these additional opportunities, they were not evenly distributed across the academic year, and participants sometimes struggled to attend. In preparation for the incoming cohort, we plan to standardize these events so participants have access to an optional whole cohort event approximately once a month.

Conclusion

The pandemic had a peculiar effect on those dedicated to online learning. For many of us, online writing instruction has been a niche skill set or talent that could meet institutional demand in a variety of ways. Then, in the blink of an eye, everyone was teaching online—or at least teaching remotely. This fact led the committee who designed the course in the 2019–2020 academic year to ask ourselves: Do instructors and other members of our community still need something like this certification?

We believe the answer is a resounding "Yes," for several reasons. First, we understand that most instructors who were suddenly forced to go remote were doing triage instruction. While the practices they were adopting were getting them and their students to the end of spring 2020, those practices were not helping students develop new twentieth-century literacy skills (Cope and Kalantzis). The certification course was needed to help instructors understand how to deliberately leverage the affordances of the digital technologies they were adopting and adapting to achieve their desired course outcomes (Cargile Cook). Second, we wanted to make sure that instructors and their students, who might have been disillusioned by that first foray into online instruction during spring 2020, understood that the experience of true online learning, as opposed to remote instruction, could be much more valuable and enriching. It was important to emphasize to instructors and institutions that online literacy/writing instruction is a field of study with a body of research and scholarship that should inform how instructors design their courses. When that research is used to shape pedagogy, the result can be meaningful and engaging for online-learning students. Third, returning to one of our original primary goals, the best people to prepare instructors for OLI are online literacy instructors, yet many instructors were being asked to adopt practices that were appropriate for more lecture-based or content-driven courses. What was needed was online experts who also knew the disciplinary content and goals of literacy courses.

The need for training, whether locally or through an organizationally supported group of OLI experts like the GSOLE certification course, is now greater than ever. Indeed, it appears that the need for the GSOLE certification course will, if anything, only be increasing.

Notes

1. For example, member pricing for the Online Learning Consortium "Online Teaching Certificate" program starts at $1,500 <https://onlinelearningconsortium.org/learn/which-teaching-certificate/>

Works Cited

Bedford, Laurie A. "The Professional Adjunct: An Emerging Trend in Online Instruction." *Online Journal of Distance Learning Administration*, vol. 12, no. 3, 2009, https://www.westga.edu/~distance/ojdla/fall123/bedford123.html

Borgman, Jessie, and Dockter, Jason. "Considerations of Access and Design in the Online Writing Classroom." *Computers and Composition*, vol. 49, 2018, pp. 94–105.

Borgman, Jesse and McArdle, Casey. *PARS In Practice: More Resources and Strategies for Online Writing Instructors.* WAC Clearinghouse, 2020. https://doi.org/10.37514/PRA-B.2020.1145.2.01

Boyd, Patricia Webb. "Analyzing Students' Perceptions of Their Learning in Online and Hybrid First-Year Composition Courses." *Computers and Composition*, vol. 25, no. 2, 2008, pp. 224–43.

Cargile Cook, Kelli. "An Argument for Pedagogy-driven Online Education." *Online Education: Global Questions, Local Answers,* edited by Kelli Cargile Cook and Keith Grant-Davie. Routledge, 2005, pp. 49–66.

Conference on College Composition and Communication, Committee for Best Practices in Online Writing Instruction. "Position Statement Of Principles And Example Effective Practices For Online Writing Instruction (OWI)." *Conference on College Composition and Communication,* 2013, http://www.ncte.org/cccc/resources/positions/owiprinciples

Cope, Bill and Mary Kalantzis (Eds.). *A Pedagogy of Multiliteracies.* Palgrave Macmillian, 2015.

DePew, Kevin. "Preparing for the Rhetoricity of OWI." *Foundational Practices of Online Writing Instruction,* edited by B. L. Hewett and K. E. DePew, Parlor Press and the WAC Clearinghouse, 2015, pp. 439–68.

GSOLE Website. "Welcome to GSOLE." *Global Society of Online Literacy Educators,* 2020, https://gsole.org/

GSOLE. "Online Literacy Instruction Principles and Tenets." *Global Society of Online Literacy Educators,* 2019, https://gsole.org/oliresources/oliprinciples

Harris, Heidi et al. "A Call for Purposeful Pedagogy-driven Course Design in OWI." *ROLE: Research in Online Literacy Education*, vol. 2, no. 1, 2019, http://www.roleolor.org/a-call-for-purposeful-pedagogy-driven-course-design-in-owi.html

Harris, Heidi and McCloud, W. "If You Build Online Classes (And Empower Faculty to Teach Them), Non-Traditional Students Will Come: One Student's Journey through the Professional and Technical Writing Program at the University of Arkansas at Little Rock." *Composition Studies,* vol. 43, no. 2, 2015, pp. 182–5.

Hewet, Beth. "International Association & Center Goals." Received by Scott Warnock, 29 Oct. 2015.

—, and Bourelle, Tiffany. "Online Teaching and Learning in Technical Communication: Continuing the Conversation." *Technical Communication Quarterly,* vol. 26, no. 3, 2017, pp. 217–22.

—, Tiffany Bourelle and Scott Warnock. *Teaching Writing in the Twenty-First Century.* Modern Language Association, 2021.

— and Hallman Martini, Rebecca. "Educating Online Writing Instructors Using the Jungian Personality Types." *Computers and Composition,* vol. 47, no. 1, 2018, pp. 34–58.

—, and Warnock, Scott. The Future of OWI. *Foundational Practices of Online Writing Instruction,* edited by Beth Hewett and Kevin DePew, Parlor Press and the WAC Clearinghouse, 2015, pp. 553–69.

Kinloch, Valerie, et al., editors. *Race, Justice, and Activism in Literacy Instruction.* Teachers College Press, 2020.

Linder, Kathryn E. and Hayes, Chrysanthemum Mattison. *High-impact Practices In Online Education: Research And Best Practices.* Stylus, 2018.

Mick, Connie Snyder and Middlebrook, Geoffrey. "Asynchronous And Synchronous Modalities." *Foundational Practices of Online Writing Instruction,* edited by B. L. Hewett and K. E. DePew, Parlor Press and the WAC Clearinghouse, 2015, pp. 129–48.

Mechenbier, Mahli Xuan. "Contingent Faculty in OWI." *Foundational Practices of Online Writing Instruction,* edited by Beth Hewett and Kevin DePew, Parlor Press and the WAC Clearinghouse, 2015, pp. 233–55.

Nielsen, Danielle. "Can Everybody Read What's Posted? Accessibility in the Online Classroom." *Applied Pedagogies: Strategies for Online Writing Instruction,* edited by Daniel Ruefman and Abigail G. Scheg, Utah State UP, 2016, pp. 90–105.

Rice, Rich and St.Amant, Kirk (Eds.). *Thinking Globally, Composing Locally: Rethinking Online Writing in the Age of the Global Internet.* Utah State UP, 2018.

Rodrigo, Rochelle. "OWI on the Go." *Foundational Practices of Online Writing Instruction,* edited by B. L. Hewett and K. E. DePew, Parlor Press and the WAC Clearinghouse, 2015, pp. 493–516.

Snart, Jason. "Hybrid and Fully Online OWI." *Foundational Practices of Online Writing Instruction,* edited by B. L. Hewett and K. E. DePew, Parlor Press and the WAC Clearinghouse, 2015, pp. 93–127.

Oswal, Sushil K., and Lisa Meloncon. "Paying Attention to Accessibility When Designing Online Courses in Technical and Professional Communication." *Journal of Business and Technical Communication,* vol. 28, no. 3, July 2014, pp. 271–300.

Yancey, Kathleen Blake. "Portfolios, Circulation, Ecology, and the Development of Literacy." *Technological Ecologies and Sustainability,* edited by H. A. McKee and R. Selfe, Computers and Composition Digital Press, 2009, pp. 1–14.

ENGL 1100 Contextualized: Designing a FYW Course for Guided Pathways

Nancy Pine

The course I describe here is a contextualized version of ENGL 1100 Composition I, a first year writing (FYW) course, designed specifically for students who declare majors in business and hospitality services programs to study composition in the context of their majors and future professions. This version of ENGL 1100 counts for FYW credit and adheres to the same learning outcomes as any other section at my institution, but it includes subject matter and the study of rhetorical situations and texts of interest and relevance to students with majors in the pathway. Developing pedagogies of contextualization for FYW through courses like this may help motivate community college students in particular to succeed in the course and facilitate transfer of their learning. The overall goal of this course is for students to recognize and value literacy learning during and beyond college, preparing them for a lifetime of reading and writing in their professional and personal lives.

Institutional Context

Columbus State Community College is an open-enrollment, two-year college in Central Ohio with two campuses, five regional learning centers in four counties, and dual enrollment partnerships with nearly two hundred high schools and career centers. The college web site reports enrollment of more than 45,000 full- and part-time students ("Fast Facts"). Columbus State considers itself the "front door" to higher education in the region ("Mission"), offering associate degrees for both degree-to-degree transfer and career programs, as well as certificate programs, and reporting "200 transfer opportunities and guaranteed admission to many institutions," including transfer agreements with more than thirty-five colleges ("Fast Facts"). Recently, Columbus State began engaging in the Guided Pathways reform movement when it was chosen as one of thirty colleges by the American Association of Community Colleges "to develop next-generation academic and career pathways designed to ensure gains in completion of both two- and four-year degrees as well as great marketability for graduates" ("Academic Chairpersons").

Business and hospitality services is one of the college's eight career and academic pathways, or metamajors, from which all incoming students choose. Students who declare this pathway may select one of the following majors: accounting; baking and pastry arts; business; business office administration; culinary; entrepreneurship; finance; hotel, tourism and event management; human resources; marketing; nutrition and dietetics; real estate; or restaurant and food service management ("Business and Hospitality Services"). Within each major are multiple programs that offer various degrees, including specialized associate's degrees as well as certificates. All of the associate's degrees, as well as some of the certificates, require ENGL 1100 in their programs of study.

A specific cohort program in the pathway called Exact Track is a partnership with nearby Franklin University. Designed for working adults, accepted students are placed in cohorts and complete a fixed sequence of courses from both institutions one or two evenings a week in person and online, to earn an Associate of Applied Science in Business Management from Columbus State and a Bachelor of Science with a double major in Business Administration and Management and Leadership from Franklin University ("Exact Track"). This program began at Columbus State's second, Delaware Campus, location, where I am stationed, but it is expanding and has been adapted for particular business partners. This contextualized version of ENGL 1100 was selected for a new Exact Track business partner cohort for inclusion in its lock-step schedule. Courses are offered on site at the business at no cost to the students, reimbursed by their employer.

ENGL 1100 is considered a gateway course at Columbus State, with the highest number of sections taught in the autumn semester. For example, in autumn 2020, just over three hundred English sections were offered, including dual enrollment. The majority of ENGL 1100 sections are taught by adjunct instructors and high school teachers. The curriculum for ENGL 1100 follows the Ohio Department of Higher Education and Ohio Transfer Module requirements, revised in 2021, to include a total of "5,000 words of text that has been thoughtfully revised and copyedited to meet the expectations of particular rhetorical situations" ("Ohio Transfer"). Within that requirement, the Columbus State English department established a standard textbook, four types of major writing project assignments with minimum word counts and grade weight ranges, a grade weight range for other work, and a standard holistic grading rubric consistent with the WPA outcomes statement for first year composition. Beyond these requirements, composition faculty are fairly autonomous in assignment creation and course design.

To date, this contextualized version of ENGL 1100 has been taught on two Columbus State campuses and one business partner site.

Creation of the Course

I was invited to develop the course starting in the Summer of 2018 as part of a Department of Education Title III grant for the College's Completion Plan specific to Guided Pathways, and I taught the first sections in autumn 2019. I received reassigned time compensation equivalent to a course release each term of course development.

I used the college web site to identify all the departments and programs in the business and hospitality services pathway and reviewed the plans of study to see which ones require ENGL 1100 and, if so, what other classes students take in each plan of study. I began communicating with pathway faculty in person and via email to learn about their subjects and fields, as well as collect their insights and feedback for the course. I first assured them that the ENGL 1100 contextualized would not replace any of the courses in their curriculum, that content would not overlap (for example, "business communication"), and that the course would "count" and transfer for FYW credit. I also shared draft course materials for feedback. In general, I requested the following information from pathway faculty to inform course development:

- What topics and texts would be useful for your students to read and write about in the course?
- What kinds of writing do students do in your classes? Would you please share sample writing assignment prompts?
- What kinds of research information do students in your program need to know? What style and format will students use to cite sources in your program? What library research databases will they use?
- What can you tell me about the norms for "good writing" in what the students will study as "discourse communities" in your field and profession (for example, goals and values, typical genres, etc.)? Would you please share sample texts students could study to understand the genres in your field?

In spring 2019, I began to develop an Open Educational Resource (OER) ebook called *Writing in Context* to support a contextualized approach to composition. For this, I received additional reassigned time as part of a college-wide OER initiative.

I taught the first ENGL 1100 contextualized sections in autumn 2019, and my colleague Deborah Bertsch and I taught sections in spring 2020. I had planned to begin assessing the course formally when offered full-scale the following academic year; however, this has been delayed due to the COVID-19 pandemic.

Theoretical Rationale

While there are a number of terms and models for course contextualization in general, when designing this course I adhered to the foundational concept that all "applications center on the practice of systematically connecting basic skills instruction to a specific content that is meaningful and useful to students" (Perin 270). For community colleges in particular, "[o]ne important 'context' for adult learning is the world of work itself and the specific tools, practices and social relations embedded in the work setting" (Mazzeo et al. 4). Therefore, I developed this version of ENGL 1100 to contextualize it for academic and work settings in the business and hospitality services pathway. Reasons offered why "key proficiencies for academic learning," such as writing, should be taught in the context of a student's academic pathway or major include (1) transferability of skills, (2) student motivation, and (3) academic skills not being taught in pathways/majors (Perin 268).

Decades of theory and research in composition studies conclude that writing knowledge and practice is situated and best understood in context. For example, Yancey et al. and other's recent research explores "the ways activity systems and contexts interact in writing transfer" ("The Teaching for Transfer Curriculum" 269). To develop this course, I combined pedagogies and curricula of Teaching for Transfer (TFT) and Writing about Writing (WAW), while emphasizing the pathway context in comparison to other disciplinary contexts across the curriculum. Composition research and scholarship demonstrate that knowledge and practices for writing are not basic, but rather a complex set of threshold concepts (Adler-Kassner and Wardle), key terms (Yancey et al.), and knowledge domains (Beaufort). When designing the course I assumed it essential that students not simply learn about isolated parts or skills in composing without the overarching, big picture: what it all means and how the parts connect in various contexts for composing, emphasizing their pathway context. If students know their "why" for composing in their pathway context, then they can work through the "how" to succeed in the course and beyond. The pathway context also facilitates students' decision-making, guiding their rhetorical choices to include discourse community and genre, while composing their writing project assignments.

Teaching to Motivate

One of the reasons to offer contextualized composition courses is that students may be motivated to engage in the work of the course due to their interest in the topics of study, seeing the relevancy of course content to their pathway majors and future careers. Therefore, designing this course, I knew that the content—what students read and write about, as well as any sites they study—could not be arbitrary; it needed to be relevant to business and hospitality services. However, "[c]ognitive theory on transfer has a long history of unresolved debates," including a question of "dosage": "how much contextualization is required to facilitate transfer of learning" (Perin 288). I had to consider the right "dosage" of pathway content with TFT and WAW pedagogies and curricula. I wanted to be sure the focus of the course wouldn't simply be reading and writing about business and hospitality services topics—studying that content—but rather studying and practicing composition concepts in the context of that pathway.

To strike the right "dosage" of pathway content, I combined the approaches of Beaufort, Wardle, and Yancey et al. and others. I applied Beaufort's approach in which "the course is structured around sustained inquiry into a subject that has both breadth and relevance" to the students ("*College Writing and Beyond: Five Years Later*"). I thought a nonfiction book would offer "breadth and relevance" and serve as a common book for the pathway students, similar to institutions where I have taught in which all incoming first year students, for example, read and discuss the same book in courses across campus. When I discussed course reading ideas with pathway faculty they indicated the value of nonfiction books in their professions, which was later confirmed by the first cohort of Exact Track students who shared examples of nonfiction books that managers or mentors had recommended they read for personal and professional development.

I received about a dozen book suggestions from pathway faculty. After piloting some of them, I have settled for now on *When: The Scientific Secrets of Perfect Timing* by Daniel Pink. It's engaging and applicable to all pathway majors—in all business and hospitality services programs—and the paperback is inexpensive. Additionally, as the book synthesizes an abundance of various kinds of primary- and secondary-source research on the topic, the students and I can find and study Pink's sources to see how various fields and disciplines approach topics (for example, business, psychology, biology, etc.).

Students use the book as a source for their first writing project assignment "Applying Theory to Experience: Personal Response to a Text" and may use it in subsequent assignments if helpful for their project. Inspired by Berthoff's double-entry notebook, encouraging students to "think, and then think again," a writer's notebook assignment requires students to think and write as they read, dividing each page in their notebook into two columns: record and respond. Drawing on field working methods from Sunstein and Chiseri-Strater, the assignment prepares students for later assignments to read not only texts but also conduct observations. For their writer's notebooks, students are also guided by prompts in the course calendar with the chapter deadlines; as a class we focus on those topics, rhetorical strategies, etc. from the book. I incorporate the book as much as possible in class discussions and activities both for introductory pathway content and as a text for studying rhetoric and composition concepts. My goal is to establish a classroom culture/community in which we actively discuss and use the book as a significant part of the class, developing a collective expertise, especially as it pertains to programs and professions in the pathway.

We finish the book halfway through the course, and after the first assignment the course content includes additional texts that the students and I bring to the course from contexts in their majors to include primary and secondary library and field research. In WAW composition courses, "the research is about language, the discussions are about language, and the goal of the course is to teach students the content of our discipline" (Wardle 784). In this course, students study and write about rhetoric and composition concepts as applied in pathway contexts. The first assignment uses the book and students' personal responses and self-studies as a motivating, pathway warm-up to the remaining WAW assignments they will complete, studying that pathway context for the majority and rest of the course. For the second and third major writing project assignment units—"Reading as a Writer: Studying How a Text Works" and "Researching Writing in Action: Case Study of a Discourse Community"— students choose a text and a discourse community to study that are related to their pathway. Students may be motivated and find relevance in studying, for example, genres used in a particular business, and students can apply composition concepts to that particular context. Within these units, group presentations, which pathway faculty reported frequently assigned in their classes, help students learn about additional texts and sites of study in their shared pathway as well.

Teaching and Learning for Transfer

Another reason to offer contextualized composition courses is to facilitate transfer of learning because "learners, even the most proficient, often do not readily transfer newly learned skills to novel settings" (Perin 268). Yancey et al. offer an overview to TFT curricula in composition studies and discuss "the complexity of transfer of writing knowledge and practice" ("The Teaching for Transfer Curriculum" 269). In designing this course, I sought to instill in students what Yancey et al. call a writing-transfer mindset with writing transfer as an outcome of the course (273-74). This course "look[s] at transfer as a process in which we want students to engage" (Skeffington 34), which includes "being much more transparent about the contextual nature of writing assignments and requirements than we are used to doing" (30) and providing opportunities for students to engage in the process of transfer in the composition course (29). The assignments in this composition course are not designed to teach students to compose in the specialized genres of their pathway majors and professions, which Wardle demonstrates is problematic (768). The assignments are WAW in the pathway context, rather than writing for the pathway. Specifically this course seeks to teach students what Perkins and Salomon call *learning for transfer*, with the instruction in composition in the pathway context "closer to the transfer performance" (30), and it is designed to foster low and high road transfer.

Low road transfer "reflects the automatic triggering of well-practiced routines in circumstances where there is considerable perceptual similarity" ("Teaching for Transfer" 25). Employing the technique Perkins and Salomon call "hugging," which means "teaching so as to better meet the resemblance conditions for low road transfer," this course teaches composition concepts in the context of pathway academic and workplace discourse communities— "hugging" them closer to the students' pathway—making connections "particularly plain" for students (28). Thus, contextualizing the course for the pathway facilitates low road transfer for students. For example, pathway faculty expressed to me that their courses require APA format, so in this course the third and fourth writing projects require APA format to support low road transfer to writing assignments in pathway courses.

However, to facilitate high road transfer, composition concepts also need to be decontextualized in the course through what Perkins and Salomon describe as the technique of "bridging" (28). In contrast to low road, high road transfer "always involves reflective thought in abstracting from one context and seeking connections with others" (26). High road transfer "require[s] explicit mindful abstraction" of "patterns and applications in other settings" to "decontextualize such patterns" and use them in other contexts (28). Therefore, in this course, while the final two writing projects require APA format, the first two writing projects require MLA format to support both low and high road transfer for each style. Students have sustained practice in two formal assignments for each style to experience transfer in the course, as well as abstracting principles about the logic of citation, transitioning from MLA format to APA. The two styles and citing sources, like all other concepts in the course, are not framed as sets of rules, but studied and found to be reflective of goals and values in particular discourse communities.

To design this course for such high road transfer, I drew on Beaufort's curriculum because I thought it was the clearest for students who would take this course.. The course content is organized around what Beaufort calls the five knowledge domains of writing—subject matter, rhetorical situation, genre, writing process, and discourse community—which she represents in a graphic as overlapping circles with discourse community subsuming the other four. For Beaufort, "mental schemata" of the five knowledge domains of writing can be used by students as "mid-level abstractions" or "mental grippers" for problem-solving in new situations to bridge from prior knowledge (17). For each assignment, the students study and apply the knowledge domains of writing, making decisions about their own chosen discourse communities, rhetorical situations, and genres that inform how and why they might compose the project the way they do.

Designing this course, I also sought to minimize negative transfer, "where knowledge or skill from one context interferes with another" (Perkins and Salomon "Teaching for Transfer" 22). Although our current composition curriculum begins with the assignment category "Writing from Personal Experience"—and most instructors assign a personal narrative or memoir for that unit—this course does not have a formal personal narrative assignment. Skeffington claims such assignments may foster negative transfer and cause issues with student perception, such as a view that class writing assignments are expressive (37). In a meeting with a group of pathway faculty from various majors, I had asked them about the role of personal writing in their courses, and they reported it is used for reflection or in assignments where students needed to demonstrate the value their skills or performances add to their team or profession (for example, performance appraisals, reports on group projects, etc). The first assignment in this course, therefore, invites students to apply a theory from a text to their personal experience—from the past, or in the present—as a form of self-study. As Beaufort writes, "transfer of learning goals need to merge with, interweave with any skills-development or knowledge acquisition goals of a given curriculum" ("*College Writing and Beyond:* Five Years Later").

I also designed this course to emphasize consistent learning goals with the pathway to facilitate positive—and minimize negative—transfer of learning from this course to pathway contexts. General writing skills are enacted in local pathway contexts because "general and local knowledge interact in human cognition" (Perkins and Salomon "Are Cognitive Skills Context-Bound?" 24). Therefore, in designing the course I took care to go "beyond educating memories to educating minds" (24), emphasizing higher order skills applicable to pathway contexts rather than only factual knowledge. For example, I noticed the concept of analysis emerged as an academic strategy that if practiced in this composition course may support student success in pathway majors, as well as across the curriculum. Writing analytically is often challenging for many students, and, as Danielewicz and others point out, terms like *analysis*, used generally, "do not help students understand how research in one field may be analyzed differently from research in another." In the assignments I reviewed from participating pathway faculty, students were frequently asked for a specific kind of case-study analysis, to apply a concept to a case, for example, and write about what the concept means or how it works. Therefore, each writing project assignment in this course invites students to make a similar analytical move, applying a theory or concept to a text or situation. Furthermore, an emphasis on analytical writing supports students' continual analysis of the five knowledge domains of writing as applied to their writing project assignments, for example, by analyzing sample texts from a particular genre in which they are considering composing their project. This strategy of analysis becomes a habit of mind in this composition course that is valued in pathway courses, as well as across the curriculum.

Therefore, to engage students in this kind of analysis, as well as the study and practice of the five knowledge domains of writing, the major writing project assignment units progress in the following way:

- "Applying Theory to Experience: Personal Response to a Text" - Students are introduced to concepts like prior knowledge and transfer of learning, reading and writing analytically, and the five knowledge domains of writing (discourse community, genre, rhetoric, process, and subject matter). For the assignment, students apply a theory from the book *When* (subject matter knowledge) to a personal experience or situation related to their pathway major.
- "Reading as a Writer: Studying How a Text Works" - Students conduct in-depth study and practice of the knowledge domain of rhetoric, using texts in pathway and other contexts. For the assignment, students apply a theory about rhetoric to analyze the rhetorical situation of a text of their choice (ideally from the discourse community they choose to study for the next assignment).
- "Researching Writing in Action: Case Study of a Discourse Community" - Students conduct in-depth study and practice of the knowledge domains of discourse community and genre, using texts and sites in pathway and other contexts. For the assignment, students apply theories about discourse community and genre to conduct a case study of a discourse community of their choice related to their pathway major.
- "Developing Your Theory of Writing: Self-Study of Writing Practices" - Students conduct in-depth study and practice of the knowledge domain writing process. For the assignment, students apply theories about writing process to conduct a self-study of themselves as writers—as they complete a writing project for the class and a project in another, ideally pathway, context—to support development of their own theory of writing.

Students have the opportunity to engage in the process of transfer of learning within this course, which includes frequent and sustained study and practice with particular genres and situations for writing. Students compose shorter texts in multiple genres and situations in various activities and then compose longer writing projects, each with opportunities for "extensive practice of the performance in question" to engage in transfer processes for "remix" or "a setback or critical incident," leading to new knowledge and writing practices for the writing situation (Yancey et al. *Writing Across Contexts* 104). Drawing on Beaufort, an informal process reflection letter assignment, which students submit with each writing project final draft submission, supports this transfer as a metacognition activity for students to reflect on their developing understanding of the knowledge domains of writing from their experience with the writing task. The last question of the process reflection also helps students brainstorm topic ideas for their final self-study writing project assignment to support their emerging theory of writing. The "Developing Your Theory of Writing: Self-Study of Writing Practices" assignment combines a WAW curriculum assignment and Yancey et al. theory of writing assignment from their TFT curriculum. Students consider what they know so far about writing concepts as applied to their pathway context by studying their practices, positioning them for transfer.

Critical Reflection

I found the most insightful and rewarding part of developing this course working with the participating pathway faculty, some of whom have continued to consult with me for issues related to teaching writing. In meetings I learned a lot about their disciplines, and I was proud to share the wealth of expertise that composition studies can offer about teaching writing to students, then applying that knowledge to develop this course supporting our shared students together. I wish they too were funded by the grant and also had received reassigned/release time to collaborate with me not only to develop the course materials, but also so we could have learned more from each other. Knowing that the participating pathway faculty volunteered, while I was compensated, I was especially sensitive to their time and labor invested as I developed the course. I didn't want to ask them to do too much, which may have limited, for example, how much I learned about their pathway to inform the contextualization of the course. Pathway faculty engagement could be especially important in creating opportunities to use techniques of "hugging" and "bridging" in their courses to support students' writing transfer beyond this composition course.

An immediate and practical challenge that needs to be addressed is enrolling the students who may most benefit from this ENGL 1100 contextualized course version. A number of students enrolled each term were in different pathways and said they didn't realize it was a "special" course version of ENGL 1100; they signed up only because of the day and time offering. These students had no interest in the business and hospitality services pathway and were perhaps less motivated than students in the pathway for which the course was contextualized. A solution the college is considering is closing registration to the contextualized ENGL 1100 versions, so that students may not register for it by themselves but only through an advisor who could share the course blurbs and other details to help students make an informed choice.

I appreciate that pathway students do have the choice of whether or not to enroll in the contextualized versions of ENGL 1100, because I have found that the students have varying interest in and commitment to business and hospitality services topics and sites of study. Because through guided pathways students are encouraged to choose a pathway when beginning their studies at Columbus State, I wonder how many students are truly "undecided" and "exploring" but end up in this or other pathways. To support their success in ENGL 1100 and beyond, I would not recommend contextualized course versions for students to test whether or not they are interested in particular pathways. With the central goals of pathway course contextualization being both student motivation and transfer of learning, I believe ENGL 1100 contextualized is best suited for students fairly committed to a major in the pathway. The Exact Track cohort with the business partner ended up not being a good fit for ENGL 1100 contextualized because of this lack of choice, with all of the students in the same program with the same major being required to take ENGL 1100 contextualized (even if they already have FYW credit). In addition, the cohort students all work for the same employer and are in this way perhaps too contextualized with security and ethical issues complicating research for the case study assignment, for example. I learned a number of the cohort students desired a regular ENGL 1100 section.

In addition, although the contextualized community college literature focuses on adult basic and developmental education, claiming such students benefit from contextualized courses, students who place near-ready for ENGL 1100 cannot currently enroll in this course because they are not paired with ENGL 0199 co-requisite (ALP) sections. If the scheduling logistics of in-person contextualized ENGL 0199/1100 pairings cannot be worked out, then perhaps online versions may be developed.

In addition to enrollment, I think this course needs more work with developing pedagogies of contextualization to support transfer of learning. Anson points out the "situational uniqueness" of writing and that "[a]daptation and success require continued situated practice and gradual enculturation," namely "situationally determined knowledge" (541-42). Students need to experience that writing knowledge and practices are situated; therefore, they need to be engaged in and learn to value the messiness of composing—the slippages in the "textbook" understandings of the knowledge domains—and they need to learn, given the situation, how to write by being adaptable, flexible, and persistent. Rosinski and Peeples demonstrate how they use problem-based learning: "Through engagement, students learn that writing is messy, open-ended, indeterminate, and iterative; they learn how to writing within such contexts; and they learn to value the process of working through/with this messiness" (15). Public pedagogies (see Holmes) that include service-learning—or other forms of experiential learning more broadly—may also present opportunities for students in this course to develop varying kinds of knowledge for composing with authentic writing situations in the pathway that would work well in a FYW curriculum.

When more sections of this course are taught, professional development for instructors will be crucial. Mazzeo and others cite research that illustrates, "While curriculum materials can be very useful, most research suggests that curriculum itself cannot promote instructional change without a complementary investment in professional development" (17). In addition, WAW and TFT curricula necessitate that instructors have some rhetoric and composition disciplinary content knowledge; however, especially at community colleges, the majority of composition courses are taught by contingent faculty with various coursework backgrounds and specializations (see Skeffington and Tinberg). Teaching for transfer would be especially challenging for instructors who are formulaic and prescriptive in their approach to teaching composition, which is especially common at institutions that teach underserved students where "teachers sometimes grab onto 'formulaic acts' to fulfill the obligations attached to composition," regulating students' literacy (Soliday and Trainor 125). In spite of these hurdles, "it is well worth the effort" to have these conversations about transfer at all institutions, including community colleges; "[t]he chief beneficiaries will doubtless be students, who will be better prepared to adapt to the fluctuating demands of college and career" (Tinberg 29). To prepare to teach this course, instructors would benefit not only from initial training workshops, but also ongoing mentoring and support their first term teaching the course, ideally through weekly meetings and frequent communication with experienced contextualized composition faculty.

These reflections occurred before the COVID-19 pandemic, which has interrupted offering this course and its assessment, but as the pandemic continues, I am reflecting on aspects of the course that may or may not translate virtually, including the case study assignment. When the course is taught again, assessment, ideally qualitative and longitudinal, can examine student motivation and the nature of transfer of learning. Are pathway students succeeding in the contextualized course version at higher rates than those in regular ENGL1100 sections? If so, why? What do students find motivating about the course? What about transfer? How do students engage in transfer of learning in this course, pathway courses, other courses, and the workplace? Are they experiencing positive transfer or negative or both? Is the transfer low road, high road, or both? For assessment and study, I think it would be ideal for students to be assigned in subsequent pathway courses a mini-self-study, theory-of-writing assignment to continually support writing transfer as well as provide data, from willing study participants, about the nature of transfer.

This data could show that a contextualized course like this does more harm than good by fostering negative transfer. Perhaps this course sends a message to students and faculty that more about writing can be taught in FYW than really can. Does the course reinforce an idea that students really "should have learned that already" in FYW and, therefore, be expected to perform more expertly in writing tasks in their pathway courses and others and their eventual workplace? Does this contextualized course make a promise that it cannot deliver? Or does the course better deliver promises already made in FYW? The field of composition studies continues to explore how to foster the adaptable and innovative lifelong literacy learners demanded in the twenty-first century, and this course pursues this goal for students in business and hospitality services programs and professions. Certainly, working together with faculty in pathway programs toward this shared goal leads to greater opportunities to support student writers.

Acknowledgments

I wish to thank the faculty who teach majors in the business and hospitality services pathway at Columbus State for generously taking their time to share their teaching and learning worlds with me as I developed the course. I also appreciate the kind and thoughtful feedback from *Composition Studies* editors Matt Davis and Kara Taczak throughout the process of this write-up. Finally, I am so grateful to my colleague Deborah Bertsch who not only provided feedback to an early draft of this project, but also supported me during the entire journey of the course's development.

Works Cited

"Academic Chairpersons." Columbus State Community College, https://www.cscc.edu/about/recruitment/chairs.shtml.

Adler-Kassner, and Elizabeth Wardle, editors. *Naming What We Know: Threshold Concepts of Writing Studies.* Utah State UP, 2015.

Anson, Chris M. "The Pop Warner Chronicles: A Case Study in Contextual Adaptation and the Transfer of Writing Ability." *College Composition and Communication,* vol. 67, no. 4, 2016, pp. 518-49.

Beaufort, Anne. *College Writing and Beyond: A New Framework for University Writing Instruction.* Utah State UP, 2007.

—. "*College Writing and Beyond:* Five Years Later." *Composition Forum,* vol. 26, Fall 2012, https://compositionforum.com/issue/26/college-writing-beyond.php.

Berthoff, Ann E. *The Making of Meaning: Metaphors, Models, and Maxims for Writing Teachers.* Boynton/Cook, 1981.

"Business and Hospitality Services." Columbus State Community College, https://www.cscc.edu/academics/business-hospitality-services/.

Danielewicz, Jane, et al. "Assignments and Expectations." *Composition Forum,* vol. 46, Spring 2021, https://compositionforum.com/issue/46/expectations-transfer.php.

"Exact Track." Columbus State Community College, https://www.cscc.edu/academics/departments/exact-track/index.shtml.

"Fast Facts." Columbus State Community College, https://www.cscc.edu/about/fast-facts.shtml.

Holmes, Ashley. *Public Pedagogy in Composition Studies.* National Council of Teachers of English, 2016.

Mazzeo, Christopher, et al. *Building Bridges to College and Careers: Contextualized Basic Skills Programs at Community Colleges.* 1 Jan. 2003. *EBSCOhost,* search.ebscohost.com/login.aspx?direct=true&AuthType=cookie,ip,uid&db=eric&AN=ED473875&site=ehost-live.

"Mission." Columbus State Community College, https://www.cscc.edu/about/mission.shtml.

"Ohio Transfer." Ohio Department of Higher Education, https://www.ohiohighered.org/transfer/transfermodule/learningoutcomes.

Perin, Dolores. "Facilitating Student Learning Through Contextualization: A Review of Evi dence." *Community College Review,* vol. 39, no. 3, July 2011, 268–295. https://doi.org/10.1177/0091552111416227.

Perkins, David, and Gavriel Salomon. "Are Cognitive Skills Context-Bound?" *Educational Researcher,* vol. 18, no. 1, American Educational Research Association, Jan. 1989, pp. 16-25. SAGE Journals, doi:10.3102/0013189X018001016.

---. "Teaching for Transfer." *Educational Leadership,* vol. 46, no. 1, Sept. 1988, p. 22. *EBSCOhost,* search.ebscohost.com/login.aspx?direct=true&AuthType=cookie,ip,uid&db=a9h&AN=8524829&site=ehost-live.

Rosinski, Paula and Tim Peeples. "Forging Rhetorical Subjects: Problem-Based Learning in the Writing Classroom." *Composition Studies.* vol. 40, no. 2, 2012, pp. 9-32.

Skeffington, Jillian K. "Enhancing Transfer from First-Year Composition: A Pedagogy of Shorter Essays." *Journal of Teaching Writing,* vol. 27, no. 2, 2012, pp. 27–45. EBSCOhost, direct=true&AuthType=cookie,ip,uid&db=mzh&AN=2019871479&sit=ehost-live.

Soliday, Mary and Jennifer Seibel Trainor. "Rethinking Regulation in the Age of the Literacy Machine." *College Composition and Communication,* vol. 68, no. 1, 2016, pp. 125-51.

Sunstein, Bonnie Stone and Elizabeth Chiseri-Strater. *Fieldworking: Reading and Writing Research.* 3rd ed., Bedford/St. Martin's 2007.

Tinberg, Howard. "Reconsidering Transfer Knowledge: Challenges and Opportunities." *Teaching English in the Two-Year College,* vol. 43, No. 1, September 2015, pp. 7-31.

Wardle, Elizabeth. "Mutt Genres and the Goal of FYC: How Can We Help Students Write the Genres of the University?" *College Composition and Communication,* vol. 60, no. 4, 2009, pp. 765-88.

Wardle, Elizabeth and Doug Downs. *Writing About Writing: A College Reader.* Bedford St. Martins, 2011.

Yancey, Kathleen Blake, et al. "The Teaching for Transfer Curriculum: The Role of Concurrent Transfer and Inside- and Outside-School Contexts in Supporting Students' Writing Development." *College Composition and Communication,* vol. 71, no. 2, 2019, 268-95.

Yancey, Kathleen Blake, Liane Robertson, and Kara Taczak. *Writing Across Contexts: Transfer, Composition, and Sites of Writing.* Utah State UP, 2014.

Where We Are

Writing in the West African Context

Linford O. Lamptey and Roland Dumavor

In West Africa and in Ghana, there exist many modes of communication beyond the verbal and written. For example, at the chiefs' palaces there exist many systems of communication; notably, symbols (ideographs) that tell the philosophies and stories of the chiefs and the people of the tribes. In the Akan language, these groups of symbols or stylized pictures are known as the Adinkra symbols. They are typically drawings, some of which depict the experiences of the clan/tribe and many others are teachings and wise sayings. As we grew up, these drawings connected us to the flora and fauna (nature elements such as birds, land, and trees) around us. At the same time, the legacies of colonialism suffuse the Indigenous culture, conflicting with its ways of knowing by blurring indigenous practices with colonizing practices. Thus, tracing pure undiluted writing systems of Africa is difficult. We can, therefore, not belittle the existence of some forms of writing in Africa in the past. However, contemporary practices of education have little to say about writing as a field.

In Ghana, as in many West African countries, it is difficult to center the study of writing because writing is micro-inscribed in the macro study of English. The study of writing forms a small section of the study of the English language. The educational systems and its students hardly recognize writing's distinctiveness or necessity. The school curricula are remnants of the colonial empire, and they inadvertently continue to maintain and promote gatekeeping structures and practices--especially in defining and teaching writing. It is not surprising that the educational institutions and stakeholders in West Africa have restricted writing to just print texts; written words are assessed based on "a test of grammar," (298) as Yancey puts it. Writing in the West African context is slow in encompassing multimodality and digital technologies in its production in the classroom. In 2017, the then senior minister of Ghana, Osafo Marfo, spoke highly in favor of the sciences over the study of language, concluded that "we can't industrialize with grammar" (Neequaye, 2017). Such a comment demonstrates that not only the arts, but that writing itself is not a priority in that country.

In this piece, we explore the West African context by focusing more specifically on writing at the high school level among the five English-speaking countries: The Gambia, Nigeria, Sierra Leone, Liberia, and Ghana. We made this choice because these five West African countries write common regional examinations organized by the West African Examination Council (WAEC). With respect to how writing is taught at the higher education level, we decided to focus on Ghana only.

Writing: Curriculum Design

West Africa has five English-speaking countries, namely Ghana, Nigeria, Sierra Leone, Liberia, and The Gambia and they, arguably, have similar curricula for various subjects at the high school level. The curriculum for English Language is divided into five main components, comprising Listening and Speaking Comprehension, Reading Comprehension, Writing, Grammar, and Literature (Teaching iv-ix). The curriculum over-relies on reception and production by students. This raises concerns about the lack of attention given to writing as a process.

Some general aims for teaching English are to "improve the communicative competence of students and give them the confidence to communicate" and "raise students' level of proficiency in English usage and their ability to communicate with other users of English" (Teaching iii). The aims are problematically stated; they give the students little to no agency in their learning. To "improve the communicative competence of students and give them..." implies that it is teachers' task to make that happen, while denying students' agency and responsibilities. This confirms Freire's banking system of education; a system that creates a giver-receiver relationship between teachers and their students where students are mere listening objects taking instructions from their subject teachers. It encourages what he describes as a situation in which contents or "empirical dimensions of reality tend in the process of being narrated to become lifeless and petrified" (52). Thus, "the knowledge of writing is a gift bestowed by those who consider themselves knowledgeable upon those whom they consider to know nothing" (Freire 53). At this level, though writing seems to enjoy some form of importance, we argue that writing would receive much more attention if it were treated as a whole entity/subject. Drawing from our past teaching experiences and knowledge, we contend that the labor in grading writing discourages many teachers from teaching writing in their English language classrooms.

Writing: Pedagogical Approaches

In this section, we explore how writing is taught in the English Language classroom at these levels. At all levels, the pedagogical approaches adopted in teaching writing focus more on writing as a product, instead of writing as product, process, recursive and nonlinear. Fulkerson describes four philosophies of composition: the Expressivists, the Mimeticists, the Rhetoricists, and the Formalists. The Expressivist values the writer and emphasizes openness, honesty, voice, and personal expressions; the Mimeticists value informational accuracy and logic while the Formalists favor the text, or the internal traits of the writing. Finally, the Rhetoricists value "effectiveness, audience awareness, persuasiveness and contextual flexibility" (Fulkerson 409-410). Of the four philosophies/ideologies of composition Fulkerson describes, the Ghanaian writing context--that is if that exists at all--tends to adapt the formalist approach, giving more attention to the text and its internal traits with little attention to the others. Although there is no open admission of the teaching philosophies, we draw our conclusions by examining the contents of writing in Ghana and to some extent, West Africa more generally. Because writing is not centered or taught on its own beyond academic requirements, it is difficult to examine writing from a central perspective.

Usually, because the teachers are considered the repository of all writing knowledge, they adopt approaches with less engagement of students in the writing process (Chokwe 541). And because much emphasis is placed on writing as a product, process activities such as brainstorming, drafting, peer review, and reflection are of little significance, while rubrics play an influential role in teaching writing. Though students are given some space for creativity, there is not enough room in writing pedagogy in West Africa for students to explore and practice their writing. This is partly because of the educational systems' overreliance on colonial and gatekeeping practices in teaching writing, with Ghana being a particular context for such an approach (Sackey 1997).

In higher education, more emphasis is placed on academic writing. The focus on grammar features prominently in teaching writing. The academic writing mainly aims to prepare students for effective communication, through writing, in the academic community (University 3). Writing practices within higher education contexts demonstrate a limited view of the reality that the most productive writing students do happens outside the classroom and beyond the walls of the academy (Yancey 300). Emerging technologies have greatly impacted the writing and writerly behavior of students. However, higher education institutions seem to be reluctant in shifting their pedagogical approaches to meet the increasing demands and needs of students outside academia.

Further, the overreliance on teaching academic writing shows that most of the students conceive writing as a non-recursive, linear process, and are not adequately prepared for the professional world, since the most common type of writing and the most valued writing, post college, are more of non-academic writing (Blythe et al. 272-273). We must be quick to admit that English language writing teachers face significant challenges: large class sizes, inadequate writing technologies, and the seemingly slow pace and reluctance of the government agencies and institutions in charge of education to review the writing curriculum.

Writing: Assessment Approaches

To give a sense of the assessment approaches adopted by writing teachers at the high school level, we examine here a marking scheme for the 2020 WAEC English paper. We use this material because the grading system for writing in the classroom is based on the WAEC marking scheme. In the West African context, assessment of writing is based on four key areas: Content, Organization, Expression, and Mechanical Accuracy. It is worth noting that Mechanics/grammar is a higher order item on the hierarchy of concerns in assessing writing. For example, in the WAEC marking scheme, Mechanical Accuracy—Grammar—receives equal importance with Content and Organization, except Expression. This goes to support our claim that pedagogical emphasis is placed on writing as a product rather than writing as a process. It could be that teachers focus on writing as a product because many educational institutions are more concerned with students' grades than what Yancey calls "use value" for writing (301). We are of the view that this approach leads to unintended consequences, as many students dread writing due to its punitive tendencies in grading. Thus, students do not feel encouraged engaging in extensive exploration of ideas/issues beyond the strict requirements, which stifle their inquiry and critical thinking. At the university level, the writing assessment story is not so different. But things have shifted: universities now have improved required writing courses for students.

To conclude, our exploration of the state of writing in the West African context shows that writing has received very little attention in scholarship. Though there are some studies done about writing in the larger African context, emphasis is placed on academic writing, a common focus of English for Academic Purposes programs (Afful 142, 147). Focusing on only academic writing as a genre fails to achieve what the Conference of College Composition and Communication calls "sound writing instruction"—an instruction that "enables students to analyze and practice with a variety of genres" (CCCC). We support Joseph Afful's call for African higher education institutions to embrace the paradigm shift and to establish writing programs that focus on writing as interdisciplinary and a social act (154). We stated earlier that it is difficult to categorize the purpose of writing and the motivations for writing in West Africa; that said, we are interested in further examining how writing in the West African educational systems promotes the "habits of mind" identified in CCCC's "Framework for Success in Postsecondary Writing."

When we do rhetorical interrogations with a focus on the evolution of writing and the responsiveness of writing sites (workplace, school, and social community), would the viability of over-reliance on academic writing hold? One of our aims in writing this piece is to problematize the teaching and research of writing in West African contexts. As scholars, concerned about what writing is and writing pedagogies in West Africa, we invite a scholarly conversation on expanding the scope of teaching writing in the West African classroom. Writing is evolving and it challenges us to look beyond the colonial educational frameworks and ideologies that drive writing pedagogies in West Africa to a more local but practical one. Emerging technologies have impacted the evolution of writing in and beyond the classroom. As educators and writing scholars from West Africa, it is our responsibility to reexamine the impact of digital technologies on the writing lives of students and explore how writing pedagogy prepares students as productive writers in various responsive writing sites. As we consider expanding the landscape of writing and writing pedagogies in ways that meet students' needs and the demands of responsive sites, we might be interested in further research that looks into interrogating and extending students' writerly productivity beyond the academy. Writing is contextual, social, and interactive and must be taught to meet such demands while responding to the ever-evolving global needs. We would be interested in among many questions, how classroom student writing impacts and informs daily interactions and meaningful negotiations, and how technology can enhance the teaching and learning of writing in West Africa. More importantly, how can we expand the landscape of writing in West Africa beyond academic writing?

Works Cited and Consulted

Afful, B. A. Joseph. "Academic Literacy and Communicative Skills in the Ghanaian University: A Proposal." *Nebula: A Journal of Multidisciplinary Scholarship*. vol. 4, no 3, 2007.

Blythe, Stuart, et al. "Professional and Technical Communication in a Web 2.0 World," *Technical Communication Quarterly*, vol. 23, no. 4, 2014, pp. 265-287.

"Conference on College Composition and Communication Position Statement: Principles for the Postsecondary Teaching of Writing." https://cccc.ncte.org/. Revised March 2015. Retrieved: 13 October, 2021.

Chokwe, M. Jack. "Academic Writing in an ODL Context: Perceptions and Experiences of First Year University Students." *Mediterranean Journal of Social Sciences*. vol. 4, no. 3, 2013, pp. 535-543.

Freire, Paulo., and Myra B. Ramos. *Pedagogy of the oppressed*. New York: Continuum. 1989/93.

Fulkerson, Richard. "Composition Theory In the Eighties: Axiological Consensus and Paradigmatic Diversity." *College Composition and Communication*, vol. 41, no. 4, 1990, pp. 409-429.

Neequaye, Yvonne. "We can't industrialize with grammar -- Senior Minister Hints at Educational Reforms". Retrieved: *http://3news.com/cant-industrialise-grammar-senior-minister-hints-educational-reforms.* 10 December, 2017. Retrieved: October 5, 2021.

Sackey, A. John. "The English Language in Ghana, a Historical Perspective," *English in Ghana*. Edited by M. E. Kropp Dakubu, GESA, 1997, pp. 126-139.

Teaching Syllabus for English Language. Ministry of Education. *www.mingycomputersgh.wordpress.com*. Retrieved: 2 October, 2021.

The West African Examination Council (WAEC). Marking Scheme for WASSCE English Language for School Candidates. 2020. *Consulted*.

University of Ghana Language Centre: Academic Writing Manuel. UGRC 110. *https://godsonug.files.wordpress.com/2016/04/academin-writing.pdf*. Retrieved: 1 October, 2021.

Yancey, Blake Kathleen. "Made Not Only in Words: Composition in a New Key," *College Composition and Communication*, vol. 56, no.2, 2004, pp. 297-328.

Something of Our Own to Say: Writing Pedagogy in India

Anuj Gupta and Anannya Dasgupta

As writing pedagogy gains distinct footholds in university classrooms in India, it is worth retracing some of its steps to the shaping influence of composition pedagogies in the United States. To begin: we met American writing pedagogy in reverse. Gupta first trained to teach writing in India at Ashoka University at the Young India Fellowship program, which is closely associated with the University of Pennsylvania (UPenn), and is now pursuing that interest as a PhD student in Rhetoric and Composition at the University of Arizona (UA). Dasgupta encountered writing pedagogy at the Rutgers Writing Program as a PhD student in literature and is now in India directing the Centre for Writing and Pedagogy at Krea University. Common to both our experiences is the usefulness of some framing concepts from American composition practice and their necessary adaptations in the Indian classrooms.

For example, conversation both as metaphor and literal aid to make academic writing easier to access is an enduring idea in American composition studies (Bruffee). In what follows, we recount our experiences of using the concept of conversation to enable academic writing in our classrooms. Each narrative details adaptations of what didn't automatically transfer to our particular contexts. These adaptations highlight a range of cross-cultural assumptions — from misaligned cultural references to the levels of prior reading and writing skills — that can be taken for granted. Overall, our work has required many more intermediate steps to make writing pedagogy workable in our socially and linguistically diverse classrooms. We learned that what seems matter-of-fact in American composition — the analogy of conversation as talk or strategy for analytic writing — has to be made accessible in our classrooms as something of our own.

Beauty of the Burkean Parlor: Anuj Gupta

While finishing my M.Phil in English literature, I stumbled upon a job opportunity that would change my life's course. I was hired to teach an academic writing course, which I would eventually manage and administer "Academic Writing at Ashoka" (Gupta), before heading to the US for a PhD in Rhetoric and Composition. For the course, I was eager to utilize exercises from the pedagogic resources shared with us. These resources had been compiled by several teachers trained in US writing pedagogy who preceded me at the program. I was particularly excited by Graff and Birkenstiens's *They Say/I*

Say: Moves that Matter in Academic Writing and its suggestion that written templates of rhetoric were modelled on oral conversations such as those in a "Burkean parlor" a metaphor drawn from the reception room of 18th-19th century Euro-American bourgeois households that hosted stimulating conversations (CriticalSkills).

Inspired, I explained in class that writing was like conversations in a parlor — only to find my students utterly confused. One hesitantly asked, "Sir, what do you mean that academic writing happens in a beauty parlour?" I was startled. In my enthusiasm, I had forgotten that in India, "parlours" and "saloons" refer to places that offer skincare and haircare services (something akin to the nail salons that are popular in the US) and not the high-brow bourgeois spaces that Burke had in mind. I decided to go out on a limb to save the situation. After all, even beauty parlours and salons are places of rich discursive exchanges that are intimate and political, even if in an informal context, as has been demonstrated wonderfully in a film called "Everybody says I'm Fine" (Bose). Instead of taking my students to Burke, I figured I'd bring Burke to my students.

I continued with the reference my students readily understood and asked, "Why do you think people go to beauty parlours and saloons?" and "What do you think they do there?" The response was "..umm, to look good?" I agreed: "Yes. They go there to look good, which brings them various emotional, social, and even professional benefits, right? That's why people go to college too, isn't it? Most people go to college to look good, to get a job, to climb the social ladder, etc. These are also reasons why people visit saloons and beauty parlours." After I said this, I realised how true this was. Most people I know, including myself, do not really go to college to participate in ancient disciplinary conversations like the Burkean metaphor implies. A beauty parlor might actually serve as a better metaphor for college than the Burkean parlor, in some ways! "Can you think of any other similarities?" I tried my luck, but my students remained silent. I changed tack. "No problem, let's speculate," I said. I pushed the metaphor — "Well the other thing that happens in parlours is that people talk. A lot! They talk to each other about all sorts of things — politics, cricket, shopping, romance, gossip! They analyze, criticize, and appreciate these topics and even laugh and cry about them. They have conversations. They listen to what others are saying. Then, they respond. After a while they leave. Some new people pop-in. And that's what Burke says happens in academic writing too!" From confusion and surprise to some degree of understanding, my students and I recreated the Burken parlor to make sense in our context. In adapting the Burkean analogy for joining conversations, we transformed and owned it.

Walking the Talk: Anannya Dasgupta

Two decades ago, at the Rutgers University Writing Program, I learned for the first time that there was a systematic pedagogy for academic writing. As evident in videos made available on the RU website that offer snapshots of my TA training, Kurt Spellmeyer talks about setting up assignment questions as conversations between authors (Spellmeyer). As described in the video, I trained to ask students questions such as: "How might the solution to the problem with globalized markets that Chua has identified be found in Bacevich's analysis of the US role in current global unrest?" This kind of essay prompt assumes that students understand enough of each author's ideas to examine the implications of what one author has to say in the expanded context of the other's topic. But, as the peer review exercise in the video demonstrates, the struggle of the writing class is that students start by writing extended summaries of the assigned readings. The writing teacher helps students, through the process of revision, learn how to join the ongoing conversation that authors like Chua and Bacevich have started and, in that process, learn to have an argument of their own.

Over the last decade in India, I have been establishing the teaching of writing at the university level; most of the students have not taken any prior classes in formal academic essay writing. Most of the faculty I hire to teach them have never taken or taught such courses either. I quickly learned that my changed context required me to go back to the drawing board and revisit the assumptions of my pedagogic training. I did not, for instance, have the luxury of assuming that all my students could write many pages of serviceable summary. As I have come to learn, the ability to summarize is necessary to follow an ongoing conversation; but to add to the conversation one has to do the work of analysis — to have something of one's own to say. To be able to teach students the work of accurate summary as the basis of convincing analysis, I had to rethink the logic of setting essay prompts from what I had learned to do at the Rutgers Writing Program.

Among videos available at the Krea-CWP youtube channel, there is one of a faculty support workshop that I conducted for the writing teachers, where we reviewed writing assignment questions (Center). As is evident from the discussion, we refocused the assignment questions from the model of direct conversation between authors to a language of connecting ideas in different readings. We are not asking students to see one author's ideas as the topic of conversation in the context or implication of another author's ideas; instead, we have made the essay prompts a different topic of conversation where the assigned readings are sources for evidence. For example, in reading Emily Martin's "Egg and the Sperm" alongside Aparna Vaidik's "From *Satyagrahi* to

Krantikari" in *Waiting for Swaraj: Inner Lives of Indian Revolutionaries Hardcover*, my pedagogical training might suggest a question like: How can Martin's idea of waking sleeping metaphors help us understand the self-formation of revolutionaries in Vaidik's narrative? Within this context for teaching writing, however, we are better served by asking: "How does a political awareness of language-use change culture?" or "What is power?" These two questions ask for a greater degree of extrapolation from the assigned readings and encourage students to use ideas and instances from Martin and Vaidik. They build on the practice of summarizing arguments from previous class worksheets, which help students avoid slipping into undirected summaries in their essay drafts. Instead of asking about the conversations in which Martin and Vaidik are engaged, we are asking students to start and direct the conversation in their essays. Along the way, students connect ideas sourced in different readings by using their own voice as they make explicit the otherwise implicit connections between the texts.

Conclusion

Making the metaphor of conversation our own in our writing classrooms helps us see the significance of adaptation as a pedagogical tool. When we adapt pedagogies, the process of adaptation itself contours theories of teaching towards practices of greater effectiveness in learning. It makes us pay careful attention to differences in context and to the particularities of our locations and classrooms. Afterall, classrooms are not homogeneous - socially, linguistically or in skill levels - either in America or in India. Adaptation empowers teachers and students to start with a known template not with the intention to replicate meaning, but to creatively expand and ultimately transform the template. A good analogy here is the way in which the English language is growing roots, and as Kothari and Snell's anthology demonstrates, becoming a "chutnified" Indian language that is distinct from the colonial notions of a standardized Queen's English. The writing pedagogy we have been developing for our classrooms is beginning to travel to the teaching of writing composition in other Indian languages as well.

What is really needed at this stage is a lot more ethnographic documentation of academic writing as it is being taught across the country. Gupta's classroom anecdote and Dasgupta's revisions of assignment questions from an actual faculty training session made available in video is our effort to give granular, experiential grounding to the discussion of pedagogical approaches that ethnographies usually make possible. The experiences that we have shared represent a miniscule sample size of teachers and classrooms that are similarly resourced and located in the complex and complicated scenario of Indian higher education. While some attempts at documenting and anthologizing more narratives of classroom experiences of teaching writing has begun (Dasgupta and Lohokare; Padwad; Roy et al.), these also serve to show the ambit of experiences that remain to be written about.

Works Cited and Consulted

Bhattacharya, Debaditya, ed. *The University Unthought: Notes for a Future*. Taylor & Francis, 2018.

Brady, John. "Investigating the Relationship between Classroom Conversation and Argumentative Writing Using Writing Moves and Types of Talk." *Acta Paedagogica Vilnensia*, vol. 40, Oct. 2018, pp. 94–110. DOI: doi.org/10.15388/ActPaed.2018.0.11890.

Bruffee, Kenneth A. "Collaborative learning and the the 'Conversation of Mankind'." *College English*, vol. 46, no. 7, 1984, pp. 635-652.

Bose, Rahul. *Everybody Says I'm Fine Haircut Scene*. 2001. *YouTube*, youtube.com/watch?v=v9pytV6Ww6s.

Center for Writing and Pedagogy. "Writing Assignment Questions that Elicit Analysis." *YouTube*, 03 October 2021. youtube.com/watch?v=2z9h4L120mU&t=895s.

CriticalSkills MU. "The Burkean Parlour Method Explained." *YouTube*, 09 March 2020, youtube.com/watch?v=faaQuZQkRZQ&ab_channel=CriticalSkillsMU.

Canagarajah, Suresh. *Resisting Linguistic Imperialism in English Teaching*. Oxford University Press, 1999.

Kothari, Rita, and Rupert Snell, eds. *Chutnefying English: The Phenomenon of Hinglish*. Penguin Books India, 2011.

Comer, Denise, and Anannya Dasgupta. "Transnational Exposure, Exchange, and Reflection: Globalizing Writing Pedagogy." *Currents in Teaching and Learning*, vol. 11, no. 2, 2020, pp. 32–54.

Dasgupta, Anannya, and Madhura Lohokare, editors. "Writing In Academia." *Café Dissensus*, no. 50, 2019, cafedissensus.com/2019/06/24/contents-writing-in-academia-issue-50/.

—."Building the Boat While Sailing It." *Café Dissensus*, vol. 50, 2019, cafedissensus.com/2019/06/24/guest-editorial-building-the-boat-while-sailing-it-writing-pedagogy-in-india/

—."A Brief and Uneven Guide to Writing Pedagogy in Higher Education in India." *Café Dissensus*, vol. 50, 2019, cafedissensus.com/2019/06/24/a-brief-and-uneven-guide-to-writing-pedagogy-in-higher-education-in-india/.

Dasgupta, Anannya. *Writing Assignment Questions That Elicit Analysis*. 2021. *YouTube*, youtube.com/watch?v=2z9h4L120mU.

Graff, Gerald, and Cathy Birkenstein. *They Say/I Say: Moves That Matter in Academic Writing*. 3rd ed., W.W. Norton and Company, 2016.

Gupta, Anuj. "Emotions in Academic Writing/Care-Work in Academia: Notes Towards a Repositioning of Academic Labor in India (& Beyond)." *Academic Labour: Research and Artistry*, vol. 5, 2021, pp. 107–36. digitalcommons.humboldt.edu/alra/vol5/iss1/7/

—. "Academic Writing Education at Ashoka University, India — A Close Look at the YIF Critical Writing Program." *Connecting Writing Centers Across Borders (CWCAB)*, 19 Mar. 2021, wlnjournal.org/blog/2021/03/academic-writing-education-at-ashoka-university-india-a-close-look-at-the-yif-critical-writing-program/.

—. "Languages → ← Realities: Some Thoughts on the Writing Courses Indian Universities Need." *Café Dissensus*, no. 50, 2019, cafedissensus.com/2019/06/24/languages-%E2%86%92-%E2%86%90-realities-some-thoughts-on-the-writing-courses-indian-universities-need/.

Martin, Emily. "The Egg and the Sperm: How Science Has Constructed a Romance Based on Stereotypical Male- Female Roles." *Signs*, vol. 16, no. 3, 1991, pp. 485–501.

Muchiri, Mary N., et al. "Importing Composition: Teaching and Researching Academic Writing beyond North America." *College Composition and Communication*, vol. 46, no. 2, May 1995, p. 175. *DOI.org (Crossref)*, doi.org/10.2307/358427.

Padwad, Amol. *Research in English Language Education in Indian Universities: A Directory*. Lulu.com, 2014.

Roy, Souradeep, Senjuti Chakraborti and Aakshi Magazine, editors. "Writing (in) the Post-Colony: Practising Academic English in Indian Higher Education." *Sanglap: Journal of Literary and Cultural Inquiry*, vol. 7, no. 1, 2020, sanglap-journal.in/index.php/sanglap/issue/view/14.

Spellmeyer, Kurt. *Teaching Expos 101*. 2010. *Vimeo*, vimeo.com/14014324.

Vaidik, Aparna. *Waiting for Swaraj: Inner Lives of Indian Revolutionaries Hardcover*. Cambridge University Press, 2021.

Transforming the Teaching of Writing from a Skills-Based Approach to a Knowledge Construction Approach in a University in Singapore

Radhika Jaidev

Introduction

The medium of instruction is English in all universities in Singapore. Typically, in engineering, science, and technology degree programmes, academic writing is taught through one or two distinct or 'stand-alone' modules delivered in the first year of students' undergraduate programmes to help them cope with the writing needs of assignments in their disciplines.

Often such modules are designed and delivered by teachers in language and communication centres like the Centre for Communication Skills [CCS] at the Singapore Institute of Technology (SIT), Centre for English Language Communication [CELC] at the National University of Singapore, and Language and Communication Centre [LCC] at the Nanyang Technological University (NTU). Some faculties in these universities may have their own small core of language teachers who specialize in teaching writing that is specific to the needs of students who take their degree programmes, but by and large, teachers at language centres such as the ones mentioned above teach academic writing to students across faculties and disciplines in these universities. This paper describes a process of transformation of the teaching of academic writing to SIT students from using a skills-based approach to one that focuses on knowledge construction (Lillis) and the development of disciplinary values (Latour and Woolgar; Lea and Street; Lea and Stierer; Yancey) at the Singapore Institute of Technology (SIT).

The Centre for Communication Skills at the Singapore Institute of Technology (CCS-SIT)

SIT was established in May 2009 as the fifth autonomous university and the university of applied learning in Singapore which is reflective of the equal emphasis given to classroom teaching of theoretical concepts and the application of those concepts at the workplace, particularly when students serve their compulsory extended work attachment that lasts from six months to a year.

The extended work attachment, referred to as the Integrated Work Study Programme (IWSP), accounts for 20 modular credits and is organized by the Centre for Career Readiness (CCR) of the university. During their IWSP, students are supervised by an academic mentor as well as a work supervisor and are required to submit bi-weekly, written, progress reports, which include the application of their disciplinary content in the projects or tasks at work. At the end of the IWSP, students are required to submit a critical reflection report of approximately 2000 words, detailing the content knowledge they brought to bear upon the work they carried out, challenges they encountered, how they overcame those challenges, what they could have done better, and how they plan to move forward and build on this learning in the future. This written reflection, along with the oral presentation of it, accounts for approximately 5 credits of the total of 20 credits and is, therefore, an important culminating writing task for all SIT students before they graduate.

SIT offers over 40 undergraduate programmes in engineering, health and social sciences, chemical engineering and food technology, infocomm technology, and design and specialized business. Approximately 95% of the students at SIT come from having completed a three-year diploma programme at one of the five polytechnics in Singapore (https://smiletutor.sg/polytechnics-in-singapore-overview-courses-admissions/); a small percentage come in after having completed either the G.C.E 'A' Level (home/examinations/gce-a-level) and/ or the International Baccalaureate (Iborganization).

In general, students who have completed their 'A' levels and IB and have written extended essays as part of their curricula, are able to cope better with the writing needs of their degree programmes. By comparison, generally, those who have taken the polytechnic route, which is the majority of SIT students, tend to be less competent in academic writing because they enroll in the polytechnics after their G.C.E 'O' Level examinations (home/examinations/gce-o-level/about-gce-o-level) and polytechnics usually focus less on academic writing and more on workplace writing (as well as a host of other workplace communication, such as interpersonal, leadership and teamwork, skills). As can be gleaned, students come into SIT with varying levels of communicative competence in academic writing and as such a significant number of them need focused instruction in it. It is precisely to address this need that the Centre for Communication Skills (CCS) was formed in 2015.

Where We Were

CCS began by offering instruction in both writing and oral presentation skills to students through distinct or 'stand-alone' modules and from 2016, assignment-specific, instruction in content modules, based on requests from content faculty, assignment-specific. Students could also seek individual consultation with CCS faculty through an online reservation system. Although both writing and oral presentation were offered in the 'stand-alone' modules, there was always more emphasis on writing as it was clear from their assignments and class work that students needed more help with their writing.

Despite the overall sense that many students needed writing instruction, not all degree programmes included a compulsory module in academic writing or any embedded writing instruction in their content modules, although almost all programmes required their students to write reports, proposals, and reflections during the course of their three or four year programmes. Thus, it was common that at certain points of the year, when students were writing their capstone, final year projects, or IWSP reports, there would be a surge in the number of those seeking help from CCS faculty through the online reservation system.

As was expected, these 'cries for help' were merely for 'quick-fix' consultations that might help them to pass the particular assignment or project and not requests to actually learn how to construct an academic paper that conformed to an academic context (Bazerman; Berkenkotter and Huckin) or the requirements of disciplinary ways of knowing and telling specific content (Ivanic; Jones et al.; Lea and Street; Lea and Stierer). Also, it did not help the situation that assessment of the assignments was based largely on the inclusion of necessary content and very little or not at all, on how the content was written.

The Transition

In 2019 some changes were made to this situation based on feedback from professionals who served on SIT advisory boards, survey findings on the views of employers of SIT graduates as well as work supervisors who oversaw SIT students on the IWSP, that our students needed to be able to write better to engage different stakeholders when they went out to work. The feedback also informed us that the transfer of writing knowledge (Eady, Machura, Jaidev, Taczak, DePalma, Mina) to the workplace, along with that of content knowledge, was necessary if SIT graduates aspired to compete with graduates from the more established local universities as well as those applying from overseas universities and advance beyond entry-level positions to senior positions in their chosen professions. More importantly, it became clear that enabling SIT students to write better should not only be the responsibility of CCS and the language and communication tutors but that of all faculty so that students would realize the gravity and urgency of investing time, effort and agency (Shapiro et al.; Tardy) into learning to write better for academic and professional purposes.

Where We Are Now

As a result of support from the senior management of SIT, 2020 saw the design and delivery of a new 4-credit module focused on teaching a first year, critical thinking version of academic writing, wherever possible, in all university degree programmes. Additionally, senior management of SIT acknowledged that for students to be able to recontextualize, repurpose, and refocus (Robertson et al.) the writing knowledge gained in the 4-credit module taken in the first year at the start of their degree programmes and apply it in new and previously unencountered contexts, purposes and audiences, writing instruction would have to be reiterated throughout students' degree programmes. Thus, what CCS had already begun doing by way of embedding assignment-specific writing instructions in content modules, but on an ad-hoc basis, was formalized as a requirement for all degree programmes across the university. It was decided that writing instruction would be embedded in at least one content module in every SIT degree programme from the second year onwards. In addition, students' writing in these content assignments would be assessed based on a set of rubrics that was agreed upon by both content and CCS faculty and weighted to contribute the equivalent of three modular credits in each academic year beginning from the second year of their programmes.

The design of the 4-credit module entitled, Critical Thinking and Communicating, was done using backward curriculum design or what Grant Wiggins and Jay McTighe refer to as "understanding by design." Basically, what we did was to work closely with content faculty and design the writing curriculum based on what students would be expected to write in their content modules and in their professions. So, we started from the point of 'desired results' (Wiggins and McTighe), namely, what are students required to write, in what formats would they be required to write, for whom, and in what contexts. At the same time, the university decided that as the university of applied learning in Singapore, we should not only infuse critical thinking in our pedagogy, we should make this effort visible. With this goal in mind, we chose to premise the teaching of these "desired results" on the Paul-Elder critical thinking framework (**Paul and Elder**) for disciplines like engineering as it lent itself well to the types of writing in that field. We worked from there to develop the content, practice exercises, activities, and assessments. The incorporation of a critical thinking framework has been useful in scaffolding the process of asking the right questions when reading academic texts, evaluating information from multiple sources and incorporating 'voice' in writing. In short, using a critical thinking framework with a process and sequence of questions has helped students to articulate their mental narratives on problem identification, solution and evaluation in concrete words.

In conclusion, by making writing instruction a requirement for all SIT undergraduates through the teaching of a distinct 4-credit module that is customized based on the writing requirements of specific disciplines, embedding assignment-specific writing instruction in content modules in subsequent years of the degree programmes to reiterate the writing knowledge acquired from the 4-credit module and premising the teaching of all writing on a critical thinking framework, we aim to scaffold and facilitate writing transfer.

Works Cited

Bazerman, Charles. *Shaping Written Knowledge: The Genre and Activity of the Experimental Article in Science*. The University of Wisconsin Press, 1988.

Berkenkotter, Carol, and Thomas Huckin. *Genre Knowledge in Disciplinary Communication*. Lawrence Erlbaum Associates, 1995.

Eady, Michelle, et al. "Writing Transfer and Work-Integrated Learning in Higher Education: Transnational Research across Disciplines." *International Journal of Work-Integrated Learning*, vol. 22, no. 2, 2021, pp. 183-197.

Iborganization. "Diploma Programme (DP)." *International Baccalaureate*, https://www.ibo.org/programmes/diploma-programme/.

Ivanič, Roz. "Discourses of Writing and Learning to Write." *Language and Education*, vol. 18, no. 3, 2004, pp. 220–245, doi:10.1080/09500780408666877.

Jones, Carys, et al. *Students Writing in the University: Cultural and Epistemological Issues*. John Benjamins, 1999.

Latour, Bruno, and Steve Woolgar. *Laboratory Life*. Sage Publications, 1987, doi:10.1515/9781400820412.

Lillis, Theresa. "Student Writing as 'Academic Literacies': Drawing on Bakhtin to Move from Critique to Design." *Language and Education*, vol. 17, no. 3, 2003, pp. 192-207.

Lea, Mary R., and Brian V. Street. "Student Writing in Higher Education: An Academic Literacies Approach." *Studies in Higher Education*, vol. 23, no. 2, 1998, pp. 157–172, doi:10.1080/03075079812331380364.

Lea, Mary R., and Barry Stierer. "Changing Academic Identities in Changing Academic Workplaces: Learning from Academics' Everyday Professional Writing Practices." *Teaching in Higher Education*, vol. 16, no. 6, 2011, pp. 605–616, doi: 10.1080/13562517.2011.560380.

Richard, Paul, and Linda Elder. *The Miniature Guide to Critical Thinking Concepts and Tools*. Rowman & Littlefield, 2020.

Robertson, Liane, et al. "Notes Toward a Theory of Prior Transfer of Knowledge and Practice." *Composition Forum,* vol. 26, 2012.

Shapiro, Shawna, et al. "Teaching for Agency: From Appreciating Linguistic Diversity to Empowering Student Writers." *Composition Studies,* vol. 44, no. 1, 2016, pp. 31-52.

Tardy, Christine M. "Appropriation, Ownership, and Agency: Negotiating Teacher Feedback in Academic Settings." *Feedback in Second Language Writing: Contexts and Issues*, edited by Ken Hyland and Fiona Hyland, 2nd ed., Cambridge University Press, 2019, pp. 64–82.

Wiggins, Grant P., and Jay McTighe. *Understanding by Design*. Association for Supervision and Curriculum Development, 2008.

—. Backward Design. In Understanding by Design ASCD. "Home." *SEAB*, https://www.seab.gov.sg/home/examinations/gce-a-level. *Smiletutor.sg/Polytechnics-in-Singapore-Overview-Courses-Admissions/*. 1998.

Yancey, Kathleen Blake. "Relationships Between Writing and Critical Thinking, and Their Significance for Curriculum and Pedagogy." *Double Helix*, vol. 3, 2015.

Writing Instruction and Writing Research in Denmark

Kristine Kabel and Jesper Bremholm

In Denmark, the educational context for children's first encounter with formal writing instruction is compulsory school, in Danish termed *grundskolen* ("foundational school"), which is mandatory and comprises the first ten years of schooling (students aged 6-15). Hereafter, students shift to vocational or general upper secondary school in new institutional settings, with the majority of students (80 percent) choosing general upper secondary school (students aged 16-18). Grade 0 is the first grade in compulsory school, and it forms a transitional year between kindergarten and school. Grade 0 has its own separate curriculum with learning goals that are recommended but not obligatory, and with regard to writing, young students should experiment with composing short texts and acquire knowledge about the alphabetic principle, writing direction, and sentence composition (Ministry of Children and Education). Hereafter, and thus in the remaining part of compulsory school (grades 1-9), students learn to communicate through writing in still more advanced ways primarily in the language arts subject Danish for which the national curriculum includes obligatory key competence goals specified for writing and multimodal text production. A multi-national analysis of the national language arts curricula in selected countries noted that, in the case of Denmark, students' writing development is conceived to "evolve in relatively linear progression, however, in increasingly contextualised, formalized and disciplinary ways" throughout compulsory school (Jeffery et al. 348; see also Kabel et al.). In recent years there has been an increased awareness among teachers and teacher educators of the need for supporting students' subject-specific writing within the entire range of K-12 school subjects. Actually, in neighboring Norway, it has been a prerequisite since 2006 that each school subject considers writing as one of five basic competences, a development also supported by developmental and research projects on how each school subject may support students' writing (e.g. Berge et al.). In the Danish educational system, similar attention has not–as of yet–been paid to subject-specific writing – despite the growing awareness of its importance.

A particular characteristic of the Danish school system also needs mentioning here: there is a long tradition of teachers enjoying a relatively extensive autonomy in all content areas, including writing (Laursen and Bjerresgaard). Thus, teachers are only obliged to follow key competence goals in grades 1-9; they are not required to apply certain instructional methods or to teach specified curricular content. Regarding writing, two regulations support the Danish teachers' autonomy: Formal grades are not introduced before grade 8 (students aged 14); the first written composition exam does not take place until grade 9 (students aged 15). However, this first (and final) written composition exam is a high-stakes exam. As a consequence, it has a strong impact on the teachers' choice of both content and instructional approach in the final years of compulsory school (Troelsen). Currently, the compositional exam puts emphasis on students' genre awareness, and in particular on their writing of journalistic opinion genres. In general upper secondary, the picture looks a bit different. In the final composition exam at this level, the students are required to master three generic forms of writing: the analytical (e.g. a literary response), reflective (e.g. an essay), and argumentative (e.g. a journalistic commentary) article.

Major pedagogical trends have contributed to the picture of what writing instruction looks like in Danish K-12 language arts classrooms today. In the 1990s, process-oriented writing pedagogy was in vogue in both compulsory and general upper secondary school in Denmark (Hetmar; Juul Jensen et al.). Although less widespread today, this approach to writing introduced a more thorough approach with response rounds integrated in much current writing instruction, and it introduced a focus on the student and their writing projects–something that also resonated with a general student-centered pedagogy in the last part of the 20th century. In the 2000s, genre pedagogy (particularly the Sydney School) was introduced in Denmark and gained support, specifically in teacher education (Mulvad). From here, it found its way to textbooks and teaching materials, and it still influences writing instruction in compulsory school. Furthered by genre pedagogy, non-fictional genres in language arts Danish received increased attention. This is reflected in the above-mentioned dominance of journalistic genres in comparison with, for example, fictional genres in the current written composition exam in the final year of compulsory school. In addition to genre pedagogy, an overarching literacy trend since the 2000s pushed forward a focus on reading and writing after the basics learned in the primary school grades. Initially, this trend was an answer to unsatisfying results in international reading assessments such as PISA, in which Denmark participated for the first time in 1991 (Mejding). Later, it developed into two sub-trends. First developed a content area reading trend reflected in a number of in-service courses for teachers, which drew primarily on socio-cognitive approaches to reading comprehension strategies (Block and Duffy). Those courses dominated in the second half of the 2000s. Second developed a disciplinary (Shanahan and Shanahan) or subject-specific trend, which drew primarily on socio-cultural and social semiotic approaches to both reading and writing (Green). Both genre pedagogy and the overarching literacy trend contributed to the more recent attention among teachers and teacher educators towards the more specific requirements when students engage with texts in still more specialised ways as part of schooling.

In addition to these influential pedagogical trends has been a years-long emphasis on the development of students' personal voice in writing. This emphasis has been especially strong in general upper secondary schools and is accompanied by a particular focus on the importance of fostering identity development through writing (Krogh). This interest in the possibilities for expressing and understanding oneself and the world through writing reflects a strong *Bildung* tradition in Denmark and the rest of Scandinavia. Today, this interest in voice and identity is part of the current picture of writing instruction. For example, the national curriculum for the subject of Danish language arts at upper secondary level now explicitly requires that the students develop a personal voice in creative writing activities, and it points to the reflective article as a format that supports such development of a personal voice (Ministry of Children and Education).

The longish history of pedagogical and curricular attention to writing in Denmark has not always been accompanied by educational writing research. A research environment in Denmark emerged in the 2000s together with the first attempts to build up curriculum research at universities. The establishment of research units at the six Danish university colleges in 2013 furthered this development. In other words, educational writing research is a new field in Denmark, and, as such, it coincides with the recent and heightened attention towards writing in school. In a Scandinavian context, Norway was the frontier when it comes to the early foundation of educational writing research in the 1980s and onwards, and it still plays a leading role today in terms of its volume of educational writing research, even though Sweden does not trail far behind (Bremholm et al.; Igland and Ongstad).[1] In Denmark, the number of research studies are still quite sparse. One early major writing research project was *Learning to Write, Writing to Learn* (2010-2014), which used a longitudinal ethnographic design to follow student writers and their trajectories in the transition from grade 9 and throughout general upper secondary. The project resulted in empirical knowledge on student writing in school subjects and novel theoretical insights about young people's individual development as writers (e.g. Elf; Krogh and Jakobsen). Currently, an ongoing research project examines early writing development across the grades 0-2 based on a textual model of writing approached as a multidimensional linguistic phenomenon (Kabel et al.). Alongside the emergence of research projects on writing, the growing interest in writing in educational contexts in Denmark is also signalled by a number of developmental projects on writing from about 2000 onwards. These projects were conducted by educational researchers and/or teacher educators, and several of them have had a notable influence on educators and writing teachers. Developmental projects have been directed at both the lower primary level (e.g., Korsgaard et al.), the upper primary level (e.g., Brok et al.) and the upper secondary level (e.g., Juul Jensen et al.).

A recent study (Holmberg et al.) on language arts PhD dissertations from the Nordic countries conducted and defended between 2000-2017 supports the picture of a new but growing educational writing research field within the last two decades. It showed that one fourth of the dissertations were within the category of writing research. Zooming out, educational writing research in Scandinavia displays – according to a current review (Bremholm et al.)—a majority of explorative and small-scale studies based particularly in sociocultural and social semiotic approaches to writing, which pave the way both for future intervention and/or large-scale studies and for cross-national studies in the region and beyond.

Notes

1. Scandinavia consists of Denmark, Norway and Sweden, countries that are culturally close due to neighbouring languages and similarities in educational systems. Scandinavia is part of the Nordic countries that besides the three Scandinavian countries consist of Iceland and Finland. The Nordic countries have fewer but still many similarities.

Works Cited

Berge, Kjell Lars et al. "Introducing Teachers to New Semiotic Tools for Writing Instruction and Writing Assessment: Consequences for Students' Writing Proficiency." *Assessment in Education: Principles, Policy & Practice*, vol. 26 no. 1, 2019, pp. 6-25, . doi: 10.1080/0969594X.2017.1330251

Block, Cathy Collins, and Gerald G. Duffy. "Research on Teaching Comprehension: Where We've Been and Where We're Going." *Comprehension Instruction: Research-based Best Practice*s, edited by Cathy Collins Block and Gerald G. Duffy, The Guilford Press, 2008, pp. 19-37.

Bremholm, Jesper et al. "A Review of Scandinavian Writing Research Between 2010 and 2020." *Writing & Pedagogy*, forthcoming.

Brok, Lene Storgaard et al. *Skrivedidaktik: En Vej til Læ*ring [*Writing Didactics: A Way to Learn*]. Klim, 2015.

Elf, Nikolaj Frydensbjerg. "Taught by Bitter Experience: A Timescales Analysis of Amalie's Development of Writer Identity in Danish Secondary and Upper Secondary Education." *Writer Identity and the Teaching and Learning of Writing*, edited by Teresa Cremin and Terry Locke. Routledge, 2017, pp. 183-199.

Green, William. "Subject-specific Literacy and School earning: A Revised Account." *Literacy in 3D. An Integrated Perspective in Theory and Practice*, edited by Bill Green and Catherine Beavis. ACER Press, 2012, pp. 5-20.

Hetmar, Vibeke. *Elevens Projekt, Lærerens Udfordringer* [*Student's Project, Teacher's Challenges*]. Danskærerforeningen, 2000.

Holmberg, Per, et al. "On the Emergence of the L1 Research Field. A cComparative Study of PhD Abstracts in the Nordic Countries 2000–2017." *L1-Educational Studies in Language and Literature, 19*, 2019, pp. 1-27. https://doi.org/10.17239/L1ESLL-2019.19.01.05

Igland Mari-Ann, and Sigmund Ongstad. "Introducing Norwegian Research on Writing." *Written Communication,* vol. 19 no. 3, 2002, pp. 339-344. doi:10.1177/074108802237748

Juul Jensen, Mi'janne, et al. *Når sproget vokser* [*Language growth*]. Dansklærerforeningen, 1998.

Kabel, Kristine, et al. "A Framework for Identifying Early Writing Development." *Writing & Pedagogy*, forthcoming.

Korsgaard, Klara, et al. *Opdagende Skrivning - en vej ind i læsningen* [*Explorative Writing – A Pathway to Reading*]. Dansklærerforeningen, 2015.

Krogh, Ellen. "Literacy og Stemme – Et Spændingsfelt i Modersmålsfaglig Skrivning" ["Literacy and Voice – A Dynamic Field in First Language Education Writing"]. *Nordisk morsmålsdidaktikk. Forskning, felt og fag,* edited by Sigmund Ongstad. Novus Forlag, 2012, pp. 260-288.

Krogh, Ellen, and Karen Sonne Jakobsen, editors. *Understanding Young People's Writing Development*. Routledge, 2019.

Laursen, Per Fibæk, and Helle Bjerresgaard. *Praktisk Pædagogik: Metodik i Folkeskolen* [*Practical Pedagogy: Instructional Methods in the Danish Public School*]. Gyldendal, 2009.

Mejding, Jan. *Den Grimme ælling og Svanerne—Om Danske Elevers Læsefærdigheder* [*The Ugly Duckling and the Swans—On Danish Students Reading Skills*]. Danmarks Pædagogiske Institut, 1994.

Ministry of Children and Education (2019). *Børnehaveklassen. Fælles Mål* [*Grade 0. Common Standards*]. www.emu.dk Accessed 1 October 2021.

Ministry of Children and Education (2021). *Vejledning Dansk A–stx 2021* [*Guidelines Danish A*]. https://www.uvm.dk/gymnasiale-uddannelser/fag-og-laereplaner/laereplaner-2017/stx-laereplaner-2017 Accessed 1 October 2021.

Mulvad, Ruth. "SFL-baseret Pædagogik" ["SFL-based Pedagogy"]. *Nordisk socialsemiotik: Pædagogiske, multimodale og sprogvidenskabelige landvindinger,* edited by Thomas Hestbæk Andersen and Morten Boeriis. Syddansk Universitetsforlag, 2012, pp. 247-276.

Shanahan, Timothy. and Cynthia Shanahan. "Teaching Disciplinary Literacy to Adolescents: Rethinking Content-Area Literacy." *Harvard Educational Review,* vol. 78 no. 1, 2008, pp. 40-59.

Troelsen, Solveig. "En Invitation man ikke kan afslå – Analyse af Afgangsprøven i Skriftlig Fremstilling med Særligt Fokus på Skriveordren" ["An Invitation You Can't Decline – an Analysis of the Final Composition Exam"]. *Nordic Journal Of Literacy Research, 4*(1), 142-166, 2018. https://doi.org/10.23865/njlr.v4.1267

Teaching of Writing in Hong Kong: Where Are We?

Icy Lee

In this short piece, I take stock of the teaching of writing in Hong Kong, highlight key issues and concerns, and suggest ways forward.

English Writing in Hong Kong

Since the sovereignty of Hong Kong was returned to China in 1997, English has remained an official language and been formally referred to as a second language, though in reality it has, arguably, the status of a foreign language. This is especially true for writing because students do not have to write in English outside the classroom. Nevertheless, English writing has a significant role to play in education. Students begin to learn to write in English from kindergarten, and by the time they reach Grade 12, they are expected to produce essays of 400 words. To get into university, they need to attain a minimum of Level 3 (seven levels in total) for the English language subject, with writing as one compulsory component requiring students to write two essays of 200 and 400 words respectively in two hours. Universities in Hong Kong are English-medium; hence, students have to produce academic writing in English.

Teaching, Learning, and Assessment of Writing at School and University Levels

Hong Kong students' lack of motivation to write in English is well documented in the literature (I. Lee et al., "Hong Kong Secondary Students' Motivation" 183; Lo and Hyland 220). English writing serves a primarily pragmatic purpose—mainly to help students pass examinations and get into university. Typical English as a Foreign Language (EFL) writing classrooms are teacher-centered, with a much stronger focus on testing than teaching. Even for the classroom writing assessment that takes place on a regular basis, it tends to stress the summative functions of assessment (with a focus on scores) rather than its formative potential (Icy Lee, "L2 Writing Teachers" 231). Teacher feedback is heavily error-focused, which easily damages students' confidence in writing and kills motivation. The Hong Kong Education Bureau has been advocating for process writing for decades; however, a majority of schools have not enthusiastically embraced it. At best, the prewriting stage is implemented, which is most frequently reflected in the use of brainstorming activities. Multiple drafting that allows students to experience drafting and revising is not a regular practice in most schools, which teachers often attribute to time constraints and students' lack of motivation to engage in rewriting.

It can be imagined that by the time students get into university, writing motivation remains low. Without the pressure of public examinations, the practical value of EFL writing has dropped significantly. Based on my informal communication with experienced university language instructors, students' willingness to make an effort in writing largely hinges on the importance their major professors attach to written language. Language instructors have heavy teaching loads and find it hard to adopt process writing. Even when process writing is incorporated, it is not easy to get buy-in from students—especially given their lack of experience with process writing at a secondary level. To provide students with additional support in academic writing, writing tutorial services, consultation sessions, and/or peer tutoring services are provided at different universities (Cynthia Lee 431; Jones et al. 2).

While feedback and assessment in primary and secondary schools are dominated by a summative orientation, universities in Hong Kong have adopted outcome-based assessment that puts a premium on the use of rubrics to guide university writing assessment. Feedback practices vary by individual instructors: primary and secondary teachers are often expected to provide detailed feedback, whereas university instructors cannot afford the time to do so due to heavy grading loads and longer student essays.

Teacher Preparedness and Preparation to Teach Writing

Second language (L2) writing teacher education is under-developed in Hong Kong. Many teachers are influenced by the apprenticeship of observation (Lortie 55-81), repeating practices adopted by their own previous teachers, such as providing error-focused feedback to students. At the university level, there has been a move to provide more English for specific academic purposes and English for specific purposes courses. At my university, for instance, while foundation courses require students to write general argumentative essays, more advanced courses involve discipline-specific genres such as product design specifications for engineering students and business proposals for business students. Language instructors are prepared to teach general academic writing, but they feel ill-equipped to teach disciplinary writing, particularly when they lack knowledge of the discipline concerned and how discipline-specific genres operate in real-world settings.

Research-Practice Gaps

Although L2 writing research in Hong Kong has grown significantly in the last two decades, insights generated from research do not seem to have filtered down to the classroom. My review of relevant literature from *Web of Science* and *Scopus* has yielded a total of 64 empirical journal articles about L2 writing in Hong Kong over the last two decades. Notably, there has been an increased amount of research conducted in the under-studied school context, particularly primary schools, that sheds light on a range of practical issues such as students' use of self-regulated strategies, technology supported writing (e.g. digital storytelling), teacher and peer feedback, and assessment for/as learning (Bai and Wang 6; Cheung 3; Man-Kit Lee 3). Research in the university context has yielded valuable findings about different aspects of academic writing, such as students' use of source texts (Li and Casanave 166), challenges of academic writing and coping strategies (Lin and Morrison 60; Xie and Lei 3). However, the research-practice gaps appear to be wide; although concerns have been raised by researchers, and in some cases solutions proposed and researched into (e.g., as self-regulated learning), in practice, viable, long-term solutions still seem out of reach.

A case in point is student motivation, which is a perennial problem in local writing classrooms. If we fail to motivate students to write, to have a real taste of the writing process, and to receive feedback that is encouraging, enabling, and empowering, and if we fail to impact schoolchildren positively at an early age before they develop ingrained fears of and resistance to writing, we are fighting a losing battle. Dominant discourses of writing in Hong Kong attribute good writing to grammatical accuracy, relegating writing to serve primarily as a vehicle for language reinforcement. Little wonder writing is a fearful and stressful activity for EFL student writers as they are bound to make tons of grammatical errors in writing. To further complicate the matter, policy discourses about writing (as evident in curriculum guides for English language education in Hong Kong schools) may send unhelpful messages about how writing should be taught and assessed. The following two paragraphs about process writing and feedback on compositions, respectively, are extracted from the 2021 curriculum guide for senior secondary for English language education (Curriculum Development Council and the Hong Kong Examinations and Assessment Authority 2021):

> To handle time constraints, teachers are encouraged to focus on ONE specific aspect of the writing process at a time (e.g. idea generation, planning, drafting or revising). They should only ask students to apply the whole process when they have gained mastery of all the strategies along the way (39-40). [. . .] When marking compositions, it is advisable to provide students with comprehensive feedback on content, accuracy, appropriateness, presentation and organisation (54-55).

If students have only one focus of the writing process at a time (e.g. brainstorming or idea generation), they are in fact not going through the entire writing process as they learn to write. In local classrooms, most teachers end up focusing on prewriting and making students correct errors based on single drafts. A good way to address time constraints, instead, is to ask for a smaller number of writing assignments but make students go through multiple drafting for each writing task (in addition to other stages of the writing process).

Comprehensive feedback on content, accuracy, appropriateness, presentation, and organization, as promulgated in the curriculum guide, means that feedback on each of these aspects is comprehensive rather than selective. This is contrary to good feedback practice advice in the literature (Ferris 7) that suggests teachers provide selective feedback on accuracy, with teacher feedback covering content, accuracy, organization, etc. in a balanced manner. When the most recent curriculum guide in Hong Kong provides the two tips cited above, I cannot but think that as far as writing pedagogy in Hong Kong is concerned, we are probably still at square one!

Closing Thoughts

The importance of school writing cannot be overstated because it helps students build a strong foundation on which academic literacy skills can be further developed. The way writing is taught and assessed in school also shapes students' beliefs and attitudes regarding writing, which have potentially strong influence on students' writing development. Indeed, motivation is what matters. There is a lot more writing teacher education can do to prepare pre-service and in-service teachers to work on motivating students to write through engaging them in the writing process, equipping them with relevant writing strategies, and providing feedback that sees teachers and students share responsibility during the writing process, as well as feedback that fosters learner agency and autonomy. There is a long way to go.

Works Cited

Bai, Barry, and Jing Wang. "Conceptualizing Self-regulated Reading-to-write in ESL/EFL Writing and Investigating its Relationships to Motivation and Writing Competence." *Language Teaching Research*, 16 Nov. 2020. Sage Journals, DOI:10.1177/1362168820971740.

Cheung, Anisa. "Digitizing the Story-writing Process for EFL Primary Learners: An Exploratory Study." *Language Teaching Research*, 23 June 2021. Sage Journals, DOI: 10.1177/13621688211027772.

Curriculum Development Council and the Hong Kong Examinations and Assessment Authority. *English Language Education Key Learning Area: English Language Curriculum and Assessment Guide (Secondary 4-6)*. Hong Kong Government Printer, 2021.

Ferris, Dana R. "Responding to Student Writing: Teachers' Philosophies and Practices." *Assessing Writing*, vol. 19, 2014, pp. 6-23, DOI: 10.1016/j.asw.2013.09.004.

Lee, Cynthia. "More Than Just Language Advising: Rapport in University English Writing Consultations and Implications for Tutor Training." *Language and Education*, vol. 29, no. 5, 2015, pp. 430-452, DOI: 10.1080/09500782.2015.1038275.

Lee, Icy. "L2 Writing Teachers' Perspectives, Practices and Problems Regarding Error Feedback." *Assessing Writing*, vol. 8, no. 3, 2003, pp. 216-237, DOI: 10.1016/j.asw.2003.08.002

Lee, Icy, et al. "Hong Kong Secondary Students' Motivation in EFL Writing: A Survey Study." *TESOL Quarterly*, vol. 52, no. 1, 2017, pp. 176-187, DOI: 10.1002/tesq.364.

Lee, Man-Kit. "Peer Feedback in Second Language Writing: Investigating Junior Secondary Students' Perspectives on Inter-Feedback and Intra-Feedback." *System*, vol. 55, 2015, pp. 1-10, DOI: 10.1016/j.system.2015.08.003.

Li, Yongyan, and Christine Pearson Casanave. "Two First-Year Students' Strategies for Writing from Sources: Patchwriting or Plagiarism?" *Journal of Second Language Writing*, vol. 21, no. 2, 2012, pp. 165-180, DOI: 10.1016/j.jslw.2012.03.002.

Lin, Linda HF, and Bruce Morrison. "Challenges in Academic Writing: Perspectives of Engineering Faculty and L2 Postgraduate Research Students." *English for Specific Purposes*, vol. 63, 2021, pp. 59-70, DOI: 10.1016/j.esp.2021.03.004.

Lo, Julia, and Fiona Hyland. "Enhancing Students' Engagement and Motivation in Writing: The Case of Primary Students in Hong Kong." *Journal of Second Language Writing*, vol. 16, no. 4, 2007, pp. 219-237, DOI: 10.1016/j.jslw.2007.06.002.

Lortie, Dan C. "The Limits of Socialization." *Schoolteacher: A Sociological Study*, University of Chicago Press, 1975, pp. 55-81.

Jones, Rodney H., et al. "Interactional Dynamics in On-Line and Face-To-Face Peer-Tutoring Sessions for Second Language Writers." *Journal of Second Language Writing*, vol. 15, no. 1, 2006, pp. 1-23, DOI: 10.1016/j.jslw.2005.12.001.

Xie, Qin, and Yuqi Lei. "Diagnostic Assessment of L2 Academic Writing Product, Process and Self-regulatory Strategy Use with a Comparative Dimension." *Language Assessment Quarterly*, 25 Apr. 2021. Taylor & Francis Online, DOI: 10.1080/15434303.2021.1903470.

Weh Wi Deh / Veh Vi Is / Where We Are: Teaching and Researching Academic Writing in the Caribbean

Vivette Milson-Whyte, Raymond Oenbring, and Brianne Jaquette

We chose this somewhat unwieldy triple-barrelled title as it reflects the complex linguistic situation of the Anglophone Caribbean, where multiple English-lexifier Creoles (such as Jamaican Creole [Weh Wi Deh] and Bahamian Creole [Veh Vi Is])—all of which developed in the colonial era out of the contact between English and myriad African languages spoken by contemporary Caribbean people's enslaved ancestors—coexist and contend with international Standard English (Where We Are). Further adding to this complex linguistic situation, the teaching of academic writing in the Caribbean reflects the region's history of competition between British (through direct colonial rule) and American (through the neo-colonial influence of American media) language variants and educational culture.

Indeed, due to the competing influences of British and American educational discourses and due to the lack of substantial "homegrown" discourses on writing instruction, academic writing courses are known at Anglophone Caribbean postsecondary institutions by various names, including: academic writing, use of English, communication, English composition, writing and rhetoric, freshman composition, English for academic purposes, critical reading and writing, and, finally, academic literacy/ies. Regardless of the name of the class or the approach taken, the development of academic writing instruction in the Caribbean region in the last few decades may be understood as a function of: (a) colonial history; (b) changing cohorts of students; and (c) exposure to developments in writing studies elsewhere (see, for example, Milson-Whyte, *Academic Writing Instruction,* and Oenbring and Milson-Whyte).

Where We Were: A Brief History of Academic Writing Instruction in the Caribbean

For our brief history, we use the example of The University of the West Indies (The UWI), the premier higher education institution in the English-speaking Caribbean. The first postsecondary academic writing course taught in the region was a survey course developed in the early 1960s with a focus on the Use of English (the actual name of the class) at the then University College of the West Indies (UCWI), which was, at the time, still an affiliate of the University of London. Modelling the course on classes then taught in England, UCWI administrators introduced the Use of English in the early years of independence of various Caribbean territories from British colonial rule in the 1960s. The focus in this course was having the largely homogenous group of high-achieving local students from upper-middle to high income groups consider general "uses of English." That is to say, this course in its original form was more of a language appreciation course than a composition course in the contemporary American sense.

By the 1970s and 80s, when the student population at The UWI started to become more diverse, there was a gradual shift to considering using language (English) appropriate for university study in general. By the late 1980s and early 1990s, with increasing democratization of education and enrollment of students from lower socio-economic backgrounds whose first language was an English-lexified Creole, UWI faculty and administrators developed parallel strands. Classes for one set of students focused on having them write appropriately in English for university study while the focus in instruction for the other set was on assisting them to write accurately—that is, write using correct English grammar, understood in a very traditional sense. There was still no consideration of including the students' creole languages in teaching.

Later, in the 1990s and beyond, the focus of UWI faculty shifted to encouraging students to develop university literacies through a course called English for Academic Purposes. This single course offered to nearly all new students on all campuses was modes-based, focusing on exposition. Students in the Faculty of Law and students in their second semester in the Faculty of Humanities also took a course in argument (understood in a traditional modes manner). While retaining an approach that would be described by US colleagues as reflecting current-traditional rhetoric (that US Composition programs had largely abandoned), faculty in Jamaica also began in this period to adopt process approaches to writing and to include writing portfolios in teaching. However, these programs were never truly process-driven, as emphasis largely remained on the product of writing. Later still, in the new millennium and based on faculty interest in and engagements with Writing Across the Curriculum and Writing in the Disciplines, UWI faculty designed courses to help students develop reading and writing skills appropriate for the disciplines in which they study—through courses deemed discipline-specific or faculty-specific (for more on this history, see Milson-Whyte's *Academic Writing Instruction for Creole-Influenced Students*).

Where We Are Now

Today, some postsecondary institutions in the Anglophone Caribbean retain general labels for courses (such as academic writing) and other institutions, such as the University of The Bahamas (UB), use course titles reflecting the influence of US composition (such as Writing and Rhetoric I / II and Advanced Composition). Elsewhere in the region, there is a move to label suites of courses as academic literacies courses (as on campuses of The UWI) or as academic literacy (as at The University of Technology, Jamaica) based on interest in academic literacies in the United Kingdom (see, for example, Milson-Whyte, "Re/Engaging Street"). Despite the era or course name and because of a general focus on excellence (rather than also on issues of equity), courses have generally focused on writing in English and on writing as a neutral endeavour.

In a context where the prevailing linguistic attitudes reflect dis-ease regarding the creoles and other non-standard languages of the region, creole languages are not usually accepted in students' writing. In general, there is really very little engagement with issues of language and identity within the context of writing instruction; the use of English remains largely unchallenged (see, however, exceptions in the work of Jones; Dyer Spiegel; and Oenbring, "The Small Island Polis"). Indeed, outsiders to the Anglophone Caribbean may be surprised that when the creole language or other aspects of students' linguistic experiences are included in the teaching of academic writing, they seem strange/revolutionary; that is to say, codemeshing and translingualism have not yet broadly taken root in the academy in the Anglophone Caribbean. Furthermore, unlike the situation with Haitian Creole French in Haiti, English-lexifier Creoles lack widely accepted government-supported orthographies (that is, codified sets of spelling). Generally, students who wish to write in English-lexifier creoles must deploy seemingly ad hoc eye dialect spellings (as we did deliberately in our title) to represent their creole language.

Where We Are Going

Our recent edited collection, *Creole Composition: Academic Writing and Rhetoric in the Anglophone Caribbean,* came out of a need for more scholarship on teaching writing in the Caribbean. While there were great ideas about teaching academic writing in the Caribbean being circulated in local spaces (that is, among faculty on campuses), there was little communication across islands. Additionally, there was a lack of scholarship that addressed the specific needs of instructors and students in the region (see, for example, Oenbring, "College Composition" and Milson-Whyte, "Academic Writing in the Caribbean")—with most of the (sporadic) research on teaching academic writing in the Anglophone Caribbean coming from the traditions of applied linguistics and/or education (see, for example, Rose). Although scholarship on rhetoric and composition in the US or academic literacies in the UK could be applied to teaching in the Caribbean, it couldn't address all of the circumstances of teaching in the region and could sometimes feel like a repetition of colonial and imperialist structures, where knowledge about the local place came from outside in a top down manner rather than from those actually working on the ground. This was a hindrance to instructors, administrations, and our students.

When writing the CFP and selecting chapters to go into *Creole Composition*, we sought to have a wide-range of contributions. For example, we wanted to represent a spread of the countries and islands that make up the region; we were interested in having scholars from diverse academic backgrounds, such as composition, literature, and linguistics; and we looked at the issues from classroom perspectives and administrative perspectives. This diversity is reflected in the organization of the book itself, which moves from reflection on the linguistic situation in the Caribbean to sections on attitudes to learning and time management amongst students, to ideas about language "errors" in writing. The encompassing scope of the book has, no doubt, contributed to its positive reception. There has been a recognition of the need for such a project, and this recognition includes winning two major awards: the Mina P. Shaughnessy Prize from the Modern Language Association and an Outstanding Book Award from the Conference on College Composition and Communication.

In the afterword to *Creole Composition*, we pointed out the need for an active and engaged regional body in the Caribbean focused on the teaching of academic writing. Fortunately, since the publication of *Creole Composition*, the still-fledgling Caribbean Association of Tertiary-level Academic Literacies Practitioners (CATALP) has become more active. Nonetheless, as we have intimated throughout this piece, the systematic study of the teaching of academic writing is still relatively new to the Caribbean. Accordingly, the opportunities for strategic partnerships between institutions and organizations within and outside the region, and for research, are extensive. (Raymond is a member of the executive committee of CATALP, and he welcomes those who may wish to discuss strategic partnerships with CATALP and/or UB.) While those of us who study academic writing in the Caribbean are limited in our resources, we share a desire to craft a uniquely Caribbean set of pedagogies that, while drawing on the best of international research in writing studies, reflects the distinctiveness of the Caribbean sociolinguistic, historical, and cultural situation.

Works Cited

Dyer Spiegel, Jacob. "Building around Nation Language: A Critical Reflection on Teaching Composition at the University of The Bahamas." Milson-Whyte, Oenbring, and Jaquette, pp. 76-104.

Jones, Carmeneta. "Teaching Literacy Skills in the Jamaican Creole-Speaking Environment: A Reflection." Milson-Whyte, Oenbring, and Jaquette, pp. 39-75.

Milson-Whyte, Vivette. "Academic Writing in the Caribbean: Searching for an Identity." *International Journal of Bahamian Studies,* vol. 27, no. 1, 2021, pp. 181-190. <https://journals.sfu.ca/cob/index.php/files/article/view/439/pdf_96>

Milson-Whyte, Vivette. *Academic Writing Instruction for Creole-Influenced Students.* University of the West Indies Press, 2015.

—. "Re/Engaging Street to Address Multiplicity in Composition Classrooms." *Against Autonomous Literacies: Extending the Work of Brian V. Street.* Spec. Issue of *Literacy in Composition Studies*, vol. 8, no. 2, 2021, pp. 136-145. <https://licsjournal.org/index.php/LiCS/article/view/857>

Milson-Whyte, Vivette, Raymond Oenbring, and Brianne Jaquette, eds. *Creole Composition: Academic Writing and Rhetoric in the Anglophone Caribbean.* Parlor Press, 2019.

Oenbring, Raymond. "College Composition in the Anglophone Caribbean: The Search for a Caribbean identity." *Journal of Global Literacies, Technologies, and Emerging Pedagogies,* vol. 4., no. 1, 2017, pp. 533-545.

—. "The Small Island Polis: Rhetorical Pedagogy in the Caribbean." Milson-Whyte, Oenbring, and Jaquette, pp. 271-284.

Oenbring, Raymond, and Vivette Milson-Whyte. "When the Writing Program Farm is a Former Plantation: Transnational Writing Program Administration in the Anglophone Caribbean." *Teaching and Studying Transnational Composition,* edited by Christiane Donahue and Bruce Horner, Modern Language Association. (forthcoming)

Rose, Pamela. "A Case for Academic Literacies: Informed Needs Analysis." *The UWI Quality Education Forum,* vol. 21, 2016, pp. 42-62.

(Re)Writing the Middle East: Tension, Engagement, and Rhetorical Translanguaging

Emma Moghabghab

What it means to teach and research writing in the Middle East today depends an awful lot on what one supposes the Middle East to be. The countries that make up the Middle East have intersecting though distinct and internally complex historical, economic, and linguistic histories. As I have touched on elsewhere (Moghabghab et al.), the "Middle East" itself is a construct that we should use with unease given the plurality of these histories (121).[1] Characterized by what Vertovec termed "superdiversity," the countries of the Middle East include not only diversity of societies but also great diversity within the groups that constitute these societies (Hodges et al. 49). Disparate colonial histories and postcolonial legacies,[2] the religious and socio-political positioning of Arabic as a regional language,[3] and the influences of globalization and translanguaging create nuanced and multilayered multilingualisms that challenge any articulation of overarching models and methods for the teaching and research of writing in the region.

At the same time, the Middle East is currently in the throes of economic and political unrest combined with violence and interspersed war in several countries; tensions that have marked the region for many years and are often reflected in the work of the region's writing teachers and scholars. Some of these include the enduring trauma in countries like Lebanon, in particular after the August 4, 2020 explosion and the country's ongoing complete economic collapse; the continuing Israeli-Palestinian conflict; the wars in Syria and Yemen; the multiple refugee crises; negotiating regional and international political relations between the various countries of the Gulf; and navigating international affairs with/in the region, to name but a few. In this ecology, the writing classroom and the discipline of rhetoric and composition become potential discursive spaces where these tensions are played out and encountered critically. As teachers and researchers of writing adapt their rhetoric and practices to create discourse communities using critical language pedagogies and postdigital rhetorics, they engage with the past and present ideological, cultural, economic, and political tensions of the region.

The earliest institutions of higher learning adopting an American liberal arts curriculum in the region date back to the middle of the 19th century. The American University of Beirut, in Lebanon, was originally founded as Syrian Protestant College in 1866 and adopted a liberal arts model in the early 20th century. In recent years, older models have been coupled with the proliferation of English-medium universities and international branch campuses in numerous Middle Eastern countries, particularly in the Arabian Gulf. However, the American "model" for writing studies does not integrate seamlessly into local cultures and communities.[4] Even terms like "English as a Second or Foreign Language" or "bilingualism" are problematized in this context where multilingual speakers negotiate varied linguistic backgrounds with competing nationalist and religious ideologies and postcolonial perceptions about the "prestige" of speaking a foreign language.[5] For instance, at the American University of Beirut, a French-language educated Catholic student and an Arabic-language educated Shia Muslim student come not only at English, but also at a shared Standard Arabic (Fus'ha), with significantly different language attitudes because of their different religious and communal backgrounds. As representative of regional diversity, the Lebanese example highlights the ever-increasing need for focused scholarship on writing studies, pedagogy, and writing centers in the Middle East also noted in Arnold et al. (11). More importantly, such scholarship needs to emerge directly from the research, expertise, and experiences of the researchers, teachers, practitioners, and writing program and writing center administrators of the region.

Prevalent assumptions in U.S.-based writing studies are complicated inside Middle Eastern writing classrooms as the value and applicability of western pedagogical models are questioned and renegotiated. When most of the student population at AUB, for example, is multilingual, speaking and learning English and/or French in both their homes and their classrooms from age 3 upwards, the concept of ESL or EFL diverges sharply from commonly accepted definitions in Western writing scholarship. One way of approaching this difficulty has been through the production of culturally relevant, custom-made textbooks. These textbooks, produced by the teachers and researchers at institutions in the region such as the American University of Sharjah, Texas A&M Qatar, Weill Cornell Qatar, and the American University of Beirut draw from common writing studies wells, but differently than many North American audiences might expect. For instance, *Pages Apart: A Reader for Academic Writing*, currently in its fifth edition and created by the instructors of the Composition Program at AUB, is considered a successful example of efforts that reconcile student needs, multicultural readings, multimodal materials, and both regional and international scholarship (Hodges et al. 51). Aided by these textbooks, students begin to consider the multiple digital, social, cultural, political, and ideological components that make up their own linguistic and rhetorical practices while also keying into the intersections and divergences between those and others in the region and in the world.

Additionally, combining this rich but divergent sociolinguistic landscape with the current affordances of digital technologies leads to the innovation of creative writing spaces that are conducive to the reterritorialization of linguistic borders at individual, communal, and national levels. One such combination can be witnessed in the emergence of projects such as the bilingual Wikipedia editing project, *2Rāth* ("AUB Communication Skills Program"). Launched in 2019, this project involves creating articles about Arab writers and poets who previously had minimal presence online. In so doing, it addresses the cultural and gender gap in Arab representation on Wikipedia and immerses students in the practical and rhetorical dimensions of digital composing. As an enactment of postdigital critical language pedagogy, this and similar projects allow teachers of writing in the Middle East to contend with the ideological force of the languages of power in all its manifestations, linguistic and otherwise. The writing classroom thus becomes an open space for students and teachers to engage the contradictions and ruptures in subjectivities that arise from a plurality of sometimes competing colonial/postcolonial histories and their associated educational, social, and cultural contexts.

More broadly, postdigital rhetorical translanguaging can offer the region a framework attuned to its particularities. Involving a critical social, cultural, and political examination of the multimodal digital performances of multilingual speakers, it fosters critical understandings and negotiations of the strategic decisions made through these dynamic processes. Considering that composition has reached a point where all writing involves digitality, postdigital translanguaging allows teachers and researchers of writing in the Middle East to navigate the complex and competing demands involved in these processes within the particular ecology of the Middle East, its history, and its multiple realities. One example of such work is the digital humanities movement that is taking on issues like intercultures, (multi)linguistic mapping, post/(de)colonial futures, computational multiliteracy studies, and countering digital hegemonies. This movement is fostered by the rise of digital humanities projects, institutes, and degree programs in multiple universities in the Middle East such as at New York University, Abu Dhabi, Hamad Bin Khalifa University, the Doha Institute in Qatar, and the American University of Beirut, among others.

On an institutional level, writing research in the region involves questions about the very nature of writing and writing instruction. These are coupled with writing programs tasked with addressing programmatic and institutional concerns such as enhancing the culture of writing within the institution, using writing to promote liberal arts instructional models, the creation and expansion of WAC and WID programs, and positioning writing centers as integral to students' critical development. In response to these concerns, this branch of the research attempts to design and implement curricula, textbooks, and programs in conversation with teachers, researchers, and administrators from both the region and North American writing studies scholarship. In relation to Writing Across the Curriculum and Writing in the Disciplines in particular, these efforts begin with developing methods to convince faculty across the disciplines to take responsibility for and apply consistent writing practice and pedagogy in their classrooms.[6] At the level of writing centers, Zimmerman underscores the momentum of this growing body of research and the efforts made to create and maintain institutional and discursive relationships between writing centers, writing programs, and the university (138).

However, writing researchers in the Middle East face numerous obstacles in attempting research projects such as accessing articles and books that are region restricted or simply too expensive to be carried by certain institutions in the region. Severe limitations on resources and access, as well as the economic difficulties of some countries, like Lebanon and Syria, are currently restricting the free flow of ideas from and in these countries, with consequences reverberating throughout the Middle East. While these might come across as mundane or logistical challenges, they represent a significant impediment to the production and distribution of locally sourced knowledge as well as to the proliferation of digital humanities research projects. Often, neither researchers who publish their work in international journals nor their colleagues have access to these very journals through their institutions. These challenges to an emerging body of literature similarly complicate efforts of community building and cross-institutional collaboration. However, this major concern is giving rise to continuous efforts to invest in locally sourced material, rely on open-access research, and activate ties across national, linguistic, and cultural borders to promote effective teaching and learning.[7]

By relying on decolonizing critical pedagogies, the promises of postdigital rhetorical translanguaging, and the proliferation of professional and scholarly ties, teachers and researchers of writing in the region continue to challenge constraints and develop models that expand the discipline and layer it with their institutional and cultural frameworks. Taking the larger tensions and characteristics of the region into consideration, writing scholarship in the Middle East complicates assumptions and renegotiates Western paradigms as it revisits, encounters, and engages complex colonial and linguistic histories and political and socio-cultural realities.

Notes

1. See Bonine et al.'s *Is There a Middle East? The Evolution of a Geopolitical Concept* for an interesting series of debates about what the Middle East is, or if it is at all.

2. See Betty Anderson's *A History of the Modern Middle East*, Norbert Bugeja's *Postcolonial Memoir in the Middle East: Rethinking the Liminal in Mashriqi Writing*, Anna Ball and Karim Matta's *The Edinburgh Companion to the Postcolonial Middle East*, Cyrus Schayegh and Andrew Arsan's *The Routledge Handbook of the History of the Middle East Mandates*, and Andrew Wilcox's *Orientalism and Imperialism: From Nineteenth-century Missionary Imaginings to the Contemporary Middle East* for an

overview of the colonial and postcolonial histories of the Middle East and their contemporary extensions.

3. As the language of the Qur'an, Arabic is tied to cultural and socio-political identity formation in the predominantly Muslim Middle East. See Yasir Suleiman's *The Arabic Language and National Identity: A Study in Ideology* as well as *Arabic, Self and Identity: A Study in Conflict and Displacement*. Murre-van den Berg et al.'s *Arabic and its Alternatives: Religious Minorities and Their Languages in the Emerging Nation States of the Middle East (1920-1950)* also offers well-grounded situated discussions of the relationship between Arabic, other languages, Islam, and Middle Eastern identity.

4. See Arnold et al.'s *Emerging Writing Research from the Middle East-North Africa Region* for relevant explorations of the historico-geographical delineation of the region and writing research and teaching.

5. See Rula Diab's "Lebanese University Students' Perceptions of Ethnic, National, and Linguistic Identity and their Preferences for Foreign Language Learning in Lebanon," Hadi Banat's "The Status and Functions of English in Contemporary Lebanon," and Fatima Esseili's "A Sociolinguistic Profile of English in Lebanon" for discussions of language learners' attitudes toward English as a foreign language in Lebanon.

6. As Hodges and Kent argue: Locally relevant ways such as hybrid writing consultants are instrumental in mediating between disciplinary "'faculty members' expectations and multilingual students' development as writers" (201).

7. Ties involve the formation of professional writing and writing center associations and maintaining regular writing and language conferences and symposia in and across the various countries of the region. Some such associations include but are not limited to the Middle East North Africa Writing Center Alliance, TESOL Arabia, and the Association of Teachers of English in Lebanon. A few examples of regional conferences and symposia are the Oman International ELT Conference, the AUB International Conference on Effective Teaching and Learning in Higher Education, and The IAFOR International Conference on Language Learning, Dubai, among others.

Works Cited

"AUB Communication Skills Program and University Libraries Collaborate on Wikipedia Education Initiative." *The American University of Beirut,* https://www.aub.edu.lb/Libraries/News/Pages/WikipediaEducation .aspx? fbclid=IwAR340DzRi0 OhPqTr-2AV2zF2j7bJzULuTC-cCGhig87Vq2tIcmG6fG7teZ0.

Anderson, Betty S. *A History of the Modern Middle East: Rulers, Rebels, and Rogues.* Stanford University Press, 2016.

Arnold, Lisa et al., editors. *Emerging Writing Research from the Middle East-North Africa Region.* Fort Collins, CO: The WAC Clearinghouse, 2017, https://doi.org/10.37514/INT-B.2017.0896.2.09

Ball, Anna and Matta, Karim, editors. *The Edinburgh Companion to the Postcolonial Middle East.* Edinburgh: Edinburgh University Press, 2018.

Banat, Hadi. "The Status and Functions of English in Contemporary Lebanon." *World Englishes,* vol. 40, no. 2, 2021, pp. 268–279, https://doi-org.ezproxy.aub.edu.lb/10.1111/weng.12513.

Bonine, Michael E. et al., editors. *Is There a Middle East? The Evolution of a Geopolitical Concept.* United States: Stanford University Press, 2011. *ProQuest Ebook Central,* https://ebookcentral-proquest-com.ezproxy.aub.edu.lb/lib/aub-ebooks/detail.action?docID=816148.

Bugeja, Norbert. *Postcolonial Memoir in the Middle East: Rethinking the Liminal in Mashriqi Writing.* vol. 40. Abingdon: Routledge, 2012.

Diab, Rula. "Lebanese University Students' Perceptions of Ethnic, National, and Linguistic Identity and their Preferences for Foreign Language Learning in Lebanon." *The Linguistics Journal,* vol. 4, 2009, pp. 101-120.

Esseili, Fatima. "A Sociolinguistic Profile of English in Lebanon." *World Englishes,* vol. 36, no. 4, 2017, pp. 684-704, https://doi-org.ezproxy.aub.edu.lb/10.1111/weng.12262.

Hodges, Amy, and Brenda Kent. "Hybrid Writing Positions within WAC/WID Initiatives: Connecting Faculty Writing Expectations and MENA Cultures." *Emerging Writing Research from the Middle East-North Africa Region,* edited by Lisa Arnold et al., Fort Collins, CO: The WAC Clearinghouse, 2017, pp. 201 – 215, https://doi.org/10.37514/INT-B.2017.0896.2.09.

Hodges, Amy et al. "Learning from/in Middle East and North Africa Writing Centers: Negotiating Access and Diversity." *The Writing Center Journal,* vol. 37, no. 2, 2019, pp. 43–60, https://www.jstor.org/stable/26922017.

Moghabghab, Emma et al. "Flash Archiving the Writing Center: Snapshots from Lebanon and Egypt." *The Writing Center Journal,* vol. 38, no. 3, 2021, pp. 119-143.

Murre-van den Berg, Heleen et al., editors. *Arabic and its Alternatives: Religious Minorities and their Languages in the Emerging Nation States of the Middle East (1920-1950).* Leiden Boston: Brill, 2020.

Schayegh, Cyrus and Andrew Arsan, editors. The Routledge Handbook of the History of the Middle East Mandates. Abingdon: Routledge, 2015.

Suleiman, Yasir. *Arabic, Self and Identity: A Study in Conflict and Displacement.* New York: Oxford University Press, 2011.

Suleiman, Yasir. *The Arabic Language and National Identity: A Study in Ideology.* Washington, D.C.: Georgetown University Press, 2003.

Wilcox, Andrew. *Orientalism and Imperialism: From Nineteenth-century Missionary Imaginings to the Contemporary Middle East.* London: Bloomsbury Academic, 2018. Suspensions: Contemporary Middle Eastern and Islamicate Thought. *Bloomsbury Collections,* http://dx.doi.org.ezproxy.aub.edu.lb/10.5040/9781350033818.

Zimmerman, Erin. "Review of *Writing Centers in the Higher Education Landscape of the Arabian Gulf; Emerging Writing Research from the Middle East-North Africa Region,* by O. Barnawi, L. R. Arnold, A. Nebel, & L. Ronesi." *The Writing Center Journal,* vol. 37, no. 1, 2018, pp. 131–42, https://www.jstor.org/stable/26537365.

On the Teaching of University Writing in Latin America

Natalia Ávila Reyes and Federico Navarro

During the last 20 years, the teaching of writing has grown worldwide as a dynamic field of international academic practice and research, as attested to by the emergence of disciplinary societies, conferences, and publications (Ávila Reyes *Multilingual Contributions;* Bazerman et al. *Conocer La Escritura;* Thaiss et al.). In the spirit of building an integrative vision of the contributions of teaching and research in writing in Latin America, this article offers an overview of what "writing studies" mean in the region.

This account is informed by previous research data of disciplinary development, but it is still inevitably partial. Latin America is a complex territory, diverse in its languages and intellectual and cultural heritage. Educational needs and opportunities, as well as socioeconomic contexts, also vary across the continent. Our positionality as scholars trained in linguistics and education and working at research universities in Chile determines a certain limitation in our perspective that may leave out valuable programs and traditions of which we still know little.

Hence, this paper builds on common nodes that have shaped the original contributions to Latin America's university-level teaching of and research on writing. On the one hand, we will report on the particularities of university systems in the region, as teaching and researching writing are situated and respond to institutional needs and opportunities. On the other hand, we will explore the central role of language and discourse studies in the disciplinary development of the field and outline the current state of scholarship with particular attention to the production of writing knowledge and theory.

Massification, inclusion, and disciplinarity in Latin American universities

The university system in Latin America ranges from teaching universities to large research universities with international influence; from small, regional institutions to metropolitan campuses with hundreds of thousands of students. Yet within this diversity, we can highlight four commonalities that help to characterize our institutional particularities. First, enrollment expansion and diversification in the region have been ongoing processes for the last 40 years (Brunner and Miranda). In some countries, the growth in private provision of higher education has been the primary mechanism for coverage; in others, the establishment of public universities in historically unattended geographic locations and an increase in funding opportunities (or the development of special admissions programs) have been instrumental for enrollment diversification (Chiroleu and Marquina; Santelices et al.). This expansion, akin to other regions globally (Hoskins and Shah), has foregrounded questions around student writing. Moreover, this growth has been concomitant with reforms that advanced accreditation and accountability imperatives as well as student-centered teaching (Ávila Reyes et al.), all essential factors in the emergence of stakeholders' interest in university reading and writing (Tapia Ladino et al.).

Second, undergraduate curricula are organized as discipline-based programs in most universities—General Education courses or leveling (propaedeutic) programs exist only in some institutions. This organization challenges the adoption of institutional responses to the teaching of writing, which may either be present at the beginning of university studies or scattered across programs. Thus, teaching writing in undergraduate education ranges from first year writing courses (Pereira) to writing courses specific to each discipline (Ávila Reyes et al.); from collaborative interventions specific to each domain (Montes and Vidal Lizama; Moyano and Natale) to tutoring programs or writing centers (Lovera Falcón and Uribe Gajardo). As a result, there is no single model or policy around university writing, and institutions are often slow to embrace institutional models and draw attention to writing outcomes (Navarro et al. "Lectura").

The third institutional factor is the time to degree in undergraduate programs. Despite reforms and homologations, undergraduate programs last between four and six years, usually leading to specific professional qualifications. Thus, writing has become relevant for the timely completion of studies and student retention because many obstacles to graduation lie in writing final, complex assignments. Therefore, research on final degree projects is widespread in Chile and the region (Calle-Arango and Ávila Reyes; Navarro et al. "Panorama Histórico").

Fourth, many of the region's most traditional and influential universities are public. Additionally, a great deal of Latin America's university enrollment is tuition-free. This feature also varies from country to country—while Argentina, Brazil, and Mexico offer a free higher education model, other countries such as Chile and Colombia have implemented fee remission programs at the national level. Thus, expanded access to higher education has foregrounded writing as a factor of learning, persistence, and graduation, which has advanced the academic development of the study of writing.

Disciplinary Origins and Evolution: Language and Discourse Studies

Following Donahue, we reject the idea that university writing is underdeveloped in places other than the North. We instead seek to acknowledge scholarship from other regions that, while not taking the same form as composition studies, responds to well-developed traditions of knowledge. Provided that not all foreign models are helpful for addressing local needs of writing teaching and research (Lillis), we need to account for the traditions that made it possible to generate local research responses to the issue of university writing in Latin America. Most practitioners and researchers come from language, linguistics, or applied linguistics units. However, other educational spaces, such as education, psychology, communications, or even speech therapy (Bazerman et al. "Intellectual Orientations"), have also responded to campus writing needs over the last 20 years. Around the turn of the century, the first scholarly developments of university writing hybridized northern theoretical frameworks (mainly WAC/WID or academic literacies) with linguistic, discursive, or cognitive theories, which were the traditions previously dealing with written communication in the region (Ávila Reyes "Locales"; Ávila Reyes "Postsecondary Writing Studies").

It is, therefore, inaccurate—and unfair—to believe that Latin American scholars just "imported" writing theory or applied it wholesale. The main disciplinary influences in foundational works on writing were psycholinguistics, sociolinguistics, text linguistics, discourse analysis, and cognitive psychology (Ávila Reyes "Postsecondary Writing Studies"). Similarly, most publications from 2000 to 2015 addressed the study of texts as linguistic products of different stages or disciplines. Although less frequent, pedagogical experiences and interventions were also among the most addressed concerns (Navarro et al. "Panorama Histórico").

Today we can see the emergence of a clearly defined group of Latin American scholars whose work has been consistently devoted to the study of writing. They are mainly based in Argentina, Brazil, Chile, Colombia, and Mexico, write in Spanish or Portuguese, and constitute a local conceptual core. In recent special issues of local journals, one out of every three research articles is an empirical study of literacy practices; meanwhile, learning and cognitive processes have almost disappeared, especially in the most recent volumes (Navarro and Colombi). The increase in studies that understand literacy as a social practice should not come as a surprise; the Latin American critical tradition has roots both in Paulo Freire's work and in the more recent heyday of Critical Discourse Analysis in the 2000s.

In sum, writing studies in the region are undergoing a steady process of professionalization. Organizations such as the Latin American Association of Writing Studies in Higher Education and Professional Contexts (ALES) or the Latin American Network of Writing Centers and Programs (RLCPE) have created spaces to advance knowledge production and join international conversations about writing.

Conclusions

The institutional characteristics and the disciplinary origin of writing studies shape a field specific to our region and epistemic heritage. We see the centrality of language in writing pedagogy—understanding it as a repertoire of expressive resources, that is, a functional perspective—as among the main potential contributions of Latin American writing studies to a more comprehensive understanding of the subject. Likewise, emancipatory perspectives on writing and diversity in higher education result from critical theory, deeply rooted in the region; they also open avenues to resignifying writing in increasingly diverse higher education contexts. We are grateful for this space in the WWA section of *Composition Studies* to offer a glimpse of the possibilities for scholarly communities to begin a two-way academic exchange, on equal grounds, understanding Latin America as a valid producer of writing knowledge and practices.

Works Cited

Ávila Reyes, Natalia. "Locales, Regionales y Cosmopolitas: Análisis Intertextual de Artículos sobre Escritura Universitaria en América Latina Hispánica." *Escrita Na Universidade. Panoramas E Desafios Na América Latina*, edited by Regina Celi Mendes Pereira, Editora da UFPB, 2018, pp. 45-82.

—, editor. *Multilingual Contributions to Writing Research. Toward an Equal Academic Exchange*. The WAC Clearinghouse, 2021.

—. "Postsecondary Writing Studies in Hispanic Latin America: Intertextual Dynamics and Intellectual Influence." *London Review of Education*, vol. 15, no. 1, 2017, pp. 21-37, doi:10.18546/LRE.15.1.03.

Ávila Reyes, Natalia et al. "Creación de un Programa de Escritura en una Universidad Chilena: Estrategias para Promover un Cambio Institucional." *Revista Mexicana de Investigación Educativa*, vol. 18, no. 57, 2013, pp. 537-60.

Bazerman, Charles et al. "Intellectual Orientations of Studies of Higher Education Writing in Latin America." *Research on Writing: Multiple Perspectives*, edited by Sylvie Plane et al., The WAC Clearinghouse & CREM, 2017, pp. 281-97.

Bazerman, Charles et al., editors. *Conocer La Escritura: Investigación Más Allá De Las Fronteras | Knowing Writing: Writing Research across Borders*. Pontificia Universidad Javeriana, 2019.

Brunner, José Joaquín and Daniel Andrés Miranda. *Educación Superior en Iberoamérica. Informe 2016.* CINDA, 2016.

Calle-Arango, Lina and Natalia Ávila Reyes. "Alfabetización Académica Chilena: Revisión de Investigaciones de una Década." *Literatura y Lingüística*, vol. 41, 2020, pp. 455-82.

Chiroleu, Adriana and Mónica Marquina. "Democratisation or Credentialism? Public Policies of Expansion of Higher Education in Latin America." *Policy Reviews in Higher Education*, vol. 1, no. 2, 2017, pp. 139-60, doi:10.1080/23322969.2017.1303787.

Donahue, Christiane. "'Internationalization' and Composition Studies: Reorienting the Discourse." *College Composition and Communication*, vol. 61, no. 2, 2009, pp. 212-43.

Hoskins, Kate and Mahsood Shah. "Chapter 1 - Policy and Practice Challenges and Opportunities for Developing Widening Participation in the Global South and North." *Bridges, Pathways and Transitions*, edited by Mahsood Shah and Gail Whiteford, Chandos Publishing, 2017, pp. 1-15. https://www.sciencedirect.com/science/article/pii/B9780081019214000014.

Lillis, Theresa. "Academic Literacies: Intereses Locales, Preocupaciones Globales? / Academic Literacies: Local Interests, Global Concerns?" *Multilingual Contributions to Writing Research. Toward an Equal Academic Exchange*, edited by Natalia Ávila Reyes, The WAC Clearinghouse, 2021, pp. 35-60.

Lovera Falcón, Pablo and Fernanda Uribe Gajardo. "Hacia Una Didáctica Crítico-Reflexiva en la Enseñanza de la Escritura en la Educación Superior." *Lenguas Modernas*, vol. 50, 2017, pp. 91-108.

Montes, Soledad and Margarita Vidal Lizama. "Diseño de un Programa de Escritura a través del Currículum: Opciones Teóricas y Acciones Estratégicas." *Lenguas Modernas*, vol. 50, 2017, pp. 73-90.

Moyano, Estela and Lucía Natale. "Teaching Academic Literacy across the University Curriculum as Institutional Policy. The Case of the Universidad Nacional De General Sarmiento (Argentina)." *Writing Programs Worldwide: Profiles of Academic Writing in Many Places*, edited by Chris Thaiss et al., Parlor Press & WAC Clearinghouse, 2012, pp. 23-34.

Navarro, Federico and M. Cecilia Colombi. "Alfabetización Académica y Estudios del Discurso." *Estudios del Discurso / the Routledge Handbook of Spanish Language Discourse Studies*, edited by Carmen López Ferrero et al., Routledge, in press.

Navarro, Federico et al. "Lectura, Escritura y Oralidad en Perfiles de Egreso de Educación Superior: Contrastes entre Instituciones y Carreras" *Revista Calidad en la Educación*, vol. 52, 2020, pp. 170-204, doi:10.31619/caledu.n52.766.

Navarro, Federico et al. "Panorama Histórico y Contrastivo De Los Estudios Sobre Lectura y Escritura En Educación Superior Publicados En América Latina." *Signos*, vol. 49, no. S1, 2016, pp. 100-26, doi:10.4067/S0718-09342016000400006.

Pereira, Cecilia. "La Lectura y la Escritura en el CBC: Memoria de la Experiencia en la Cátedra de Semiología." *Primer Congreso Nacional: "Leer, escribir y hablar hoy". Universidad Nacional del Centro de la Provincia de Buenos Aires, 28 de septiembre al 1 de octubre de 2006*, 2006.

Santelices, Verónica et al. *Equidad en la Educación Superior*. Ediciones UC, 2018.

Tapia Ladino, Mónica et al. "Milestones, Disciplines and the Future of Initiatives of Reading and Writing in Higher Education: An Analysis from Key Scholars in the Field in Latin America." *Ilha do desterro*, vol. 69, no. 3, 2016, pp. 189-208, doi:10.5007/2175-8026.2016v69n3p189.

Thaiss, Chris et al., editors. *Writing Programs Worldwide: Profiles of Academic Writing in Many Places*. Parlor Press & WAC Clearinghouse, 2012.

Writing Instruction in Australia

Susan E. Thomas

"Writing Instruction" in Australia usually means one of two things: creative writing or TESOL, both having rich histories and traditions and usually offered as graduate courses in departments of Education or Linguistics. Academic writing, however, with few exceptions, is an all-but-invisible practice in undergraduate education. It draws attention only when it falls short, at which point the response is to fix what's wrong at the surface level rather than consider the broader needs of student writers. For this reason, Australia's version of compositionists, academic language and literacy (ALL) experts, are usually located in learning and language centers, regarded as (re)mediators for academic casualties (Percy). From an institutional standpoint, theirs is a deficit discourse, a "study skills" approach, divorced from disciplinary contexts and focused on redeeming or rehabilitating "weak" students (McKenna). And while progressive scholars have launched remarkable initiatives over the past thirty years, advocating for more embedded approaches (Chanock; Clanchy; Percy 2011; Skillen et al.), including Writing Across the Curriculum/WAC (Petelin) and writing centers (Emerson; Thomas), these are usually short-lived, overcome by the prevailing deficit remediation model.

Since the 1970s, there have been strong arguments for moving academic writing into the mainstream of Australian higher education. John Clanchy, Kate Chanock and Valerie Burley, Claire Woods and Paul Skrebels, Anne Surma, Carolyn Webb, Roslyn Petelin, Jan Skillen, Lisa Emerson and Rosemary Clerehan, Alisa Percy, and others have advocated for embedded approaches to writing instruction in Australian universities, which American compositionists would recognize as a WAC approach. But Australian universities have neither a strong liberal arts education tradition nor a general education requirement. There is no history of first year writing nor institution-wide approaches to writing in/across the disciplines, despite brilliant, if short-lived, initiatives at various institutions. Writing centers are the exception rather than the rule, and accredited writing courses are relatively recent elective additions to degree structures (where they exist at all). The Australian Qualifications Framework (AQF) underpins "national regulatory and quality assurance arrangements" for higher education Australia-wide. Describing distinctive features of each degree type (i.e., bachelor's, master's, doctoral), the AQF specifies communication proficiency as a required outcome for all tertiary programs, both as a generic learning outcome and a specified skill. For a bachelor's degree, the AQF states that graduates will have:

...well-developed cognitive, technical and communication skills to select and apply methods and technologies to: analyze and evaluate information to complete a range of activities; analyze, generate and transmit solutions to unpredictable and sometimes complex problems; transmit knowledge, skills and ideas to others. (13)

In keeping with these broader strategic directions – or possibly as a consequence of them – Australian universities commonly include the ability to write and/or communicate effectively in their list of desired graduate attributes. However, there is usually no corresponding writing/communication instruction to support this outcome, and despite employers' general satisfaction with new graduates' performance, graduates' written skills usually do not meet employer expectations (Graduate Careers Australia).

This disjuncture becomes even more concerning as Australian higher education expands and diversifies under a policy of "widening participation," which seeks to have 40% of all Australians 25–34 years old holding achelor's degrees by 2025, combined with a stated goal for 20% of the undergraduate cohort in 2020 to come from low socioeconomic backgrounds (Gale and Parker). The higher education expansion agenda requires equity principles to support all students to achieve the required outcomes and equip graduates to progress in their careers; however, the development of corresponding writing programs to support such students has not kept pace with policy, leaving universities unable to meet increasing student demand for writing instruction. And despite being attracted to Australian universities by sophisticated marketing campaigns, culturally and linguistically diverse students often face a reality far different from the anticipated experience (Tian). With few exceptions, they are expected to assimilate on their own and take language acquisition classes at their own expense if their writing needs exceed the scope of short programs offered through learning centers or libraries. But with learning and language centers stretched to their limits in response to the latest "literacy crisis" (*The Australian*), which exposes contract cheating as a last resort for struggling international students, the time has come to acknowledge the limitations of deficit remediation approaches to writing instruction.

However, rearticulating writing instruction as a social act—a fundamental and global good for *all* students—will require a major paradigm shift. The challenge for Australian educators will be developing sufficient political momentum and influence for embedded, research-based writing programs to be effectively and consistently developed across the country. The history of American professional organizations for writing program administrators serves as a useful precedent for how collective activism can shift discourses around academic writing from remediation to integration. But before progress can be made, Australian WPAs must consider the history of Australian higher education and the political and social forces that have shaped it, not least the concepts of "path dependency," (Davis), a seeming inertia to maintain the British educational system's status quo, and "cultural cringe" (Phillips), which is often interpreted as a blatant Australian refusal to admit inferiority of any kind, including the need for writing instruction.

As former Vice Chancellor of the University of Melbourne Glyn Davis explains, the tendency of Australian institutions to cling to the familiar can be attributed to the concept of "path dependency" that has seen Australian universities conform to a single model:

> We choose a path and thereafter it shapes our choices—the 'deep lane insists on the direction', as T.S. Eliot wrote in 'East Coker'. The further we go, the more we commit to this direction; the further behind fall the other choices, those paths not taken. Over time, this seems the only road possible. For universities in Australia, the path chosen early still guides our bearing. A distinctive Australian idea of a university, developed in colonial society, has influenced all universities created since 1850.

In early 2004, I would encounter path dependency firsthand when I was hired by the University of Sydney to design and implement a first year writing program in the English Department. Confronted with institutional challenges, pressures, and mindsets eerily reminiscent of those in nineteenth-century American universities, I had seemingly stepped back into Fred Newton Scott's milieu. And while my knowledge of Australian higher education was admittedly limited, my understanding of the history of writing instruction in the United States, particularly the seemingly universal struggle between tradition and progress, made me well-placed to recognize the conditions that would make a writing program all but impossible in an Australian Department of English. Despite American and Australian higher education histories sharing common milestones, their respective responses to the effects of post-WWII massification on university enrollments, namely their approaches to language and literacy education, have been starkly different. While composition courses came into their own in America following WWII, to cater to a rapidly diversifying student population, Australian universities made no such changes to their curriculum, despite also having a more diverse student population. While "path dependency" might be mostly to blame, one must not overlook "cultural cringe," which has become a familiar Australian catch-phrase after Melbourne schoolmaster A.A. Phillips coined the term in 1950. Rollo Hesketh writes:

The term has come to refer to Australians' inherent lack of faith in their own culture, often at the popular level. This is divorced from the originally intended meaning, which was explicitly linked to "high" culture. Phillips wished to create a national culture that conceded no inferiority to Britain, and indeed was unembarrassed to be Australian: "temper, democratic; bias, offensively Australian." (https://meanjin.com.au/essays/a-a-phillips-and-the-icultural-cringei-creating-an-iaustralian-traditioni/).

Phillips acknowledges Australia's tendency to compare itself with Britain, the United States, and Europe, partly due to its origins as a convict settlement. But the cringe is also understood as a stubborn refusal to admit inferiority to any other nation or culture. Therefore, in addition to path dependency, the resistance of Australian universities to implementing a general education requirement or embedding writing instruction in the mainstream curriculum may point to a deeper reluctance to admit any perceived shortcomings in Australian universities—or their students. While working to establish the writing program in the Department of English, I was frequently reminded, "this isn't America," and "we've survived just fine for 150 years without 'Freshman Comp.'"

The academic writing program at the University of Sydney had followed the typical path in an Australian university, having been rejected by the mainstream but finding traction as a program in a learning and teaching unit. However, unlike short-lived writing initiatives in other universities, the program became the Department of Writing Studies in 2017. The first of its kind in Australia, the Department houses a thriving writing program, writing minor, writing center, and de facto WAC program. In 2020, a major in Writing Studies was approved, along with a senior academic hire. But despite these successes, current restructure proposals in the Faculty of Arts and Social Sciences have called for the merging of small departments with larger ones, recommending the amalgamation of Writing Studies and English. So after twelve years of demonstrable success, first as an independent program and then as an independent department, this field of dreams (O'Neill et al.) seems destined to join other Australian writing initiatives in the ever-growing minefield of dreams (Everett and Hanganu-Bresch).

Works Cited

Chanock, Kate, and Valerie Burley, editors. "Integrating the Teaching of Academic Discourses into Courses in the Disciplines. Proceedings from the National Language and Academic Skills Conference." 1994: Mebourne: La Trobe University Language and Academic Skills Unit.

Chanock, Kate. "What Academic Language and Learning Advisers Bring to the Scholarship of Teaching and Learning: Problems and Possibilities for Dialogue with the Disciplines." *Higher Education Research and Development*, vol. 26, no.3, 2007, pp. 269-280.

Clanchy, John. "Language in the University." *Education News*, vol. 16, no. 4, 1978, pp. 20-23.

Clanchy, John. "The Higher Illiteracy: Some Personal Observations." *English in Australia*, vol. 37, 1976, pp. 20-47.

Davis, Glyn. "The Australian Idea of a University." *Meanjin Quarterly*, 2012, https://meanjin.com.au/essays/the-australian-idea-of-a-university/. Accessed 22 November 2021.

Emerson, Lisa. "Developing a 'Kiwi' Writing Centre at Massey University, New Zealand." *Writing Programs Worldwide: Profiles of Academic Writing in Many Places*, edited by Chris Thaiss, Gerd Bräuer, Paula Carlino, Lisa Ganobcsik-Williams, and Aparna Sinha, The WAC Clearinghouse, 2011, pp. 43-53.

Emerson, Lisa, and Rosemary A. Clerehan. "Writing Program Administration Outside the North American Context." *The Writing Program Interrupted: Making Space for Critical Discourse*, edited by Donna Strickland and Jeanne Gunner, Boynton/Cook, 2009, pp. 166-174.

Everett, Justin, and Cristina Hanganu-Bresch, Cristina, editors. *A Minefield of Dreams: Triumphs and Travails of Independent Writing Programs*. The WAC Clearinghouse and University Press of Colorado, 2017, https://wac.colostate.edu/books/perspectives/minefield/. Accessed 22 November 2021.

Gale, Trevor, and Stephen Parker. "Widening Participation in Australian Higher Education." Report submitted to Higher Education Funding Council for England (HEFCE) and The Office for Fair Access (OFFA), Leicester, UK, https://www.ncsehe.edu.au/publications/widening-participation-australian-higher-education/. Accessed 22 November 2021.

"Graduate Careers Australia." *Graduate Outlook 2014: Employers' Perspectives on Graduate Recruitment in Australia*. http://www.graduatecareers.com.au/wp-content/uploads/2015/06/Graduate_Outlook_2014.pdf. Accessed 22 November 2021.

Hesketh, Rollo. "A.A. Phillips and the 'Cultural Cringe': Creating an 'Australian Tradition." *Meanjin Quarterly*, vol. 72, no. 3, 2013, https://meanjin.com.au/essays/a-a-phillips-and-the-icultural-cringei-creating-an-iaustralian-traditioni/. Accessed 22 November 2021.

McKenna, Sue. "Changing Discourses of Academic Development at a South African Technikon 1991 to 2002." *South African Journal of Higher Education*, vol. 17, no. 2, 2003, pp. 60-67.

O'Neill, Peggy, et al., editors. *A Field of Dreams: Independent Writing Programs and the Future of Composition Studies*. USU Press, 2002. https://digitalcommons.usu.edu/usupress_pubs/135. Accessed 22 November 2021.

Percy, Alisa. "A New Age in Higher Education or Just a Little Bit of History Repeating?: Linking the Past, Present and Future of ALL in Australia." *Journal of Academic Language and Learning*, vol. 5, no., 2, 2011, pp. 131-144.

—. "From the Margins to the Centre: Reflections on the 'Past-Present-Future' of Literacy Education in the Academy." Special Issue on Writing Across the Curriculum in Australia and New Zealand, edited by Karen Vered, Susan Thomas, and Lisa Emerson, *Across the Disciplines*, vol. 16, no. 3, 2019, pp. 9-23. https://wac.colostate.edu/docs/atd/australasia/percy2019.pdf. Accessed 22 November 2021.

Petelin, Roslyn. "Another Whack at WAC: Reprising WAC in Australia." *Language and Learning Across the Disciplines*, vol. 5, no. 3, 2002, pp. 98-109. http://wac.colostate.edu/llad/v5n3/v5n3.pdf. Accessed 22 November 2021.

Phillips, A.A. "The Cultural Cringe." *Meanjin*, vol. 9, no. 4, 1950. https://meanjin.com.au/essays/the-cultural-cringe-by-a-a-phillips/. Accessed 22 November 2021.

Skillen, Jan. "Teaching Academic Writing from the 'Centre' in Australian Universities." *Teaching Academic Writing in UK Higher Education: Theories, Practice and Models*, ed. Lisa Ganobcsik-Williams, *Palgrave Macmillan*, London, 2006, pp. 140-153.

Surma, Anne. "Defining Professional Writing as an Area of Scholarly Activity." *TEXT: Journal of Writing and Writing Courses*, vol. 4, no. 2, 2000, http://www.textjournal.com.au/oct00/surma.htm return to text. Accessed 22 November 2021.

The Australian Qualifications Framework, Second Edition, 2013. https://www.aqf.edu.au/sites/aqf/files/aqf-2nd-edition-january-2013.pdf. Accessed 22 November 2021.

"The Who, Why and How of Student Cheating at Australian Unis." *The Australian*, 2018.https://campusmorningmail.com.au/news/the-who-why-and-how-of-student-cheating-at-australian-unis/. Accessed 22 November 2021.

Thomas, Susan. "The WAC-Driven Writing Center: The Future of Writing Instruction in Australasia?" Special Issue on Writing Across the Curriculum in Australia and New Zealand, edited by Karen Vered, Susan Thomas, and Lisa Emerson, *Across the Disciplines*, vol. 16, no. 3, 2019, pp. 9-23. http://wac.colostate.edu/docs/atd/australasia/thomas2019.pdf. Accessed 22 November 2021.

Tian, Yang. "Take the Money and Run: how Australian Universities Let Down Their Chinese Students." *The Guardian*, 2019. https://www.theguardian.com/commentisfree/2019/sep/02/take-the-money-and-run-how-australian-universities-let-down-their-chinese-students. Accessed 22 November 2021.

Webb, Carolyn. "Language and Academic Skills Advisers: Professional Ontogenesis." Keynote Address presented at the Changing Identities: National Language and Academic Skills Conference, University of Wollongong, 2001. https://learning.uow.edu.au/LAS2001/LAS2001/plenary.pdf. Accessed 22 November 2021.

Woods, Claire, and Paul Skrebels. "Students and an Undergraduate Program in Professional Writing and Communication: Altered Geographies." *TEXT: Journal of Writing and Writing Courses*, vol 1, no. 2, 1997. http://www.textjournal.com.au/oct97/woods.htm. Accessed 22 November 2021.

Book Reviews

Literacy and Pedagogy in an Age of Misinformation and Disinformation, edited by Tara Lockhart, Brenda Glascott, Chris Warnick, Juli Parrish, and Justin Lewis. Parlor Press, 2021. 255 pp.

Reviewed by Christine Wilson, North Central College

The meaning of *critical literacy* depends on one's vantage point as its definition and application can be flexible. Still, regardless of one's disciplinary background or educational perspective, it is important to note that critical literacy is not a definitive skill; it is an evolving, multi-dimensional process of layered reading comprehension, contextual analysis, and honest reflection. In the simplest sense, it is a lens through which to view content. As of late, that lens has been made political according to the authors of *Literacy and Pedagogy in an Age of Misinformation and Disinformation*.

Published under the Parlor Press Working and Writing for Change series, this book is a larger response to the 2017 special issue of *Literacy in Composition Studies* titled "Literacy, Democracy, and Fake News." Building upon this groundwork developed by fellow teacher-scholars and activists, *Literacy and Pedagogy in an Age of Misinformation and Disinformation* still set out with formidable goals of providing a free (PDF only), 18-chapter volume that tackles a great deal in depth and breadth almost too much). The text covers a host of interconnected processes: software literacy, quantitative literacy, historical literacy, civic literacy, media literacy, academic literacy, and rhetorical literacy. The editors also included six chapters devoted to practitioner interviews representing leaders from *Americans of Conscience Checklist*, Twitter, *Wired*, *Goalbook*, the *Other98*, and an international baccalaureate program coordinator. On top of all this, the volume devotes an especially rich chapter to campus librarians, two chapters to discussing the fraught curriculum work of our K-12 colleagues, and two chapters to the plight of refugees and immigrants. Suffice to say, the editors and authors created an extensive compilation of updated theories, tested assignments, and focused dialogue on information literacy, especially as it pertains to first year writing.

Candidly, I understand the editors' ambition and immediacy. Over my near decade of teaching, what were once sparse comments doubting authority, has now manifested as a deliberate and defiant attitude in and of itself. As Eric Leake aptly put in his chapter from this book: "At issue now is not so much an unwillingness to question authority but a readiness to flatten all authority, to make no distinctions among claims to authority, so that news from *The New York Times* appears to be as legitimate, or even less so, as new from the *Christian Times Newspaper*" (74).

As suggested in the editors' introduction, gone are the days of applying our graduate learned (and outdated) traditional critical literacy skills to all of our 21st Century worldly problems. While they serve as an excellent foundation, we as composition instructors and fellow readers must go further to help novice rhetoricians navigate an insatiable, click-bait media landscape—one where the self-serving goal is mining personal data, over the traditional selfless objective to inform the citizenship. All to say, the volume's authors continually and correctly emphasize that literacy is not, and will never be, a conclusive skill. It is a learned process that will evolve as technology will always outpace the studied researcher. So, educators must learn to be even more comfortable proactively preparing for the authorless unknown, rather than always reacting to last year's technology trend. This text readies those tools.

In the introduction, the editors also suggest a handful of ways to read their volume. As previously mentioned, the editors took on several themes, making the chapter order uneven. Ideally, the volume would have kept like-minded terms or topics together. Nevertheless, where the text falls short in organization, it excels in practical content. That is not to say the text overlooks academic research; each chapter is grounded in rich theory spanning predominately across the fields of education, composition, literacy, and public policy discourses. Still, the treasure-trove of tested practices, all in one place, proves invaluable for the busy reader. Excerpts, or in some cases the entire length, of the aforementioned practitioner interviews could be assigned as supplemental classroom readings. Though every chapter contributes new information to the field, six chapters offer particularly noteworthy research and resources for readers.

Angela Laflen's work in chapter three, "Quantitative Literacy in the Composition Classroom: Using Infographics Assignments to Teach Ethical and Effective Data Use" was extremely illuminating. Laflen did an excellent job of slowing down and decompartmentalizing the almost instantaneous speed of infographic trickery by including not one, two, but three smartly scaffolded assignments—with student examples—as means to best support fellow instructors. As most of my students subscribe to what Sundar demystified in his earlier work, "cool is [not] credible" Laflen's took his research miles forward in practicality and practice.

In chapter six, Thomas Girshin and Tyrell Stewart-Harris write about their own take on Princeton's first year seminar "Great Books: Ideas and Arguments," co-taught years previously by Cornel West and Robert George. Their own Ithaca College course reading list is one to reference for future syllabi covering a host of communication modes, centuries, and racially informed political causes.

While life pre-2016 is briefly mentioned throughout the volume, only one chapter grounds its whole argument and challenges the idea that 'post-truth' is not remotely new. Author Drew Virtue's discussion of historical literacy in

"Historical Literacies: McCarthyism, Edward R. Murrow, and the Television" proved especially useful, as a main critique of the volume is a disproportionate focus on the Trump Administration. For as much as the book takes on, the majority of chapters focus on practical problems spanning the last five years. While the previous authors, Girshin and Stewart-Harris, allude to the disingenuous communication strategies of President Nixon and President Clinton, by and large, most authors focus on President Trump. Virtue notes, explicitly, these conflicting forces were at play long before President Trump took over and will be exploited long after. His chapter addition effectively filled a gap.

Chapter ten, "I am a Refugee and I am OK: Instructor Identity in Resisting Classrooms," includes two writing assignments grounded in transnational pedagogy. As a first year instructor, whose teaching theme is "place," I have forwarded this entire chapter to my department. Lava Asaad's writing strikes a compelling balance of vulnerable and authoritative. She addresses freedom of speech in the classroom, apathetic rhetorical practices, and students' impulsive resistance head on: "I am using 'resisting' here not in its positive meaning as circulated in social media. Rather, I am using it in the sense of students who challenge literacy, or misuse it, for their own pre-constructed ideologies" (130). For Asaad, the political is personal and she rightfully challenges her students to reflect on their own, often underdeveloped and unwitting, political identity. Her reading list, prompts, and learned experience are rich, honest, and humbling.

In Chapter twelve, Genevieve García de Müeller and Randall W. Monty's "'Don't Give Me Bullshit": Constructing a Framework of Response to Fake News" share their idea of assigning students to screenshot a sample of their own "everyday writing" and code for 1) the rhetorical situation, 2) "textisms", and 3) worknet pedagogy (156). Interestingly, this practice was then scaled up by asking a student to code a previous piece of academic writing. Learning and framing ethos in terms of the self, compared to the other, cut to the core of understanding credibility; it was a very shrewd practice.

In chapter sixteen, "Keeping Truth Alive: Literacy, Libraries, and Strategies in an Age of Misinformation," Nicole Allensworth shares six classroom activities devoted to information literacy, not to mention an appendix of resources that should be posted in every Blackboard course. Finally, Melissa R. Sande and Christine M. Battista's call to action is a compelling note to conclude this review. "Developing Critical Consciousness: Literary Theory, Process Pedagogy, and Information Literacy" rightfully asserts: "If students are truly to understand IL [information literacy] as a process with relevance in every discipline and relevance to them as citizens, it must extend beyond first year writing and be reinforced continually in other writing-intensive and upper-level courses" (181). Throughout their chapter, Sande and Battista confront a hole not only in the volume, but also in our discourse literature: there is little interdisciplinary study or classroom collaborations regarding information literacy. While most first year instructors are trained rhetoricians, we, as faculty, all rely on sources written in and out of the academy. Just as fellow disciplines support student writers, they must support them as critical readers and researchers. I sincerely appreciate Sande and Battista's addition and hope it serves to inspire more cross-campus collaborative efforts.

In closing, this readily accessible volume advances the teaching of information literacy by acknowledging that its underpinnings are fluid. Compared to a studied writing process, we as fellow citizens are experiencing these tectonic societal and communicative shifts right along with our students. To the authorless software, we are all data consumers. Still, the book's contributors motivate educators to do what we do best: inspire change. It provides readers, especially those on the frontlines in first year writing, with a bounty of classroom resources and cultural reassurance.

Naperville, Illinois

Works Cited

Sundar, S. Shyam. "The MAIN Model: A Heuristic Approach to Understanding Technology Effects on Credibility." *Digital Media, Youth, and Credibility*, edited by Miriam J. Metzger and Andrew J. Flanagin. The MIT Press, 2008, pp. 73–100.

PARS in Practice: More Resources and Strategies for Online Writing Instructors, edited by Jessie Borgman and Casey McArdle. Fort Collins, CO: The WAC Clearinghouse/Boulder, CO: University Press of Colorado, 2021. 367 pp.

Reviewed by Omar Yacoub, Indiana University of Pennsylvania

PARS in Practice: More Resources and Strategies for Online Writing Instructors is an extension of *Personal, Accessible, Responsive, and Strategic: Resources and Strategies for Online Writing Instructors* (2019) where Borgman and McArdle introduced the PARS approach to online instruction— personal, accessible, responsive, and strategic. In this edited volume, Borgman and McArdle draw from a wide range of experiences reported by different writing instructors using, reflecting on, and extending the PARS approach. The book is divided into four major sections: Design, Instruction, Administration, and User Experience, and it includes a foreword, an introduction, a conclusion, and an afterword. Each of the four major sections consists of five chapters that approach the theme from various perspectives.

The first PARS book concluded with an emphasis on students' user experience; however, this book starts with the claim that PARS, juxtaposed with the user experience approach, achieves the goals for online writing instruction. The editors stress that the PARS approach is not a "checklist" but a "holistic approach" that addresses the complex nature of online writing instruction (Borgman and McArdle 4). As Harris indicates in the foreword, the various experiences and case studies shared in these chapters by a diverse body of authors (graduate students, adjunct faculty, and tenured professors) are what contribute to the practical richness of this book.

The first section, "Design," includes five chapters that address different challenges pertaining to course design and presents recommendations through and beyond the PARS approach. The author of the first chapter, Crawley, explains how she strategizes her online first year composition course at a community college through applying Shipka's Statement of Goals and Choices to select her online learning tools. Despite some challenges, including heavy workload, Geary, in chapter two, presents his experience of redesigning his accelerated technical writing course at a community college using the PARS approach. In chapter three, Stewart presents a case study of a graduate online course teaching hybrid pedagogy to online writing instructors. She explicates her use of Garrison's Community of Inquiry framework to achieve the goals of the PARS approach, specifically strategic and user-centered course design. In chapter four, Sibo explains, through the PARS approach, the efficacy of small group discussions between students as a tool to help them make connections and build knowledge with less literacy load. Karabinus and Dilger, in chapter five, provide an explanation of implementing the grid approach, inspired by the PARS, to teaching first year writing courses. The grid approach is based on three units and three assignment options for every unit. This section applies and extends the PARS approach in different contexts for the sake of course design development.

Section two, "Instruction," includes five chapters that discuss and recommend pedagogical practices for online writing instructors. Chapter six, by McClure and Mahaffey, presents the nuances of why, when, and how to use videos to achieve the goals of the PARS approach in online writing instruction. Laflen and Sims write chapter seven to discuss the affordances of using a labor-based grading system as a strategic and responsive instruction method in online classes. Even though this grading system responds to the needs of the diverse student population of online classes, the authors acknowledge its limitation in online settings and provide strategies for a successful implementation. Moreover, Pandey, in chapter eight, addresses the importance and challenges of building a community in online classes through pedagogical humor. After identifying the challenges of using humor in the online classroom, the authors of the chapter recommend certain places—such as individual conferences, ice breakers, and instructional videos—where appropriate humor can be implemented. Reflecting on her experience teaching an online technical writing class in chapter nine, Pengilly first addresses the issues of accessibility and usability in technical writing courses and then provides practices and tools to make courses strategic and accessible with the explicit teaching of accessibility and the challenging of pedagogical practices that promote ableism. In the last chapter of this section, Evans uses her personal experience as an instructor and an online student to address how she negotiates the difficulties that come along last-minute online teaching assignments, like having no guidance into the teaching and the design of the course or having poor templates of the course design. She then explains the use of the PARS model in addition to other recommendations to resolve issues created by "just-in-time" online teaching (167). This section is ultimately informative of many pedagogical practices that address different issues pertinent to online writing instruction.

Section three, "Administration," discusses how administrators can apply the PARS approach for the success of the program through instructors' practices and students' learning. Based on empirical data, Thomas et al.'s participants in chapter eleven reported a high importance of finding personal connections with instructors in their online courses. In addition to providing practical strategies to make courses and administration personal, they explain how personal connections between administrators and instructors and between instructors and students build a community that contributes to the success of online writing instruction. In chapter twelve, Hilliard explains the application of the PARS approach in her writing program administration experience. Starting with the aspect of building a community, she offers details of the application of each element of the PARS approach with extended implications, such as advocating for instructors' agency and practices including a face-to-face digital pedagogy day. In addition, Jackson and Olinger use chapter thirteen to offer a practical view of a mini training course designed to prepare instructors to teach online writing courses. The authors ask and answer seven questions to explain how other administrators can design responsive and strategic professional development opportunities for their instructors. Furthermore, based on the assumption that most instructors have web experiences, including booking flights and shopping online, Snart, in chapter fourteen, calls for administrators and instructors to consider developing themselves as strategic web designers, creating a successful user experience for students. The last chapter, by Wilkes, reflects on and reports data from the author's teaching of an online graduate seminar where she used the PARS approach to design the course *and* as the content of the course. Her graduate students, who were preparing to teach online first year writing courses, reported positive learning outcomes. This section particularly targets administrators to prepare their instructors to effectively teach online, which successfully happens through building a community.

Section four focuses on user experience (UX) as inclusive of all the elements of online writing instruction and as the grounds on which the PARS approach is established. Retzinger, in chapter sixteen, addresses the disconnection between some online writing instructors' experiences and the nature of online writing courses. The author makes a connection between his experience as an online bass student and online writing instruction, making recommendations for instructors and administrators to think outside of their disciplinary boxes for the sake of creating a user experience for students. Next, chapter seventeen, by Getto, provides a definition of successful user-experience course designs as those applying the elements of the PARS approach. This is thoroughly explained by presenting the development of an online technical writing course tapping into other topics such as usability testing and maintenance. Specifically focusing on usability testing as a strategy for online course design and instruction, Bartolotta dedicates chapter eighteen to present one usability test in addition to explaining how instructors can set up other usability tests. This promotes a user-experience approach as the author positions students as the testers of their courses rather than the instructors. In Chapter nineteen, Stone presents a case for redesigning a face-to-face community-engaged course into an asynchronous online course. The author, following the PARS approach, refers to students' needs as the "sweet spot" that should be considered when designing online courses (317). Finally, the last chapter, Ledgerwood, creates a connection between HyperDocs, the PARS approach, and multimodality, promoting a user-centered approach to online writing instruction. The number of ideas surrounding user experience in online writing instruction for this section echoes Borgman's and McArdle's argument that "online courses [are] complex ecosystems of activity" (273).

To sum up, this edited collection responds to the growing need for online writing instruction caused by the COVID-19 pandemic. The authors of the chapters implement, extend, analyze, and reflect on the PARS approach in their design, instruction, and administration of online writing courses. In addition, this collection presents a wide range of voices, including professors, instructors, and graduate students working in different online writing contexts such as technical writing, first year writing, and community-engaged writing courses. Moreover, even though the chapters do not follow a specific organizational pattern, they all follow a pattern that starts with presentations and discussions of their experiences followed by recommendations for readers to implement and extend their practices. This is translated in the editors' conclusion highlighting the "Moving Day" as a chance for all readers to take this further to new courses, student populations, and institutional contexts (Borgman and McArdle 353). The book plays the role of go-to resource that is full of successful practices, digital tools, and recommendations for instructors teaching writing online with or without institutional or administrative support.

Indiana, Pennsylvania

Works Cited

Borgman, Jessie, and Casey McArdle. *Personal, Accessible, Responsive, Strategic: Resources and Strategies for Online Writing Instructors*. The WAC Clearinghouse, 2019.

Garrison, D. Randy. *E-learning in the 21st century: A Community of Inquiry Framework for Research and Practice*. Taylor & Francis, 2016.

Shipka, Jody. *Toward a Composition Made Whole*. University of Pittsburgh Press, 2011.

The Anti-Racist Writing Workshop: How to Decolonize the Creative Classroom, by Felicia Rose Chavez. Haymarket Books, 2021. 216 pp.

Reviewed by Siara Schwartzlow, University of Wyoming

> Active racist behavior is equivalent to walking fast on the conveyor belt. The person engaged in active racist behavior has identified with the ideology of White supremacy and is moving with it. Passive racist behavior is equivalent to standing still on the walkway. No overt effort is being made, but the conveyor belt moves the bystanders along to the same destination as those who are actively walking. Some of the bystanders may ... choose to turn around. . . . But unless they are walking actively in the opposite direction at a speed faster than the conveyor belt—unless they are actively antiracist—they will find themselves carried along with the others.
>
> —Beverly Daniel Tatum, *Why Are All the Black Kids Sitting Together in the Cafeteria?" And Other Conversations About Race*, 91

We've been doing it wrong—workshopping in our writing courses, I mean. Or if we're being honest with ourselves, we've been doing all of it wrong: reading lists, in-class discussions, homework. Our current practices are a disservice to every one of our students, but especially our students of color. We've tried, of course, but our collective attempts at inclusivity and culturally responsive pedagogy pale in comparison to the complete overhaul Felicia Rose Chavez, emboldened by experience, has implemented into her classroom.

See, Chavez is angry—and rightfully so. All her life, she's been judged, criticized, controlled. And when she finally found her voice, it came out roaring. It came roaring at a white-washed literary canon; at white professors looking for her input as the token person of color in the room; at institutions treating her and other brown-skinned people like the Others; at offering scholarships not on merit, but on the promise of satisfying racial quotas; at classroom procedures catering to white students and shutting her—her culture, her history, her voice—out. Now, she's using her voice to effect real change, building on ideas previously presented by anti-racist composition scholars like Iris D. Ruiz and Asao B. Inoue. In this book, Chavez expertly blends hard-hitting anecdotes with simple suggestions for improvement, making *The Anti-Racist Writing Workshop* a valuable resource for anyone looking to strive toward more equitable practice.

Before I begin, I should admit that at times, I questioned whether almost two hundred pages were truly necessary to communicate the simple steps

Chavez recommends. And while it's true that the exposition tends to drift nonlinearly, the text ultimately benefits from Chavez's snarky, emboldened tone and reflective storytelling because they both remind us that this project isn't just theory. It's real people affected in real ways. At times, it feels like we're peeking into Chavez's freewrites embedded in the pages of this book. It's certainly possible. After all, at the heart of her methodology is a trust in oneself, a reliance on instinct, a willingness to write first and edit later. Perhaps that's why her words are so powerful. Perhaps she edited for clarity but refused to edit her truth.

Early on, Chavez traces her educational experience at various institutions. As a student, Chavez writes that she tried to create change but was ultimately shut down by the people around her who were comfortable with the status quo. These were the individuals who confronted her about the frequency of her requests for inclusive reading lists, told her to stop mentioning race so often in her essays, and removed her as a volunteer reader for the campus's literary journal because of her open concerns about bias among its staff. In the end, Chavez's willingness to share these stories with her readers boosts her ethos as someone who's been through the system and who would have benefitted from the types of changes she presents in the coming chapters.

Before she launches into the specifics, Chavez takes a moment in the introduction to clarify the differences between traditional and anti-racist workshop models. Echoing Inoue's idea that "academic discourse...privileges middle class white students," she explains that the traditional workshop model involves white workshop leaders, a white-centered literary canon, and the "right" way to write, measured with rubrics against white standards (8). Students in these classrooms provide textual interpretations that the instructor measures against the "right" answer. Here, instructors assume their students' background knowledge. During a traditional workshop in this sort of classroom, student writers must sit silently and listen to their classmates rip their work apart , criticizing their word choices and unrelated tangents that remind someone of something else. They can't speak up to defend their work because, well, rules are rules, right?

Comparatively, the anti-racist model, or "aggressive activism," in Chavez's perspective, pits instructors as allies to and recruiters of writers of color (14). This model encourages leaders to pull texts from contemporary writers and create a living anthology that accepts contributions from students. Here, students define academic vocabulary without interference from the instructor. And when it comes time to workshop the writer, importantly, is not silenced. In fact, the whole goal of the workshop is for the participants to carry out a dialogue with each writer. It becomes a two-sided conversation guided by your questions. It's a radical change. And it's an equitable one.

Next, Chavez directly confronts the problems in the current model of workshopping in an enlightening way, beginning with concepts that many of us may have never considered: from the use of the word *literary*, which has essentially become synonymous with *white*, to the master-slave dichotomy that is embedded in reading famous white authors' texts and working to replicate them. Essentially, all the rules we're probably used to need to go.

In the remaining chapters, Chavez shares her experience by detailing how she lays the groundwork for an anti-racist classroom that also takes into account inclusive approaches to student engagement, reading practices, and writing expectations. Particularly effective is her focus on emotional enrichment for writers, which she refers to as *mothering*. Using classroom stories to which many readers can certainly relate, Chavez juxtaposes her approach against the traditional, product-based mentality that says students need to struggle, be torn down, and then built back up. Masculine. Tough. Not at all like the humanist approach Chavez prefers—one that celebrates individuals, their experiences, their attempts, and their growth en route to the sort of social reconstruction Ruiz calls for in her work.

Equally effective is the impetus Chavez shares for revising the literary canon, which, as she explains, perpetuates white supremacy. With sentiments similar to Ruiz's emphasis on "incorporating lost histories in writing curricula," Chavez offers simple solutions, such as presenting a digital anthology of contemporary, marginalized writers—people of color, people with disabilities, and gender-nonconforming individuals (12). Students can contribute to it, too; not only do students get to hear from marginalized voices, but also power and authority are distributed among the class. It's responsive. Relevant. Nothing at all like the prescribed list of homogenous writers most workshops favor.

Chavez also takes a unique approach to classroom language. Specifically, she refuses to stand at the head of the room and lecture on prescribed definitions of craft-related vocabulary such as *voice* or *exposition*. Instead, she encourages students to collaborate and create their own definitions, terms and conditions that they use during workshops. Student-led discourse isn't necessarily new, but Chavez's approach highlights the importance of avoiding assumptions about our students' background knowledge. Essentially, her approach ensures that no one is left behind.

Near the end of the book, Chavez returns to her storytelling expertise to share how she came upon *The Liz Lerman Critical Response Process,* a method that Chavez credits as foundational to her work. Lerman's approach, originally intended for dancers, has four steps: participants offering "statements of meaning," artists asking questions, respondents posing "neutral questions," and participants offering "permissioned opinions" (137-38). When applied to writing, these steps upend the traditional model. During her student-led workshops, no one is silenced, participants avoid "it's good" or "I didn't get it" statements, and writers have control.

Some readers may wonder how Chavez could possibly assess students within the model she proposes. Disagreeing with Inoue's claim that writing assessment is more important than pedagogy, she offers "discovery-based assessment," centered on growth and change rather than rubrics and benchmarks (Chavez 169; Inoue 9). The process involves reflection in the form of freewriting and daily check-ins about goals and feedback. Under this form of assessment, students harness and observe their own growth, which tells them much more than a number on a grading scale ever could.

Overall, Chavez does a remarkable job explaining what it's like to be a person of color in a college-level writing course today. She uses history and anecdotes to illustrate a perspective that's surely foreign to many white professors and students sharing space at institutions across the country. While some may argue that these stories deviate from the step-by-step process we as educators must consider implementing, the pieces are all here, and as Chavez recommends, we can take portions, or implement all of her process, from top to bottom. It's up to us. What's not an option is to do nothing at all. As Chavez says, "To do nothing is to stand still and submit to white supremacy. Take action" (150).

Brodhead, Wisconsin

Works Cited

Inoue, Asao B. *Antiracist Writing Assessment Ecologies: Teaching and Assessing Writing for a Socially Just Future.* Parlor Press, 2015.

Lerman, Liz, and John Borstel. *Liz Lerman's Critical Response Process: A Method for Getting Useful Feedback on Anything You Make, from Dance to Dessert.* Dance Exchange, 2003. Print.

Ruiz, Iris D. *Reclaiming Composition for Chicano/as and Other Ethnic Minorities: A Critical History and Pedagogy.* Palgrave Macmillan, 2016.

Tatum, Beverly Daniel. *"Why Are All the Black Kids Sitting Together in the Cafeteria?" And Other Conversations About Race.* Basic Books, 1997.

Speaking Up, Speaking Out: Lived Experiences of Non-Tenure-Track Faculty in Writing Studies, edited by Jessica Edwards, Meg McGuire, and Rachel Sanchez. Utah State University Press, 2021. 243 pp.

Reviewed by Stacy Wittstock, University of California, Davis

It should come as no surprise to anyone working in or around the field of writing studies that the number of non-tenure-track faculty (NTTF) teaching and working in US colleges and universities has steadily increased over the last several decades. In an oft-cited statistic, the American Association of University Professors (AAUP) reported that as of 2016 over 70% of instructional positions in US higher education were off the tenure track (see also Giordano et al.; Kahn et al.; Kezar et al.; Maisto and Street; MLA Office of Programs; Welch and Scott). Writing studies has a long and rich tradition of scholarship on NTTF, including the CCCC-sponsored journal *Forum: Issues about Part-Time and Contingent Faculty*. Likely because of the many constraints placed on NTTF regarding research and publication, scholarship focusing on NTTF has most often been written *about them* rather than *by them*. A recent edited collection, *Speaking Up, Speaking Out: Lived Experiences of Non-Tenure-Track Faculty in Writing Studies*, addresses this gap by presenting fifteen chapters written exclusively by scholars who, at the time of writing, were teaching and working off the tenure track. Edited by Jessica Edwards, Meg McGuire, and Rachel Sanchez, all NTTF themselves, this collection centers on the voices of NTTF, allowing them to tell their own stories, speak their own truths, and reclaim their own narratives.

The fifteen chapters include qualitative and mixed-methods research studies, theoretical frameworks and metaphors for understanding the realities of NTTF work, and reflective narratives about authors' experiences. Each chapter evokes a sense of vulnerability through storytelling—a rhetorical move that lends credence to the title's use of the term "lived experiences." A number of common themes emerge across the chapters, many of which should be familiar to anyone interested in conversations around academic labor in writing studies. One common refrain among authors is feeling undervalued, looked down upon, or exploited by their institutions, programs, and tenure-line colleagues. For example, chapters by Rachel Azima, Lilana M. Naydan, and Megan Boeshart Burelle and Elizabeth J. Vincelette each describe working conditions at the intersection between the institutional devaluation of writing centers and the liminal space of contingency. Several authors express feeling demoralized at being as equally qualified as their tenure-track colleagues but having limited job protection and being paid considerably less, even when doing similar tasks like research, administration, and committee work. In her chapter, Heather

Jordan contends that the idea that academia is a meritocracy is a harmful myth that creates an unsustainable environment for both NTTF and tenure-track faculty. A longing for a sense of community and collegiality also permeates the chapters, in addition to a palpable sense of frustration with the lack of professional development and teacher training available to NTTF.

The collection is separated into 4 parts: Definitions, Critical Perspectives, Lived Experiences, and Next Steps. "Part 1: Definitions" highlights the difficulty of defining NTTF given that they often occupy an array of different positions and titles with varying levels of institutional protection. Azima, a Professor of Practice and Writing Center Director, explains the ways that perceptions of her status as NTTF and the service-oriented view her institution held of the writing center impacted her work. Similarly, Naydan spotlights the challenges in defining NTTF whose work encompasses more than teaching, particularly those who work in writing centers. Peter Brooks proposes training NTTF in theories from student affairs in order to help them learn productive ways to support students while coping with the emotional labor such work involves. Erica M. Stone and Sarah E. Austin compare their differing experiences as NTTF, with one holding a full-time, renewable appointment at a military college while the other was a part-time adjunct at several institutions. All told, instead of clarifying definitions, this section is helpful in that it further highlights the lack of clear common characteristics among NTTF—a reality that makes finding common solutions equally difficult.

"Part 2: Critical Perspectives" offers frameworks for understanding NTTF experiences. Lacey Wootton develops a gendered metaphor for NTTF work by comparing the myth of women "having it all" during the second-wave feminist movement to the complex positionalities and working conditions of NTTF who are institutionally encouraged to expand their labor outside of teaching. Brendan Hawkins and Julie Karaus present the results of participatory action research with fellow adjuncts aimed at understanding conceptions of "contingent spaces" (92); their results demonstrate that adjuncts, who are often denied space both physically and communally, have little to no professional community to call their own and often feel as if they do not belong.

"Part 3: Lived Experiences" provides narratives of the working lives of NTTF. Burelle and Vincelette explain how vague job descriptions hampered their work as NTTF directing a writing center, leaving them with unclear labor boundaries and few ways to account for their administrative work on their promotion portfolios. In a conversational narrative, Jessica Cory and John McHone describe their hectic NTTF household where she holds a full-time NTTF position and he adjuncts at several nearby institutions. Angie McKinnon Carter, Christopher Lee, and Linda Shelton explore the ways that the lack of security and stability for NTTF can lead to feeling silenced and voiceless, while Denise Comer provides an honest account of her experiences as an administrator (albeit NTTF herself) who did not initially understand and support unionization efforts of another NTTF group. Finally, this section ends with an emotional and philosophical narrative (with a bonus bread recipe) from Seth Myers, who examines "body and affect" through his career as NTTF and co-founder of the Conference on Community Writing (178).

In the final section, "Part 4: Next Steps," authors provide some thoughts on how to address the inequities experienced by NTTF outlined throughout the book. Dauvan Mulally presents a qualitative study of portfolio-assessment groups in her institution and posits that such groups might provide NTTF opportunities for community, professional development, and collegiality. Nathalie Joseph and Norah Ashe-McNalley contend that collaboration can make publishing more manageable for NTTF by describing their own fruitful and amiable relationship as research collaborators. Jordan pushes back on this suggestion by pointing out that the institutional expansion of NTTF work beyond teaching serves to increase their workload without offering them the benefits their TT colleagues receive for the same work. As a reader, I found this section to be somewhat nebulous in that it does not offer much in the way of consensus-driven suggestions or solutions; however, this is perhaps because as the narratives throughout the book demonstrate, the needs of NTTF faculty are exceedingly diverse. In this way, the collection reveals not only the distributed and divergent experiences that NTTF have, but also the related lack of coherent or centralized next steps in addressing inequities related to their work.

As I read this book, I found myself resonating on a deep, personal level with many of the experiences outlined by the authors in this collection. Like Sanchez, I took what for me turned into a three-year "bridge appointment" when I was hired to teach as contingent faculty by the department from which I earned my MA (9). I experienced the same contradiction of immense gratitude—"We're so lucky; it could be so much worse" —with a quiet knowledge that my appointment benefited the institution far more than it did me (11). As a contingent faculty member and then later a PhD student facing an increasingly uncertain job market, I have also experienced the same fears expressed by Wootton; that if I don't take advantage of every opportunity, be it underpaid work or unpaid service, those prospects might vanish forever. Even for the opportunities I have taken, as when I accepted a WPA position as a coordinator in my MA institution's writing center, my status as contingent, combined with the institutional undervaluing of writing centers noted by several authors, led to the position being abruptly cut, leaving me scrambling to find full-time work.

This collection emphasizes that despite their often monolithic treatment in scholarship, NTTF experiences actually vary widely. They are known by a variety of titles, hold a variety of professional identities, and experience the labor associated with writing programs in a variety of ways. The support (or lack thereof) that they receive often hinges on their perceived value to their institutions and can both determine and be determined by their status in relation to their colleagues. But as the editors note in the introduction, one commonality among all NTTF is that they "are consistently defined by what [they] are not" (3). Overall, this collection contributes a comprehensive representation of the range of experiences and identities of NTTF, helping to move the conversation forward by developing a better account of the diverse needs of this community of faculty through those experiences. As writing studies labor scholar and activist Seth Kahn has highlighted in "The Problem of Speaking for Adjuncts," well-intentioned tenured or tenure track faculty can easily speak for or over NTTF. This collection offers a valuable and much-needed alternative by lifting the voices of NTTF to speak for themselves.

Davis, California

Works Cited

American Association of University Professors (AAUP). "Data Snapshot: Contingent Faculty in US Higher Ed." *AAUP Updates*, 11 October 2018, https://www.aaup.org/news/data-snapshot-contingent-faculty-us-higher-ed#.YMBNnjZKjPA

Forum: Issues about Part-Time and Contingent Faculty. Conference on College Composition and Communication (CCCC), https://cccc.ncte.org/cccc/forum/issues

Giordano, Joanne Baird et al. "TYCA Working Paper #9: Contingent Labor and Workload in Two-Year College English." *Workload Issues Committee, Two-Year College English Association (TYCA)*, April 2021, https://ncte.org/wp-content/uploads/2021/04/TYCA_Working_Paper_9.pdf

Kahn, Seth. "The Problem of Speaking for Adjuncts." *Contingency, Exploitation, and Solidarity: Labor and Action in English Composition*, edited by Seth Kahn, William B. Lalicker, and Amy Lynch-Biniek, The WAC Clearinghouse; University Press of Colorado, 2017, pp. 259-270, https://doi.org/10.37514/PER-B.2017.0858

Kahn, Seth et al., editors. *Contingency, Exploitation, and Solidarity: Labor and Action in English Composition*, The WAC Clearinghouse; University Press of Colorado, 2017, https://doi.org/10.37514/PER-B.2017.0858

Kezar, Adrianna et al. *The Gig Academy: Mapping Labor in the Neoliberal University*. Johns Hopkins University Press, 2019.

Maisto, Maria, and Steve Street. "Confronting Contingency: Faculty Equity and the Goals of Academic Democracy." *Liberal Education, American Association of Colleges and Universities (AACU)*, vol. 97, no. 1, 2011, https://www.aacu.org/publications-research/periodicals/confronting-contingency-faculty-equity-and-goals-academic

MLA Office of Programs. "Preliminary Report on the MLA *Job Information List*, 2017–18." *The Trend: Research and Analysis from the MLA Office of Programs*,

21 June 2019, https://mlaresearch.mla.hcommons.org/2019/06/21/preliminary-report-on-the-mla-job-information-list-2017-18/

Welch, Nancy, and Tony Scott, editors. *Composition in the Age of Austerity*. University Press of Colorado, 2016.

Sixteen Teachers Teaching: Two-Year College Perspectives, edited by Patrick Sullivan. Utah State University Press, 2020. 324 pp.

Reviewed by Bethany Sweeney, Des Moines Area Community College

Aimed at "anyone teaching reading and writing, grades 6-14" (14), *Sixteen Teachers Teaching* is a collection of contributions by two-year college teachers and students that offers a wealth of practical, research-grounded insight, information, and encouragement for instructors who envision their classrooms as a site in which students build their reading and writing skills for both their own good and the good of the larger community. Editor Patrick Sullivan and his contributors take seriously the charge to see the community college as a "social justice institution" (4), and while they are rightfully invested in making that vision as expansive as possible, they do it in such a way as to give readers a toolkit that will allow them to make pragmatic, justice-inspired changes in their own teaching spaces, whether those are housed in K-12 or in higher education. The volume is organized into five parts, each of which contains chapters written not only by well-established two-year college instructors and scholars deeply enmeshed in the work of education, but also by two-year college students who offer insights into their experience with effective and inspiring teaching and learning in the classroom.

The first part of the collection serves as a primer on the challenges and joys of teaching writing at the two-year college. Readers who know well those ups and downs and readers who may be entirely new to them alike will benefit from perspectives that highlight the broad range of student experience present at the two-year college and the need for teachers to, in the words of student contributor Bridgette Stepule, "embrace flexibility" (66). Darin Jensen's "Dispatches from Bartertown: Building Pedagogy in the Exigent Moment" recognizes the particular challenges faced by the largest group of instructors in the two-year college—adjunct instructors—and offers a concrete sense of principles that can help sustain those in contingent positions as they navigate the community college environment and do the all-important work of education while having to hustle to make even basic ends meet. Sullivan's interview with well-known scholar and teacher Helene Adams Androne stresses the importance of "teaching in the plural," a pedagogical approach that recognizes that "American identity is inherently pluralized and, therefore, much of what we do will and should deliberately reflect that" (58). Together, all of the perspectives in the section emphasize the complexity of the community college classroom and the need to approach that classroom with a wealth of flexibility and passionate engagement while not downplaying the challenges that instructors and students alike face on a daily basis.

The second part of the collection narrows in on the importance of a theory-driven practice of instruction motivated by the central value of compassion. In her chapter "Compassionate Writing Instruction," Brett Griffiths reminds us that compassion should not be treated as "the antithesis to standards" (72), but rather as a central component of writing and reading instruction that will enable students to thrive. Both Jeffrey Klausman and Jeffrey Andelora assert the importance of bringing scholarly engagement and classroom experience together to meaningfully inform praxis. Similarly, both of the section's student contributors, Darlene Pierpoint and Kevin Rodriguez, emphasize the need for teachers to bring both engagement and structure to the classroom, arguing for the importance of passion that is channeled into clear teaching goals that recognize the backgrounds and experiences of the students receiving instruction. Read together, the contributions in this section compellingly argue that truly effective instructors take the perspectives of both students and scholars seriously.

When the volume takes up the question of equity and social justice in its third section, it provides both practical tools for how to make classrooms more equitable and antiracist and reminds instructors of the importance of reflecting on the way in which our own privilege impacts the classroom spaces that we create. Scholars Holly Hassel and Hope Parisi emphasize our need to recognize the skills and strengths our students bring to the table and to adapt our classrooms and pedagogy to those skills. Parisi further points to the need to turn absences—in attendance, in submitted assignments, in particular rhetorical fluencies—into presences, explaining that "in community college settings, the *getting here* and *coming back* are large recurrent moments for celebrating what student presence means" (166, emphasis in original). Student Lauren Sills echoes that emphasis, reminding readers that community college students are motivated to be present and to create and benefit from the unique kinds of community that two-year colleges have to offer.

The third section of the volume also includes a much-needed reprint of an article first published in *Teaching English in the Two-Year College* in 2016: "The Risky Business of Engaging Racial Equity in Writing Instruction: A Tragedy in Five Acts," with a postscript specifically added for this collection. Within it, Taiyon J. Coleman, Renee DeLong, Kathleen Sheerin DeVore, Shannon Gibney, and Michael Kuhne discuss the significant challenges they encountered when they attempted to create a two-year college English department centered on racial justice and accountability; their postscript notes that their work to share those challenges has resulted in pushback that "really should not have been surprising as we're telling tales 'outside the house,' sharing long-kept secrets, and mostly asking a still-white-supremacist field, college comp instruction in America, to tell the truth about that ongoing colonizing violence, and to help us end it" (195). Rather than a warning against the perils of doing such work—though their chapter outlines those compellingly—their work serves to highlight how critical it is for writing instructors to commit to equity and form local and national coalitions to decolonize classrooms and transform them into spaces of racial justice. After all, as the authors argue, "while doing equity work is hard, not doing equity work will continue to produce misery and trauma" (175).

The final section of the collection narrows in to examine recent shifts in the teaching of developmental reading and writing. Two chapters by Jamey Gallagher and Peter Adams, explore the development of the Accelerated Learning Program, or ALP, model for integrating writing and reading support into the college-level classroom, explaining how the approach has evolved over the last two decades and providing practical examples of how to structure ALP classrooms and assignments. Student Jamil Shakoor pushes against the growing trend to do away with as many remedial offerings as possible, using his personal experience to emphasize the importance of giving students who are not traditionally prepared for college time to gain skills and adjust to its rigors. And in her chapter "Second-Chance Pedagogy: Integrating College-Level Skills and Strategies into a Developmental Writing Course," Joanne Baird Giordano explains what she learned through the process of creating a developmental course that integrates reading and writing, namely that developmental students thrive when they are given college-level work and supported throughout their process of engaging with it. The section would have benefited from a chapter that more directly engaged with the concerns outlined by Shakoor about losing remedial opportunities at the two-year college. Despite that, and though coming from sometimes notably different perspectives, all chapters in the section emphasize how important it is for writing instructors not to make assumptions about students but to challenge them to thrive and to help them build the skills and support networks that they need to do so.

Though each section of the text is thematically organized, one of the strengths of the collection is the way that chapters from each section interweave with each other to emphasize a set of common themes: the importance of reading and writing instructors integrating scholarly engagement into their pedagogy (and vice versa), the need to provide flexibility and rigorous support to students, and the centrality of joy and compassion to the creation of effective teaching. The scholarship included in the volume also strives to demonstrate the principles it lays out for the classroom within its own writing: authors not only foreground their own race-, class-, gender-, and sexuality-based contexts; they also integrate the discourse that springs from those contexts into the work of their writing, calling readers' attention to the fact that notions of "standard English" reproduce hierarchies of oppression. They provide examples of assignments rooted in the theoretical interventions they expound.

They demonstrate a commitment to equity and justice even as they argue for those values. Though the voices of up-and-coming scholars and teachers are not specifically highlighted, the volume successfully centers the experiences and contributions of students: student voices are integrated into each section, reminding readers that teaching is about learning and co-creating as much as it is about sharing expertise.

Ultimately, this collection effectively encourages reading and writing instructors to integrate scholarship, pedagogy, and service in the quest to educate students and build stronger and more democratic communities. As Leah McNeir's address to new English teachers puts it, "above all else, strive to encourage a passion for learning, open-mindedness, and exploration in your students and use your course's content as a tool for this aim" (285). This volume offers readers a timely and essential toolkit for putting that set of goals into action.

Carroll, Iowa

Work Cited

Coleman, Taiyon J., et al. "The Risky Business of Engaging Racial Equity in Writing Instruction: A Tragedy in Five Acts." *Teaching English in the Two-Year College*, vol. 43, no. 4, 2016, pp. 347–370.

Empowering the Community College First-Year Composition Teacher: Pedagogies and Policies, edited by Meryl Siegal and Betsy Gilliland. University of Michigan Press, 2021. 328 pp.

Reviewed by Katherine Daily O'Meara, St. Norbert College

Community colleges have seen their fair share of precarity—an issue that has been brought into even sharper focus recently through the lens of the COVID-19 pandemic. A *New York Times* article from April 2021 notes that while all types of colleges and universities have been negatively affected by COVID-19, it is community colleges that have been disproportionately impacted: a 9.5% decrease in enrollment is cited, a drop that is "more than double the loss experienced by four-year schools" (Saul). A November 2020 article from *Inside Higher Ed* notes that enrollment for community college freshmen is down by 19%, with the hardest-hit population of "underrepresented minorities" decreasing by nearly 30% (St. Amour). And even before pandemic times, vast educational reforms in curriculum and placement, widespread budget cuts, and the financial incentivization for colleges "to get more students through a course of study (transfer, certificate, or degree) more quickly" has meant that community college teachers face substantial challenges that inform the ways they approach pedagogy and interact with programmatic and institutional policy (Siegal and Gilliland 5).

But despite emergency transitions to (and then sustained engagement with) online platforms, despite waning enrollments, and despite decreased funding, first year composition (FYC) teachers at community colleges continue to do good and meaningful work. The new edited collection *Empowering the Community College First-Year Composition Teacher: Pedagogies and Practices* sheds a necessary light on the teachers who are at once resilient and nimble, despite the challenges of a changing landscape. Editors Meryl Siegal and Betsy Gilliland provide readers with a collection that "provides a broad look at contemporary community college FYC that inspires teaching and learning and, at the same time, endeavors to present the complexity of community college FYC in higher education" (11).

Precarity sometimes proves to be the catalyst for meaningful work to get done in response to—and often in spite of—challenges. Teachers of community college FYC rise to these challenges by asking: How does the changing landscape affect our pedagogical decision-making? Are our current programmatic structures, course designs, and writing curricula as effective and equitable as they can be for an undeniably diverse student population? How can we best contribute to all students' success considering local material conditions? What skills (writing or otherwise) are the most practical and transferable for the students in our FYC classes? How can we listen to one another and learn from our individual but collective experience? Siegal and Gilliland's collection showcases the innovation, collaboration, and wily resilience of this teaching population in four thematic parts, comprising sixteen engaging chapters.

The "Introduction: Why FYC Teachers' Perspectives Are Important," offers necessary context and exigence, and Siegal and Gilliland note the shifting trends in offering first year composition courses (e.g., moving away from past models of remediation/developmental writing in an effort to accelerate students through programs expediently) and the widespread conviction that "The [community college] student is a customer focused on getting in, getting through, and getting out" (7). They assert that teachers are an integral and inextricable asset to creating institutional change and seek to amplify these expert voices in the parts that follow.

In "Part 1: Refining Our Pedagogy," four chapters contribute to the ongoing discussion of refining one's pedagogy and offering sound practice in community college FYC. In this section, readers explore studies that investigate student agency in constructing the writer's identity through reflective writing; improving reading comprehension and retention in online formats; empowering multilingual students through socio-cognitive classroom practices; and the metalinguistic knowledge students possess through writing-about-writing frameworks. Common threads in part one include meeting diverse student populations where they are at, and maximizing their diverse experiences and knowledge to make the composition classroom "work" for them.

"Part 2: Teaching Toward Acceleration" includes three chapters that share how meaningful classroom practices occur even in accelerated formats. These chapters explore the transformative value of contract grading as anti-racist praxis, focusing on student responsibility and time management; relationship- and community-building not only to inspire mutual trust among students but also to improve academic literacy; and scaffolding writing-intensive projects for students with disabilities, demonstrating ways to make college writing curricula truly accessible. Part 2 shares multiple stories of community college FYC offering innovative and dynamic approaches to assessment, classroom engagement, and student advocacy and support.

Each of the three chapters in "Part 3: Considering Programmatic Change" does just that: When faced with changes at the program level (ostensibly to meet students' evolving personal and/or career exigencies), community college FYC teachers adapt to these challenges with students' best interests at the heart of their decision-making. In this section, readers engage with discussions of how to provide meaningful, humanities-informed instruction to STEM students; how to facilitate student success in synchronous online instruction to students in rural areas (and how to assess within these constraints); and how CTE (Career and Technical Education) professional writing approaches can motivate students to rise to the challenge and rigor of college-level writing expectations.

This section makes visible the adaptability and agility of community college FYC teachers, who innovate even in the face of changes to material conditions. Part 3 demonstrates the transfer of skills, knowledge, and expertise among disciplines, as well as between academia and the real world.

"Part 4: Considering Curriculum: Research and Policy" is the longest thematic section, boasting six chapters that each present a different approach to "researching issues in FYC instruction, student success, and educational policy" (Siegal and Gilliland 14). Readers can engage with topics that include advocating for the diversity of multilingual learners; an ethnographic approach to understanding how community and two-year colleges support international students; and how departments respond to educational reform and policy change. This section concludes with chapters that discuss corequisite teaching models; how faculty perceive changes to FYC programs, including curriculum reform and placement protocols; and a look into what the processes of a community college institutional research (IR) offices do for students and faculty alike. Researching and connecting what happens in the classroom with overarching policy allows community college FYC teachers to understand diverse student needs and work toward institutional practice that is equitable for all students.

In their "Conclusion: Listening to Teachers," Siegal and Gilliland discuss practical applications of the previous chapters, encouraging readers to take a cue from the collected authors and pursue research, classroom practices, and programmatic initiatives that further the common community college goals of access and equity. The striking and effective balance of focus on what happens at the classroom level, combined with the big-picture view of community college FYC's positionality in the larger institution, is a highlight of the edited collection. The conclusion also offers a robust selection of questions for reflection and review for every chapter, as well as a glossary of key terms, encouraging readers to engage with the studies even more meaningfully and inviting more teachers to join the conversation.

Siegal and Gilliland believe in teachers. Despite all challenges, teachers are resilient, they are collaborative, they are visionary. This book situates teachers at the center of every discussion and amplifies their dexterity and adaptability. *Empowering the Community College First-Year Composition Teacher* "is an effort to bring grassroots faculty perspectives back to the curriculum, showcasing faculty knowledge, expertise, and creativity in designing and implementing excellent instruction in FYC" (10). The book champions community college FYC teachers and the tenacious work they have been doing all along, and *all* educators will be empowered by the work shared in this collection.

De Pere, Wisconsin

Works Cited

Saul, Stephanie. "The Pandemic Hit the Working Class Hard. The Colleges That Serve Them are Hurting, Too." *The New York Times*, 2 Apr. 2021. nytimes.com/2021/04/02/us/politics/covid-19-colleges.html

Siegal, Meryl, and Betsy Gilliland. *Empowering the Community College First-Year Composition Teacher: Pedagogies and Policies*. University of Michigan Press, 2021.

St. Amour, Madeline. "Who's Up, Who's Down and Why." *Inside Higher Ed*, 19 Nov. 2020. insidehighered.com/news/2020/11/19/community-college-enrollments-down-nationally-not-everywhere

Style and the Future of Composition Studies, edited by Paul Butler, Brian Ray, and Star Medzerian Vanguri. Utah State University Press, 2020. 274 pp.

Reviewed by Roberto S. Leon, University of Maryland College Park

Interest in style continues apace in composition studies. *Style and the Future of Composition Studies* builds on the well-trod and copious path set by T.R. Johnson and Tom Pace's collection *Refiguring Prose Style: Possibilities for Writing Pedagogy* (2005) as well as previous work from the editors of this collection, including Paul Butler's *Out of Style: Reanimating Stylistic Study in Composition and Rhetoric* (2008); Mike Duncan and Star Medzerian Vanguri's collection *The Centrality of Style* (2013); and Brian Ray's *Style: An Introduction to History, Theory, Research, and Pedagogy* (2015). In those works, contributors historicize and define style, as well as articulate the pedagogic value of deliberately attending to style. *Style and the Future of Composition Studies* extends this previous work by presenting ways in which "style effects change" (3) in various areas of interest to composition studies researchers and teachers, including transfer studies, writing ethics, professional writing, linguistic justice, digital rhetoric, genre studies, legal writing, and creative writing.

Attention to language often must compete with research that focuses on writing with a wide-angle lens, a lens in which writing is understood as a part of a genre system and an activity system. This competition can either lead to a productive tension that contextualizes style—as we see here in *Style and the Future of Composition Studies*—or that leads to the type of eclipse we see in the brilliant but incomplete *Naming What We Know: Threshold Concepts of Writing Studies* (2015), where language and style are taken only as "Words Get Their Meanings from Other Words," "Writing Involves the Negotiation of Language Differences," and perhaps "Habituated Practice Can Lead to Entrenchment." Much more can and should be said about style. For example, what threshold concepts could scholars of style bring to the table?

Style and the Future of Composition Studies is not explicitly organized around threshold concepts. However, this collection is organized around four "key actions" that style performs (5). It might just be the Univers and Garamond typefaces, but these "key actions" read a lot like threshold concepts and might be productively read as such: "Style Mediates Relationships" (Concept 1: Writing is a Social and Rhetorical Activity); "Style Conveys Identity" (Concept 3: Writing Enacts and Creates Identities and Ideologies); "Style Forms Strategy" (Concept 2: Writing Speaks to Situations through Recognizable Forms"); and "Style Creates and Transcends Boundaries" (this last key action recalls several threshold concepts). *Style and the Future of Composition Studies* is ultimately not a footnote to *Naming What We Know* (though the thought is intriguing).

It does, however, provide a wide variety of stylistic studies to enable new lines of inquiry regarding these issues of audience, identity, genre, and boundaries. The first section, "Style Mediates Relationships," forefronts questions regarding writer-reader relationships ("Writing Addresses, Invokes, and/or Creates Audiences," in *Naming What We Know* parlance). For example, in chapter one Andrea Olinger looks at how an undergraduate in psychology negotiates the different style preferences of her two professors, a cognitive psychologist who writes for the public and a clinical psychologist who writes for academia. In almost all regards, the professors' advice and lists of preferences are at cross-purposes ("don't use 'I'" vs. "use 'I'"; "eliminate 'jargon'" vs. "sound sciency,'" etc. [29]). As the student developed a heterogeneous style to take up both perspectives, Olinger notes that the student came to realize that even her professors did not follow their own style rules on all accounts. She came to recognize how style is dynamic and co-created by writers and their readers (31). Olinger uses this case study to argue that more attention to style can provide further insights for transfer studies. While the transfer studies Olinger cites focus on style as synonymous with grammar and mechanics and therefore devalue style or reduce style to ill-defined lists of rules (like the infamous "Be clear" that T.R. Johnson takes up in chapter three), an attention to style as a separate construct can illuminate other discontinuities and thresholds writers experience as they develop writing expertise.

Turning from transfer and developmental stages to ethics, Melissa Goldthwaite's chapter on epistolary style asks how we can help students recognize how writers encourage metonymic listening through their style. Goldthwaite looks at Chimamanda Ngozi Adichie and Ta-Nehisi Coates's epistolary fiction through the lens of Krista Ratcliffe's *Rhetorical Listening: Identification, Gender, Whiteness*. Through their stylistic choices, Adichie and Coates invoke and address multiple audiences and cast the reader as someone with authority to respond and counsel. Here, style is described in terms of "pronoun usage, sentence type and variation, repetition, imagery, and juxtaposition" (37–38). Goldthwaite concludes by providing prompts for helping students learn how to listen rhetorically. In chapter four, Tom Pace provides a series of professional writing assignments based on Erasmus's *De Copia* to further show how students can be made aware of style as it mediates between audience and purpose.

This concern for audience and relationships carries over into the second section, "Style Conveys Identity." The section opens with an analysis of Spike Jonze's film *Her* by Cydney Alexis and Eric Leake. Their analysis highlights the weight of style in establishing and maintaining social relationships. Laura Aull and Zak Lancaster's chapter on stance is particularly useful. Focusing primarily on metalanguage (transitions, signposts, etc.), Aull and Lancaster describe stance as a matter of attitude, epistemology, and interactional words, phrases, and other expressions. These stances will reasonably differ across genres and disciplines (102). Through facilitating stance awareness, Aull and Lancaster show a way to instruct writers to see style as part of larger rhetorical situations, rather than simply as a fixed, formalistic construct.

Other chapters emphasize the injustices of perceived identity. Jimmy Butts, for example, explores what we mean when we associate a particular style with stupidity. "The future of writing," Butts writes, "is inherently couched in an understanding of whatever gets labeled or underestimated as stupid" (115). Through juxtaposing examples of those we are quick to label and those who we defend, Butts suggests that we should ultimately "look past our stupidity with kindness and embrace a more perfect view of pluralities and possibility" (129). Eric House similarly takes on questions of linguistic justice—an issue that should be relevant to all readers and teachers—using the hip-hop cipher as an example of translingual practice and pedagogy. House suggests combining this improvised call-and-response practice with Genius, a collaborative annotation website primarily for lyrics. Many other possible pedagogical applications are shared in this and the other chapters—this is not just a theoretical collection.

The third section, "Style Forms Strategy" takes on similar themes, but shifts the focus from interactions toward larger, more pervasive strategies. Take Almas Khan, who draws on applied legal storytelling to consider how humans are represented or "embodied" in writing. In the following chapter, "What Style Can Add to Genre," Anthony Box considers style as metalanguage, cohesion, and coherence, to suggest that style provides more "nuance and control" than genre alone can offer (195). Laura Aull also returns to consider markers of civil, ethical, listening discourse. And Jaron Slater ponders on the transdisciplinary, sublime aspects of style.

The collection ends with "Style Creates and Transcends Boundaries," a theme foreshadowed in the first chapters of each section. Jon Udelson leads off with a discussion of what we might call boundary-guarders and boundary-crossers between the disciplines of writing studies and creative writing studies. Style is an ideal boundary object, a point of contact between these two fields. Mike Duncan follows with a discussion of stylometrics and authoring. William FitzGerald then closes up shop by considering progymnasmata for teaching verbal style (drawing on Jeanne Fahnestock's *Rhetorical Style*), with notes on craft and de-composition.

The ebb and flow of these themes—style and relationships, style and identity, style and strategy, and style and boundaries—emphasizes the flexible arrangement of these chapters. As Butler, Ray, and Vanguri put it in their introduction, "These categories could easily be combined or rearranged to reveal even more possibilities" (5). For example, chapters could be alternatively grouped for style and genre (chapters six, ten, twelve, and fifteen); style and social justice (chapters two, three, seven, eight, and eleven); and style as a boundary object (chapters one, four, five, and nine). By allowing multiple paths and groupings, this collection reflects the potential of style to contribute to the future of composition studies writ large.

Ultimately, *Style and the Future of Composition Studies* fulfills its promise to introduce ways in which style and the study thereof can effect change. This book will be an important resource for researchers and instructors looking to update themselves on style scholarship and consider how style can speak to change in the many subfields of composition and across disciplinary divides.

College Park, Maryland

Works Cited

Adler-Kassner, Linda, and Elizabeth Wardle. *Naming What We Know: Threshold Concepts of Writing Studies*. Utah State University Press, 2015.

Butler, Paul. *Out of Style: Reanimating Stylistic Study in Composition and Rhetoric*. Utah State University Press, 2008.

Duncan, Mike and Star Medzerian Vanguri, editors. *The Centrality of Style*. The WAC Clearinghouse/Parlor Press, 2013.

Fahnestock, Jeanne. *Rhetorical Style: The Uses of Language in Persuasion*. Oxford University Press, 2011.

Johnson, T.R., and Tom Pace, editors. *Refiguring Prose Style: Possibilities for Writing Pedagogy.* Utah State University Press, 2005.

Ratcliffe, Krista. *Rhetorical Listening: Identification, Gender, Whiteness*. Southern Illinois University Press, 2005.

Ray, Brian. *Style: An Introduction to History, Theory, Research, and Pedagogy*. Parlor Press/The WAC Clearinghouse, 2015.

Contributors

Timothy Ballingall is an instructional assistant professor in the Department of Liberal Studies at Texas A&M University at Galveston, where he teaches technical and professional writing. His work can be found in *Peitho* and *Praxis: A Writing Center Journal*. He received his PhD in Rhetoric and Composition from Texas Christian University.

Kristin Bennett is a PhD candidate in Writing, Rhetorics, and Literacies at Arizona State University. She researches the intersections between rhetoric, disability studies, and technical and professional communication across institutional discourse. Her work has appeared in *IEEE: Transactions on Professional Communication* and is forthcoming in the *Journal of Business and Technical Communication*.

Jesper Bremholm is a senior researcher at the Danish National Centre for Reading. His fields of expertise include disciplinary literacy, textbook studies, writing development, and ethnographic and mixed-method approaches to the study of literacy. Formerly, he has been a teacher educator and an associate professor at Aarhus University.

Felicita Arzu Carmichael is an assistant professor of writing and rhetoric at Oakland University, where she teaches rhetorics of race, introduction to writing studies, contemporary issues in writing studies, and first year writing. Her research and teaching center race, technology, inclusion, and place-embodiment. Her work has appeared in *Technical Communication Quarterly*, *WPA Journal*, and *Constellations: a cultural rhetorics publishing space*.

Amy Cicchino, PhD is Associate Director of University Writing at Auburn University. Her research takes up writing program administration, digital multimodality, and writing across the curriculum, and it has been featured in publications like the *International Journal of ePortfolios,* the *Online Literacy Open Resource,* and *WPA: Writing Program Administration*.

Richard Colby is the Assistant Director for Writing and a teaching professor at the University of Denver. He has co-edited two collections and written several articles on gaming and the teaching of writing for *Computers and Composition, Computers and Composition Online, in media res,* and *Communication Design Quarterly.*

Rebekah Shultz Colby is a teaching professor at the University of Denver. She has co-edited *The Ethics of Playing, Researching, and Teaching Games in the Writing Classroom* and *Rhetoric/Composition/Play through Video Games*. She has also published articles exploring how to use games to theorize and teach rhetoric and writing.

Anannya Dasgupta directs the Centre for Writing and Pedagogy at Krea University, where she is also an associate professor of literature in the Division of Literature and the Arts. Prior to this, she set up the Centre for Writing Studies at O.P. Jindal Global University and taught at Shiv Nadar University, where her journey in writing pedagogy in India began. She trained in writing pedagogy at the Writing Program at Rutgers University, where she also earned her doctorate from the Department of Literatures in early modern literature. Among her publications are *Magical Epistemologies: Forms of Knowledge in Early Modern English Drama* (2020) and a book of poems, *Between Sure Places* (2015). She has also co-edited, along with Madhura Lohokare, a collection of essays titled *Writing In Academia* (2019). Her current work is focussed on developing writing pedagogies for the Indian classrooms from school to the university level. She has conducted several workshops on academic writing for teaching faculty, research scholars, college students, and high school students.

Kevin E. DePew, Associate Professor of English at Old Dominion University, teaches various courses from English Composition to Online Writing Instruction and Multilingual Writing Pedagogies for graduate students. He, with Amy Cicchino, administrates GSOLE's Certification Course. In addition to studying online literacy instruction, he examines antiracist pedagogies in face-to-face and online courses.

Roland Dumavor is a graduate student and a first year writing instructor in the Writing, Rhetoric, and American Cultures Department at Michigan State University. His research interests include social/criminal justice, WPA, multimodality, African/Black digital rhetorics, cultural rhetorics, environmental rhetorics, and Indigenous rhetorics. His focus in scholarly work is framed by Black/African and Indigenous experiences, theories, praxis, methodologies, and approaches.

Anuj Gupta is a graduate student in the Rhetoric, Composition and the Teaching of English Program at the University of Arizona. He works at the intersection of composition studies, applied linguistics, and digital humanities. He is interested in researching the relationships between emotions and writing through multiple perspectives. He is currently studying how graduate students experience academic writing anxieties and also exploring computational methods to study how media texts use emotions to persuade the public. In the past, he has worked as a writing program administrator to help build one of India's first college-level writing programs at the Young India

Fellowship at Ashoka University. He is passionate about helping develop the writing pedagogy community in India, transforming composition studies research to integrate well-being as a curricular focus, and implementing digital and computation techniques as research methods.

Carrie Hall is an assistant professor and WPA at the New York City College of Technology in Brooklyn. She studies the politics of paying attention: how people learn to pay attention (and to perform paying attention) and how different performances of attention get valued in academia. She can be found on her website, "The Boredoms" at drcarriehall.com.

Brianne Jaquette is an associate professor of English literature and culture at Western Norway University of Applied Sciences (Høgskulen på Vestlandet) in Bergen, Norway. Her work on composition and literature can be found in the *Journal of the Midwest Modern Language Association*, the *International Journal of Bahamian Studies*, *Tulsa Studies in Women's Literature*, and *Pedagogy*.

Radhika Jaidev is the Director of the Centre for Communication Skills (CCS) at the Singapore Institute of Technology (SIT), where she also teaches academic literacies with a focus on critical thinking to undergraduates while driving a university-wide Writing-in-the-Disciplines (WID) program. Her research is in writing transfer in the disciplines as well as in the workplace.

Matthew S. S. Johnson is Professor of English and Director of First-Year Writing at Southern Illinois University, Edwardsville. He specializes in rhetoric-composition, digital literacies, and video game studies/ludology, often focusing on the relationship between work and play. He is Reviews Editor for the *Journal of Gaming and Virtual Worlds*.

Kristine Kabel is Associate Professor and PhD at the Danish School of Education, Aarhus University, Denmark. Her main research interests are subject-specific literacy, student writing, and writing development, particularly in the context of first-language education. Moreover, she is a steering group member in the Nordic Research Network on Literature Education.

Linford Lamptey is a doctoral student of English at Miami University, Ohio. He has his master's degree in rhetoric from Michigan Technological University. His research interests center on writing and digital compositions, and he explores the intersections between writing, the digital, decolonial, and African rhetorical practices.

Icy Lee is a professor in the faculty of education at The Chinese University of Hong Kong. Her main research interests are second language writing and second language teacher education. She was a former co-editor of the *Journal of Second Language Writing* and is currently Principal Associate Editor of *The Asia-Pacific Education Researcher*.

Roberto S. Leon is a PhD candidate in the Language, Writing, and Rhetoric Program at the University of Maryland, College Park. His interests include histories and theories of rhetoric and composition, comparative rhetoric, professional/technical writing, second language writing, and writing program administration.

Brad Lucas is Associate Professor of English at Texas Christian University, where he teaches courses in composition, technical communication, research methodologies, and the rhetorics of social protest. He is author of *Radicals, Rhetoric, and the War*, and his recent work has appeared in *Rhet Ops: Rhetoric and Information Warfare*.

Vivette Milson-Whyte is Head of the Department of Language, Linguistics and Philosophy at The University of the West Indies in Jamaica. She is the author of *Academic Writing Instruction for Creole-Influenced Students* (UWI Press, 2015) and co-editor of the MLA and CCCC award-winning *Creole Composition: Academic Writing and Rhetoric in the Anglophone Caribbean* (Parlor Press, 2019).

Emma Moghabghab is an instructor in the Communication Skills Program at the American University of Beirut, where she also served as Assistant Director of the Writing Center. Her past work has appeared in *The Writing Center Journal* and the *Writing Lab Newsletter*. She is ABD in Composition and Applied Linguistics at the Indiana University of Pennsylvania, where her current research focuses on postdigital rhetoric, composition, and power.

Federico Navarro is Associate Professor at the Universidad de O'Higgins. He is the former chair of the Latin American Association of Writing Studies in Higher Education, ALES. He has led several funded research projects on writing and is the series editor of the *International Exchanges on the Study of Writing: Latin American Section* at The WAC Clearinghouse.

Raymond Oenbring is Professor of English at the University of the Bahamas, where he serves as Writing Program Coordinator. He received his PhD from the University of Washington, Seattle.

Katherine Daily O'Meara is Director of Writing Across the Curriculum and Assistant Professor of English at St. Norbert College in De Pere, Wisconsin. She teaches courses in rhetoric and composition, professional writing, and linguistics. Kat is an institutional ethnographer whose research includes WPA, WAC/WID, online writing instruction, and second-language writing.

Nancy Pine is an associate professor of English at Columbus State Community College, where she teaches composition courses. She is the author of the Open Educational Resource (OER), *Writing in Context,* and articles in publications including *Teaching English in the Two-Year College* and the *Journal of Basic Writing.*

Natalia Ávila Reyes is an assistant professor of education at Pontificia Universidad Católica de Chile. She is interested in writing across educational levels and in the disciplinary emergence of writing studies in Latin America. Her most recent research explores university students' experiences with writing in contexts of increasing diversity.

Siara Schwartzlow is a graduate student at the University of Wyoming. Her interests include equitable pedagogy and instructional coaching. When she's not studying, she teaches middle school English Language Arts and writes fiction for children and adults.

Jason Snart is Professor of English and Chair of Literature, Creative Writing, and Film at the College of DuPage in Glen Ellyn, Illinois. His research focuses on hybrid teaching, learning, and development. His most recent book, *Making Hybrids Work: An Institutional Framework for Blending Online and Face-to-Face Instruction in Higher Education*, was published in 2016 by NCTE. In 2020/21 Snart was awarded a League for Innovation Excellence award and also won the Outstanding Full-Time Faculty award at College of DuPage.

Bethany Sweeney has taught writing, literature, and history at Des Moines Area Community College since 2014. She has a PhD in literature from the University of California, Santa Cruz. Her research interests focus on American countercultures, science fiction, writing studies, and equity at the two-year college.

Susan E. Thomas is Founding Director of the Faculty of Arts and Social Sciences Writing Hub and Writing Program and former Associate Dean Teaching and Learning at the University of Sydney, Australia. Her current research focuses on navigating change in writing program administration and designing inclusive writing programs. Susan is the current president of the Council of Writing Program Administrators.

Scott Warnock, PhD is Professor of English and Associate Dean of Undergraduate Education in the College of Arts & Sciences at Drexel University.

Warnock has authored numerous books, articles, chapters, and webtexts about writing and digital technology. He was the president of the Global Society of Online Literacy Educators from 2018 to 2020.

Christine Wilson is an active teacher-scholar and is currently an adjunct assistant professor of English at North Central College in Naperville, Illinois. Her pedagogical interests include writing transfer, information literacy, and the role of writing centers. She has taught first year writers for the last ten years.

Stacy Wittstock is a PhD candidate in Education and Writing, Rhetoric, and Composition Studies at the University of California, Davis. Her research interests include writing program administration, developmental writing and writers, institutional ethnography, and the intersections between faculty identity and contingent labor in writing programs.

Omar Ahmed Yacoub is a PhD candidate (ABD) in the Composition and Applied Linguistics program at the Indiana University of Pennsylvania. His research interests are in composition studies, writing transfer, and STEM writing. He also has experience working as a writing center research assistant and tutor.

PARLOR PRESS
EQUIPMENT FOR LIVING

Now with Parlor Press!

Studies in Rhetorics and Feminism
Series Editors: Cheryl Glenn and Shirley Wilson Logan

New Releases

Writing Spaces: Readings on Writing Volume 4

Running, Thinking, Writing: Embodied Cognition in Composition
by Jackie Hoermann-Elliott

English Studies Online: Programs, Practices, Possibilities, edited by William P. Banks and Susan Spangler

Feminist Circulations: Rhetorical Explorations across Space and Time, edited by Jessica Enoch, Danielle Griffin and Karen Nelson

Pedagogical Perspectives on Cognition and Writing, edited by J. Michael Rifenburg, Patricia Portanova, and Duane Roen

MLA Mina Shaughnessy Prize and CCCC Best Book Award 2021!

Creole Composition: Academic Writing and Rhetoric in the Anglophone Caribbean, edited by Vivette Milson-Whyte, Raymond Oenbring, and Brianne Jaquette

Check Out Our New Website!

Discounts, blog, open access titles, instant downloads, and more.

www.parlorpress.com

Composition Studies **Discount:** Use COMPSTUDIES20 at checkout to receive a 20% discount on all titles not on sale through January 15, 2022.

www.ingramcontent.com/pod-product-compliance
Lightning Source LLC
Chambersburg PA
CBHW031317160426
43196CB00007B/573